Breaking Boundaries

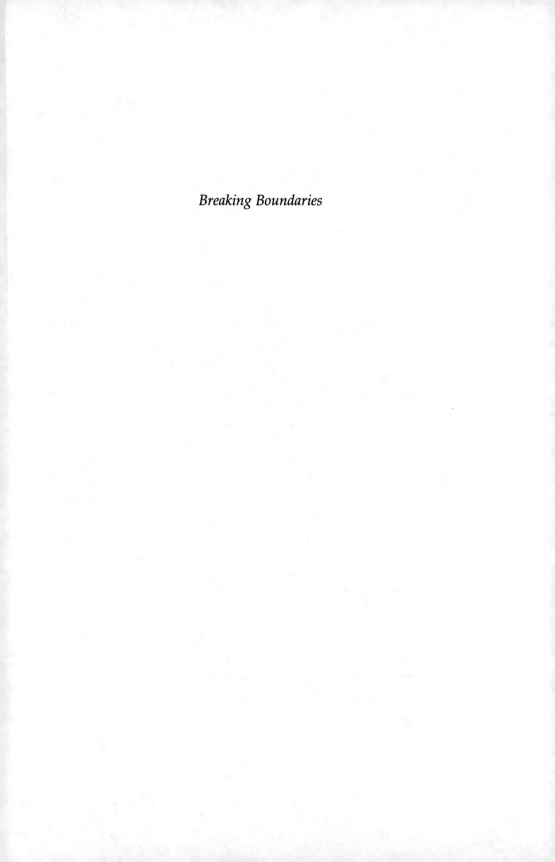

Breaking Boundaries

Latina Writing and Critical Readings

Edited by

Asunción Horno-Delgado

Eliana Ortega

Nina M. Scott

Nancy Saporta Sternbach

The University of Massachusetts Press

Amherst

Copyright © 1989 by The University of Massachusetts Press

All rights reserved

Printed in the United States of America

LC 88–17141

ISBN 0–87023–636–9 (pbk)

Set in Linotron Palatino at Keystone Typesetting

Printed by Thomson-Shore and bound by John Dekker & Sons

Library of Congress Cataloging-in-Publication Data

Breaking boundaries : Latina writing and critical readings / edited by
Asunción Horno-Delgado . . . [et al.].

p. cm.

Bibliography: p.

ISBN 0–87023–636–9 (pbk. : alk. paper).

1. American literature—Hispanic American authors—History and
criticism. 2. American literature—Women authors—History and
criticism. 3. American literature—20th century—History and
criticism. 4. Hispanic American women—Intellectual life—20th
century. 5. Women and literature—United States—History—20th
century. 6. Hispanic Americans in literature. I. Horno Delgado,
Asunción, 1956–

PS153.H56B74 1989

810'.9'9287—dc19   88–17141

CIP

British Library Cataloguing in Publication data are available.

To Latina writers
whose work
has inspired this book

Contents

Contents   ix

Preliminary Considerations

Breaking Boundaries has as its primary intention just what the title implies: to reevaluate the paradigmatic and often divisive categories set forth by the literary establishment, whether those be cultural, linguistic, literary, academic, political, or sexual. We focus on an already extensive and rich body of literature written by Latina women, yet virtually unrecognized by institutions of power (universities, departments, publishing houses, media), although, fortunately, there are some exceptions. As scholars, we do not consent to the discriminatory practices that perpetuate this marginalization. It is part of our effort, then, to make this literature less than marginal, to give it visibility and accessibility so that a larger audience can come to know it.

We came together as a panel at the Tenth Symposium of Spanish and Portuguese Bilingualism held at the University of Massachusetts at Amherst in November 1986. It was then that we decided to work together as editors to make a book of those papers. With the exception of Nicholasa Mohr's "Puerto Rican Writers in Puerto Rico, Puerto Rican Writers in New York: A Difference Beyond Language," all of the papers were written specifically for this book by authors who have been working in this field.

Whereas it is not possible to make available to readers the entire scope and complexity of Latina writing within the parameters of this one book, we do aim to contribute to a better understanding of the historic and literary processes that give rise to this literature. For this reason, we have chosen a socio-historical approach in both these preliminary considerations and the essay by Sternbach/Ortega. It proved impossible to deal with all the issues concerning Latina discourse, but our book does represent a wide variety of approaches to the Latina texts under discussion. We do hope that exposure to these texts, as well as access to the bibliography, will act as stimuli to encourage further reading of, and research on, Latina

xi

literature. And in spite of constraints of time and space, our effort was twofold: to include representative writers and to introduce some lesser known names.

Latina literature is most often excluded from curricula in English and Spanish courses because of its bilingual or "interlingual" nature. To make all entries completely accessible to a non-Spanish-speaking reader, we have provided translations. But because translations can often be intrusive, we have limited their place to footnotes. The very need for these translations underscores the unfortunate monolingual nature of U.S. society. In Latin America, however, given the neo-colonial situation, bilingualism (that is, having to learn English) becomes a necessary factor for professional, political, and commercial transactions. The dominant culture expects this, yet, in spite of the obvious political implications of U.S.–Latin American relations, feels no obligation or need to learn Spanish. Nor does it seem to have any interest in learning the language of its approximately twenty-five million Latino and Latina inhabitants.

We initially discussed the idea of publishing this book in Spanish, the language of many of the original papers. However, as we are dealing with a literature produced in the U.S., we chose English as the means to make this work available to an Anglo audience who would not otherwise have access to it. This act does not diminish the possibility of translation into Spanish and other languages as one more effort to portray "minority" experience in the U.S.

We have structured this work chronologically. Chicanos were the first Latino group historically present in what is now U.S. territory. As Luis Valdez has declared: "We did not, in fact, come to the United States at all. The United States came to us."[1] In this context we have begun our book with Chicanas, for they were the first to establish a literary heritage in the U.S. Texts of Puerto Rican women writers follow. We have placed them in the second section, for they reflect a historic situation that peaked during the mid-twentieth century. This literature, sometimes referred to as "Nuyorican,"[2] reflects the migration and immigration experience of rural and working-class Puerto Ricans to the New York and Northeast areas. A third section of our book concerns itself with Cuban women writers, most of whom came to the U.S. after 1959 as a result of the Cuban revolution. Like the other two groups, those who were raised here generally write in English or bilingually, whereas those who came as adults probably choose Spanish. The last section of the book attempts to address the sometimes problematic status of some Latin American women writers who are permanent residents of the U.S. and who have, to some degree, identified with the above-mentioned groups.

Perhaps because of the complexity of Latina writing, critics to date have tended to focus on one or another of these groups, i.e., specific studies of specific Latinas. This is the first book of literary criticism where Latina writers of all these groups are considered simultaneously. Our reason for such a grouping was based on the socio-historical realities that unite them on literary and political issues, as evidenced by their appearance in several publications such as *Third Woman, Revista Chicano-Riqueña, Nosotras,* and *Imagine.*

Each part begins with one or two *testimonios*[3] of a representative Latina writer from that group since each writer's concrete experience is the basis for our accurate understanding of the full process of U.S. Latina writing. These *testimonios* also bridge the gap between theory and practice.

Finally, the bibliography of literary works and criticism, although current and up-to-date, will already need revision by the time this book is published, further evidence of what Yvonne Yarbro-Bejarano has called an "effervescence"[4] in this fast-growing field. There is no reason to assume that this level of production will not continue.

There is no one single critical approach to Latina literature, as the essays in this book will demonstrate. As editors, we have not attempted to intrude on the ideological framework of the authors' critical approach. Each essay, therefore, expresses the view of its author independently of the editors. The questions raised by these literary works and their critical readings indicate the need for a legitimized space for Latina writing in literary, academic, and publishing circles. Yet these questions cannot be answered in isolation, for that very isolation contributes to the continued marginalization of the works themselves. With this book, we hope to add to the body of existing criticism that calls for new parameters in both readings of and analytic approaches to Latina writing.

NOTES

1 Luis Valdez, "Introduction," *Aztlán: An Anthology of Mexican American Literature* in *Fiesta in Aztlán: Anthology of Chicano Poetry,* ed. Toni Empringham (Santa Barbara: Capra Press, 1981), 11.

2 This term grew out of the fact that New York was the locus of the greatest number of Puerto Rican immigrants. Yet it should be pointed out that Puerto Ricans live all over the U.S. This is also a term with political implications of a separate identity from the U.S. and from the dominant culture of the Island. Not all Puerto Rican writers in the U.S. have adopted this term. Similarly, not all Mexican American writers will identify themselves as Chicanos, a term with political connotations stemming from the Chicano movement of the sixties.

3   "A verbal message, preferably written in order to reach a wide audience, although it may be oral in origin. Its explicit intention is to provide proof of or truth to a social fact that has already occurred. Its interpretation is guaranteed by the speaker while declaring her/himself actor/witness to the events s/he narrates." Renato Prada Oropeza, "De lo testimonial al testimonio: Notas para un deslinde del discurso-testimonio," in *Ideologies and Literature: Testimonio y Literatura*, ed. René Jara and Hernán Vidal, no. 3: 11.

4   Yvonne Yarbro-Bejarano, Introduction to Helena Maria Viramontes, *The Moths and Other Stories* (Houston: Arte Público Press, 1985), 7.

Acknowledgments

Many people assisted directly and indirectly with the making of this book, and we wish to thank all our friends who provided love, support, and sustenance during the summer of 1987. Although it is not possible to name all those friends and colleagues who offered their time, special mention must be made of those who have helped to render this idea into a concrete reality. We owe our profound thanks to the writers and our colleagues, the contributors to this book, who, on very short notice, dropped other projects in order to participate in this one with original essays. As this book is a direct by-product of the Tenth Symposium on Spanish and Portuguese Bilingualism, we wish to acknowledge Juan Zamora for having enthusiastically endorsed the idea of the panel that gave birth to this book, and to Asunción (Chonín) Horno-Delgado for having organized it. Additional thanks go to Nina Scott for her editing skills and especially to Nancy Saporta Sternbach for assuming an extra burden of work on the text during a number of months when the other editors were unable to complete as much work as they had anticipated. Pauline Collins' initial bibliographical work, unpaid and written on her own time, greatly assisted us in the first stages of the project. Janet Gold's willingness to provide her translation services, notwithstanding our pecuniary situation, is testimony to her dedication and commitment to this subject. R. C. Allen and Alberto Sandoval read earlier drafts of some of the essays, providing careful and insightful comments to the manuscript. Without the critical comments of our Latina students in the Five-College Area, especially those of *La Unidad* and *Nosotras*, this manuscript might have been less grounded in the reality of everyday Latina life. We thank them for sharing their perspective with us and helping us to learn how to read Latina literature. Finally, we owe a special tribute to Eliana Ortega, who first pioneered Latino/a literature in the Five-College Area and has taught it now for almost a decade, and to Nancy Saporta Sternbach, who introduced it to the Smith College curriculum.

The Editors

Toward a Critical Practice
of Latina Writing

At the Threshold of the Unnamed: Latina Literary Discourse in the Eighties

ELIANA ORTEGA AND NANCY SAPORTA STERNBACH

Puerto Rico es una curva
hacia mí misma
. . . . .
ETNAIRIS RIVERA[1]

Y si la patria es una mujer
Then I am also a rebel and a lover of free people
and continue looking for friction in empty spaces
which is the only music I know how to play
SANDRA MARÍA ESTEVES[2]

I am Chicana
And I turn to you,
my sisters of the flesh
I cry to your cities,
Buenos Aires, Caracas, Bogotá,
Lima, Mejico, Rio and Montevideo.
I am Chicana
Our seed was the same,
born of an Indian womb
victims of the rape.
SYLVIA GONZALES[3]

I am what I am I am Boricua as Boricuas come from the isle
of Manhattan
ROSARIO MORALES[4]

Estoy de pie, de frente a mi destino.
De pie junto a mis voces de silencio,
junto a la verde espera que enraíza
y me crece por dentro.
AMELIA DEL CASTILLO[5]

Inside

I am here. (do
you hear me?) hear
me. hear me.
I am here. birthing
(yourself) is
no easy task.
I am here. (pleading)
I am here. (teasing)
I am here. (taunting)
I am here. (simply)
I am here.

ALMA VILLANUEVA[6]

Conventional readings of "minority" literature in the U. S. have traditionally tended to emphasize each ethnic group's search for identity. Such
readings imply that the critic either doubts or questions the existence of a
national or ethnic identity in said literature and, therefore, in its writers. In
our view, rather than this supposed search for identity, the above-cited
poems specify a paradigm of self-affirmation in the Latina writer, a self-
perception and a self-definition that stems from her rootedness in her
heritage and in her historical circumstances. If there is a "search" in this
writing, we contend that it must be defined as a search for the *expression* or
articulation of that identity, but not for her identity itself.

The question of identity arises as a result of the negation, marginalization, and silencing of Latinas' history by official discourse, that is, the
dominant culture's version of history. As we embark upon a reading (and
in some cases, a re-reading) of Latina literature, those silenced voices and
their history must inform our analysis.

In 1848 and in 1898, respectively, part or all of Mexican and Puerto
Rican national territory was confiscated as a result of expansionist policies
of the United States. Since that time, the Latino community has been
documenting that experience through a wide range of literary and artistic
expressions. Although the first recorded accounts tended to be male-
authored, women's participation in all aspects of cultural life has always
been significant, although their published works have appeared much
later than those of their male counterparts. It was more than a century
after the first of these annexations, in 1985, that the first book-length
works of criticism concerning Latinas appeared in print. This essay seeks
to explore the literary, social, political, and economic components that
give rise and shape to a Latina literary discourse. At the same time, we

shall examine the issues related to the reception of this discourse as a cultural product that confronts, questions, and denies the regulatory norms and values of U.S. society.

Not surprisingly, there has been both resistance to and ignorance of this literary discourse from the various institutions of the dominant culture. Even in feminist criticism, where one expects broader paradigms than in the male establishment, little, if any, attention is given to Latina literature. A revision of the most progressive anthologies and criticism in the last five years reveals a failure to include a Latina perspective. This systematic exclusion of a Latina voice makes it impossible even to begin to catalogue those anthologies. It is only possible here to list the works in which the literary production of Latinas is mentioned.[7]

THE LITERARY CANON

The task of creating, promoting, and establishing literary canons is informed and carried out in the academy. Most feminist scholarship, according to certain theorists, takes place in the literary realm,[8] suggesting the importance of feminist criticism in establishing new paradigms for the study of culture in general and literature in particular. Indeed, in the last two decades, feminist literary scholars have engaged in a questioning of established canons and have insisted on the insertion of women's literature into the curriculum. From the academy, then, and as feminists, we approach this essay with a certain trepidation in recognizing the contradictions inherent in the canonization of Latina literature. We resist the notion of becoming "canon-makers," as if by merely wishing it, we could, for this endeavor has implied discriminatory practices toward works of art by anyone who, in Paul Lauter's view, is not white, male, and of the privileged class.[9] Furthermore, once canons are established, the merit of any works they embody is put beyond question.[10] Major critics have recognized the immutable quality of the canon in spite of the changing social circumstances that originally put works in it.[11] As a result, canonized works become subsumed into a static monolith and as a consequence, works by women, people of color, and working classes are rarely considered universal enough to be valued as "good taste" or "great books."

If the United States literary canon, established in the twenties, continues a tradition of including only authors who have access to the literary means of production and distribution, works by Latinas will fall outside these definitions. The question remains whether or not these works, part of a young and dynamic corpus of literature, could benefit from the immutability implied in the canon. Failing to recognize them as worthy of inclusion, however, continues to relegate them to marginal status. Within the legitimization process of any literary work is its recognition by critics in their roles as both anthologists and teachers,[12] or canon-makers. The implicit and explicit contradictions in the canonization of literary works such as these can be treated in one of several ways. Although Eliana Rivero has proposed "different rules and canons for a cultural, literary and artistic manifestation which requires its own parameters of judgement,"[13] the late Joseph Sommers argued adamantly for the establishment of Latino literature in Spanish and English department curricula,[14] a process that implies the incorporation of these works into two canons. In this light, we consider this literature a vital component of the literary history of both the United States and Latin America which should therefore be included in both. We can only theorize about why Latina literature is so rarely taught in either English or Spanish departments in the U.S.[15] What follows, then, is not in a hierarchy of order, but rather some of the contributing factors we signal as interfacing this exclusion.

It has been a common practice to view Latina(o) literature as sociology rather than as a literary production. As such, it has been the object of more ethnological studies than literary ones.[16] When, indeed, it is acknowledged as literature, one of the obstacles cited that impedes its systematic study is the nature of the language in which it is written. Its bilingualism furnishes a pretext for Spanish and English departments to dismiss it; Spanish professors condemn the "mangling" of the language, a phenomenon they grace with the word "Spanglish." Further, as a literature produced in the United States, it is theoretically beyond the purview of the countries they study. This attitude not only ignores the factors that contribute to a Latina(o) presence in the U.S., but also refuses to connect Latinas(os) to the larger Latin American community. English departments, in contrast, consider that bilingualism makes Latina(o) literature inaccessible to non-Spanish speakers. Nevertheless, their failure to acknowledge Latina(o) presence and cultural production reaffirms the concept that U.S. culture, and hence its literature, is only white and middle-class. In both cases, the use of "sub-standard" language is given as reason enough not to consider it legitimate literature. Each would like to relegate it to the other, but neither wants it and neither claims it.

One of its only homes seems to be in Ethnic Studies departments.[17] Yet these same departments, which flourished during and because of the sixties' academic commitment to the Civil Rights movement, are now themselves threatened. With the advent of a national political scene that has veered sharply to conservatism, many of these programs have been debilitated and now find themselves with a precarious academic status. Questioning of the curriculum, the issue of "relevance" that characterized the birth of these departments or programs, and the idealism of that era can be contrasted with the current policy of returning to a "basic" curriculum or a renewed interest in the "classics."[18] In these conservative times, a "minority" literature, which has always experienced difficulties in being "integrated" into both academia and its canons, will find even less acceptance than before. "Cultures of resistance to capitalism,"[19] such as the Latino culture that ardently defies and challenges such a system, will find their works marginalized by that same system.

HISTORY OF LATINAS

Since Latina literature is written primarily within the sociopolitical sphere of the U.S., it is classified as U.S. literature by the Library of Congress. It certainly seems appropriate, therefore, to study it within that context. Nevertheless, it can hardly be dismissed as simply or exclusively North American since it also portrays the reality that forms part of Latin American history. The literary production of Latinas is by women who belong to several different national origins. Because of the tendency to group Latinas(os) as a single entity, it may be useful to examine the historical circumstances that have contributed to their literary presence in the U.S.

With the exception of those Mexicans residing in what was then Mexican territory in 1848, each of these groups has one or several periods of migration to the United States. As a result of the policies of Manifest Destiny, what is today the Southwest of the United States was usurped from Mexico. Mexicans living in this area were offered either citizenship or the "choice" of "returning" to Mexico. For them, there was never a migration. Nevertheless, other Mexicans have crossed the border in the aftermath of the Mexican revolution, during World War II, and at times of extreme economic hardship that continue into the present. Efforts by Chicano historians of the last twenty years as a result of the Chicano movement have helped to create a revisionist view of this imperialist political process.[20]

Puerto Rican immigration is the result of both economic pressures and political status. From the time that Spain ceded Puerto Rico to the U.S. in 1898 at the end of the Spanish-American War, its status as a colony has punctuated the various waves of immigration from the Island, peaking during its times of economic crisis after World Wars I and II, or in times of the U.S. technological expansion in the fifties. In 1952, the establishment of the *Estado Libre Asociado* (Free Associated State or "Commonwealth") was imposed on Puerto Rico. Some historians view this political maneuver as a consequence of the penetration of foreign capital onto the Island, a strategy that, in its origin, was called "Operation Bootstrap."[21] From then on, there has been a constant flux between Puerto Rico and the U.S. that has also been caused by economic need. The same is true of the Dominicans, another Latino group from the Caribbean that share certain social and economic experiences with the Puerto Ricans.

Cuban emigration, a result of the 1959 Cuban Revolution, is the most recent one of these large Latina(o) groups. Unlike previous migrations, this one is not primarily of the working class. Eliana Rivero has noted that some educated exiles cannot be grouped as ethnic minorities but rather constitute a group of " 'dissident intellectuals' [who] . . . belong to the Latin American tradition of 'sojourner writers' " with a long tradition of residence in the U.S.[22] She further distinguishes between what she has called "native Hispanic" and "migrated Hispanic" groups. These Cuban intellectuals, along with other Latin Americans who came here in mid-life, are "migrated Hispanics," in contrast to their children, those born here or who emigrated early in life, and for whom English is the language of their education. The latter would be considered "native Hispanic" in Rivero's schema.

In more recent years, the Central American community, required to emigrate as a result of the conflagration of their homes, falls into the category of migrated Hispanics. They are joined by another group of Latinas(os) producing a literature in the U.S., exiles from all over Latin America, particularly from countries where U.S.-supported military dictatorships forced their departure in the seventies. The majority of those who write are predominantly from middle- and upper-middle-class backgrounds. Some came seeking political asylum; others chose self-exile, as in the case of intellectuals linked to academia. In each of these groups, further distinctions may be perceived on the basis of class and political identity.

Clearly, the discourses emerging from each of these different nationalities and spates of migrations are vitally different. In spite of certain common denominators, the concept of a monolithic "pan-Hispanism,"[23] so vigorously espoused by the government, does not do justice to this diversity. The use of the term "Hispanic" to categorize Latinos distorts the origin and roots of these populations, preventing and excusing the dominant culture from understanding, respecting, and taking into account all the complexities of a culture other than its own. Therefore, the presupposition that all peoples of Latino origin are "Hispanic" fails to take into account the ethnic components of Latin America. Even when that ethnicity is considered, it is presumed to be the only feature of that group; that is, race, class, and gender are not examined. It also assumes that all "Hispanics" are linguistically Spanish-dominant or Hispanic-surnamed, in spite of the fact that many fourth-generation Chicanos, for example, are English-dominant. Another unexamined element is the degree of political participation and an allegiance to political identity as essential components of a people's history. The failure to incorporate all these elements into an analysis of Latino cultures is tantamount to neutralizing these groups, or the dominant culture's tendency to "push to the margins of experience whatever it cannot explain."[24] This lack of comprehension lies behind the concept of the "melting pot"; in order to maintain its cultural, racial, and linguistic hegemony, labeling serves the dominant culture by separating each of these peoples from itself and from each other. The same errors applied to the categorization of Latinos are also apparent in reference to Latina women, who are essentialized as a single nationality, race, and class, as we shall discuss below.

LATINA UNITY

Despite the complexities of Latinas residing in the U.S., their discourse reveals certain commonalities; these voices share an awareness of their insertion into a history of colonization and neo-colonialism. Because they are perceived as "women of color," they have appropriated this term in an act of self-naming with little regard to their actual degree of *mestizaje*,[25] for the term "woman of color" implies an identification with the working class.[26] When they are joined by Latin Americans residing in this country, it is because the latter are willing to identify politically in those terms. In spite of this unity, however, a palpable diversity is apparent with the cultural ingredients of each nationality: Indian, Black, or European, compounded by differing degrees of proficiency in Spanish, education, and class. Nevertheless, as a result of the upward mobility implicit in the educational process, it is frequently in educational institutions where these diverse groups have met and sometimes united on political issues.

The unity of Latinas in the eighties began to be perceived in the collectives and alliances born with the decade, a confluence of the liberation movements of both the United States and Latin America. The collections *Cuentos: Stories by Latinas* and *Compañeras: Latina Lesbians*[27] are good indicators of this process. They unite as storytellers or as participants in oral histories those women who took part in the Civil Rights movement, the Chicano movement, Gay liberation, or the progressive and revolutionary movements of Latin America, and whose views have been informed by the Women's Movements of the U.S. and Latin America. In 1987 we are seeing a virtual blossoming of a discourse by Latinas, or what one of their critics, Tey Diana Rebolledo, has recognized as their "com[ing] into their own."[28] In spite of the emergence of this literature and of the efforts by some critics to keep this work alive, there still prevails the resistance to acknowledge it for the reasons discussed above. In this stage of definition, it appears to us that we are at the threshold of the unnamed.

Accepting the premise that literary production is a part of the historical process, we may conclude that those groups with the longest residency in the U.S. will also have the most fully developed literature and criticism. The one hundred and forty years between the initial literature and book-length works of criticism devoted to women corresponds to what feminist theorists have described as a process of reconstruction of the disciplines. Criticism by and about Chicanas in María Herrera-Sobek's *Beyond Stereotypes: Critical Analysis of Chicana Literature* and in Marta Sánchez' *Chicana Poetry*, both published in 1985, represent the stage that theorists Marilyn Schuster and Susan Van Dyne have called Phase 4 of this reconstruction, or "the study of women on their own terms." Factors such as a longer literary tradition, an earlier insertion of the Chicano population into academia, and the emergence of a significant number of Chicano-managed publishers, both in literary presses and in journals, have contributed to the seeming paradox of a first work of criticism so highly placed. Not coincidentally, however, is the fact that this is the stage Schuster and Van Dyne signal as the first to give attention to race, class, and cultural difference.[29]

Before placing women on their own terms, Phase 4 must be preceded by the previous work of all the other phases completed in order to establish the location of the literature and criticism of Puerto Rican, Cuban, Dominican, and other Latin American women. This has not occurred to date, except as isolated articles published mainly in non-mainstream journals.[30] Both Puerto Ricans and Cubans, then, appear to fit into Phase 2, "the exceptional few," and in some cases Phase 3, a "protest of existing paradigms," characterized by anger and a desire for social justice. Although in majority literature this phase has been known to incorporate the "few and famous," in the Puerto Rican and Cuban examples, the few who write are hardly famous, being a part of a "marginal" literature. When we place Dominicans and Central Americans into the schema they would tend to fall into Phase 1, "a womanless literature."[31] This is not the case, however, with the permanent residents of the Latin American literary establishment who often hold jobs in prestigious academic institutions. Their literature is the object of studies, dissertations, and panels at conferences on a par with, or beyond, the Chicanas. They are in Phase 4 as well.[32] None of these literatures or criticisms would fall into what Schuster and Van Dyne call Phase 6, a "balanced" curriculum with transformed paradigms. Women writers from all these groups can and do form alliances with, and draw on, traditions from those groups established with a longer history, that is, Chicanas and Puertorriqueñas. It is within that alliance that we can begin to speak of a Latina literature.

THE SPECIFICITY OF LATINA WRITING

In spite of what Sommers contends is the hostile climate for minority literature in the late seventies, there has been a virtual explosion of Latina writing in the eighties. The following analysis provides a framework in which to examine this apparent anomaly.

A Latin American example may prove useful as an initial frame of reference. We have observed that the years of the greatest political repression and conservatism are precisely the time of the greatest proliferation of Latin American women's organizations and creativity (such as recent examples in Argentina and Chile prove). The conception and growth of organizations such as labor unions, feminist alliances, mothers' groups, and religious organizations, plus regional, national, and international conferences and *Encuentros*, with subjects as diverse as feminism and women's literature, have taken place in spite of the presence of severe dictatorships. One possible theory about the emergence of women into a public sphere during times of repression stems from the fact that in all instances, normative cultural life had been interrupted or destroyed. As outsiders to that public or cultural sphere, women perceived, and took advantage of, the fractures within the system and began to establish themselves, appropriating a newly-defined space in the public arena. In a similar fashion to their Latin American sisters, Latina writers also found a space within the fractures of the political climate of United States culture of the eighties, when many social programs disappeared, when the radicalism of the sixties movements had been co-opted, and when the dominant Anglo-American culture was empowered more than ever through Reaganism. A substantial number of these authors belonged to that generation of Latinas educated in the sixties, benefiting from the access to higher education available at that time to some minorities. Two decades later, the fruits of that education are the few Latina writers in university faculty positions and a maturation of a literary discourse, formulated by a group who finds it imperative to speak and, thus, define its Self. In the same way that Latin American women profited from the feminist strategy of positioning themselves in those spaces, these writers have also situated themselves in between the cracks of the operative literary systems.

The previous existence of a feminist discourse also encouraged and facilitated the insertion of Latinas into a literary sphere.[33] We postulate that even those Latinas who eschew the term feminist are, to some degree, affected by its significance on both theoretical and practical levels. The critics of Latina literature are primarily women, many of whom have applied feminist theory in their analyses. On the everyday level, many Latinas are involved in communities of women, spaces where they share their written work and experiences with each other. For example, poetry readings featuring a variety of women's voices provide what Yolanda Mancilla has called a "spoken mirror"[34] wherein to reflect and contemplate one another.

In their solidarity with women writers, the "few and famous" men of these Latino groups—editors of journals and publishers of this literature—understood early on the importance and centrality of the Latina voice. In the critical studies of the two major literatures that appeared in 1980, the authors of both books included Latina works.[35] Some Latinas believe that this interest parallels a more general one for women writers, as is evidenced by the honeymoon between women's literature and the publishing industry, and manifested by new publications initially by white women, then Black women, followed by Native American and Asian-American women, and now Latina women. It is not a new phenomenon for editorial decisions to be influenced by the fluctuations of the market according to the laws of supply and demand, incorporating the trends of imposed tastes for the consumption of reading lists with "new and worthy books." In spite of the vicissitudes experienced by women's studies programs and departments in the academy, in the publishing world women's literature is a "commodity," particularly when it is the production of a group often depicted as "exotic." What the academy marginalizes as "other," the market exploits as profit.

In spite of these reasons, and perhaps because of them, a clearly distinguishable discourse of Latinas is continually in the process of constructing itself through its literature. Just as Latina history is varied and yet culturally unified, so, too, is Latina writing. By "Latina writing," we not only mean the literature of Chicanas and Puertorriqueñas but also the literary production of those women from other groups who identify with them and their struggle. This implies that literature by Latina women will depict, but not limit itself to, the reality, experiences, and everyday life of a people whose working-class origin serves as a springboard to understanding cultural contexts. By cultural contexts, we refer to those Alejo Carpentier considered central for an analysis of Latin American literature: racial, economic, ethnic, political, social, chronological, culinary, ideological, luminous, and stylistic.[36] Within those contexts, the Latina writer will often prioritize the lives of women who have, like themselves, carved an existence out of the immediate experience within a woman's space. More specifically, their recognition and celebration of what we call "a matriarchal heritage" can be expressed in remarks such as Ana Castillo's: "We all have our *abuelita* poems."[37] It is not infrequent in Latina discourse to pay tribute to a "long line" of female ancestors.[38]

This woman-context centers not only on the *abuelita*. In Latina writing, the entire extended family of women—mothers, daughters, sisters, aunts, cousins, godmothers, lovers, neighbors, fortune-tellers, *curanderas* (healers), midwives, teachers, and friends, especially girlhood friends— makes up a cast of characters. When we speak of a family of women, we also imply a restructuring of the traditional patriarchal family. Since many of these women are from immigrant or exile families—a condition that often causes the split of a traditional nuclear family—the writers have often displaced a central patriarchal figure, replacing it with a woman-headed and woman-populated household.

Not surprisingly, then, the mother-type appears with great regularity in Latina literature. On the one hand, there is a celebration of, or tribute to, the mother, while on the other, a confrontation of two cultures and two generations frequently takes place on the mother-daughter terrain. In contrast to the mother's messages about the need to learn English and to be educated in the system, there exist her own misgivings about the assimilation process and subsequent loss of cultural values. Regardless of a Latina writer's choice of heterosexual or lesbian relationships, more often than not a cultural conflict is epitomized in relationship to sexuality, especially for second-generation Latinas who came to maturity during the so-called sexual revolution. The act of choosing and practicing her sexuality, and then writing about it, is often perceived as either an assimilation of the Anglo-gringo way of life or a loss of Latina values and culture. The situation is not simply a cultural one but rather a microcosm of all the ways in which culture is constructed dialectically in the intersection with race, class, and gender. Barbara Smith's contributions to the understanding of these cultural intersections in regard to Black women can also be applied to a discussion of Latinas:

> None of us have racial or sexual privilege, almost none of us
> have class privilege, maintaining straightness is our last re-
> sort. Being out, particularly out in print, is a final renunciation

of any claim of the crumbs of tolerance that non-threatening, ladylike black women are sometimes fed.[39]

When Latina theorists such as Marcela Lucero consider the issue, it becomes, in her words, the problematic of the "tri-cultural person in a triple-bind oppression." Consciousness of, and writing about, a Latina Self who is neither an "Anglo woman nor a Chicano man" constitutes counting feminism as one of the three cultures a Latina must take into account as one more structure of ideological domain. For this reason, as late as 1987, the discourses of Latina writers must still confront the false representation of their reality and reveal to themselves who they really are.[40] Rather than being able solely to define themselves, they have found themselves defined by others, particularly by the mass media, in false representations that Carmen Tafolla has called either "left-over stereo-types from old cowboy movies" or "tropical bombshell/s/."[41]

These portrayals, set forth for Latinas by dominant ideology and often labeled "difference," are constantly questioned by them. Latina feminist literature has unmasked the real meaning of such utterances as "vive la différence." What appears to be a celebration of diversity is actu-ally a celebration of what, for Michele Barrett, is "division, oppression, inequality, internalized inferiority for women [*of color* especially] in con-temporary capitalism"[42] (our emphasis). Like "difference," the much-used concept of "diversity" also becomes a euphemism for racism when it is imposed by outsiders, as is evident in such rituals as "Festivals of Diversity," in which women of color are exhibited as exotic dolls in native costume. If diversity is perceived *only* in racial or ethnic terms, without questioning the relations of, and to, power structures, then it also be-comes a celebration of oppression and continues the marginalization of the "diverse" people in question by assigning them a framed space and date in which to perform. Thus, literary and artistic expressions of "di-verse people" can easily be discounted as insignificant, as Lauter has discussed.[43]

Another form of challenge to the official hegemonic ideology evident in Latina literature is the exposure of what Belsey and others have called "its partial truths." For Belsey, this discourse is a "set of omissions, gaps rather than lies, smoothing over contradictions";[44] Latina discourse, on the other hand, fills in the omissions, flourishes between the gaps, and exposes its contradictions. Nowhere is this more evident than in the mass media, where the portrayal of the Latina has tended to be either as an angel or a whore. While white women were also similarly stereotyped. Latinas tend to be depicted in such marginal characterizations as criminals and servants, or their wives and companions. Forced to view themselves only in this manner, Latinas are denied the promised American dream of upward mobility. Their literature has therefore insisted first what they are *not* and then affirmed what they are, who they are, and their place in this historical space.

According to Margo Culley's discussion of women's diaries, it was when the self emerged as a subject that women initiated diary writing; that is, they began to write.[45] Latina inscription into a literary discourse is the result of complex processes that are both historical and personal. According to Belsey, the cultural construction of subjectivity, that is, the consideration of oneself as a speaking subject, is an issue central to feminism.[46] Therefore, in order to decode a Latina discourse, understanding the sociocultural construction of Latina subjectivity is imperative. Belsey posits that bourgeois ideology's function is to construct people as subjects so that they feel they have a free will in moving through the social practices, interactions, and configurations of "reality" when, in fact, such free will is non-existent. Nevertheless, for a subject who is not part of the dominant ideology, construction of the self is a far more complex negotiation. In constructing herself as a subject, a Latina must dismantle the representation of stereotypes of her Self constructed, framed, and projected by the dominant ideology. Because language and images are key factors in the construction of subjectivity—for they permit full access to the socio-symbolic order[47]—the Latina, a bilingual person, will experience a more arduous task, for the self must be inscribed into two symbolic orders: English, the language of the hegemonic culture, and Spanish, the mothertongue. The positioning of this speaking-I into two symbolic orders signifies that she will constantly be negotiating her alliances with one or both of these orders. Since one of those languages is culturally devalued by the Anglo establishment, as is Spanish, the subject may appropriate an imposed negative perception of herself and turn against herself internally, as expressed by Lorna Dee Cervantes: "Let me show you my wounds: my stumbling mind, my / 'excuse me' tongue, and this / nagging preoccupation / with the feeling of not being good enough."[48] At the same time, the Latina subject is engaged in a continual recovery of female cultural subjectivity, as expressed in Rosario Morales' "Birth":

> I wish I were in my own home, not here with his family. Or at
> least with my mother who would touch me, who would know
> how sad I was, how my chest hurt from the iron ache of loss.[49]

As a result of the fact that the speaking-I does configure and articulate herself in two languages, Latina writing is bilingual. Even when, as speakers, they are not totally bilingual, the majority of their discourses are informed by a Spanish mothertongue. For this reason, perhaps, members of the dominant culture familiar with this literature tend to note bilingualism as its most salient feature, disregarding any other characteristics, themes, or messages it may contain.[50] Although it is true that many of these texts are to some degree bilingual, it is also true that a great majority of them are in English and therefore fully accessible to monolingual English speakers. While bilingualism is objectionable in this Latina writing, dominant cultures, on the other hand, can and do appropriate bilingualism for their own purposes to demonstrate "sophistication," internationalism, or as an exaltation of the exotic.

Bilingualism is often devalued in that it is viewed as the product of a schizophrenic mind straddling two cultures. In actuality, it is the linguistic expression of a hybrid reality, or what we interpret as the epitome of cultural *mestizaje*. For Juan Bruce-Novoa, there is a synthesis of two languages into a third that he has called "interlingual."[51] This third language, like other languages, has its own rules of expression, albeit in noncompliance with the grammatical structures or the linguistic codes of the Spanish and English from which it derives. It is the expression of what Efraín Barradas has called a "society in transition."[52]

Yet language is only one feature of Latinas' necessity to continually cross boundaries, question, and often break conventions. Whether Latina writers express themselves in English, Spanish, or interlingual, they live in a society defined by male paradigms; for this reason, Latina literature frequently confronts sexual inequality in both Anglo and Latino cultures. As creators of a literature seeking social and political change, a denunciation of inequality is one of their priorities. What follows often takes the form of a call to action in order to create a more equal relationship for all members of their society. In this regard, some Latinas may express an ambivalence about revealing the sexism evident in their culture, fearing that this will be used as a divisive element against their people. Nevertheless, they refuse to let this be a deterrent to silence them. Thus, while confronting sexism, they also challenge the racism implicit in the dominant culture's perception of Latino men, as is revealed in Tafolla's chapter, "Myths, Machos and the Movies: Will the Real Chicana Please Stand Up?" In this chapter, she examines the new English use of the word *macho*, a derogatory expression signifying "sexist," in contrast to the original Spanish, meaning "male." In concluding that they are false cognates, Tafolla exposes the continual stereotyping of her culture, while at the same time not compromising her feminism.[53]

Other Latina writers who participated in revolutionary or liberation struggles dedicate a significant amount of their writing, especially in poetry, to addressing their men. Some of the works reveal great anger as the speaker rails against the double standard, while others insist that the total liberation of their peoples is—or should be—an essential ingredient in these movements. In this sense, they demanded to be *compañeras*, partners with equal rights and responsibilities, as Bernice Zamora has written in "Notes from a Chicana 'COED'":

> And when I mention
> your G.I. Bill, your
> Ford Fellowship, your
> working wife, your
> three *gabacha guisas*
> then you ask me to
> write your thesis
> you're quick to shout,
> "Don't give that
> Women's Lib trip, mujer
> that only divides us, and we have to work
> together for the *movimiento*
> the *gabacho* is oppressing us!"[54]

Essential here, as in much Latina poetry, is the preoccupation that Latino culture will accuse women involved in their own liberation of imitating Anglo feminists, thereby causing divisiveness among Latinos.

Because Latinas live in a context of having to juxtapose several oppressions simultaneously, articulating their anger and breaking those silences constitute pithy components of their literary discourse. In Luz Vásquez' words, they are "the angry storytellers."[55] At the same time, another constant of their work is their view of themselves as preservers of history, documentors of their own lives, as well as those of their community.

It is possible to envisage the debilitation of the Latina subject as a result of continually having to struggle with tokenism, holding the fabric of many lives together, denouncing injustices in the worlds they inhabit, and eking out a living between the cracks or in the fractures of two systems. Rather, as she affirms her Self, the Latina writer engages in a dialectic and dynamic process, transforming those aggressions directed at her into her own strength, a process that approximates Miguel Algarín's concept of "dusmic" poetry.[56] In Tafolla's words, "the attempted victim of racism, machismo, and other bi-world 'isms' emerges as a whole person."[57] The Latina writer is a good example of how Latina subjectivity, when rooted in her history and collective being, produces a woman whose psyche is intact, contrary to the schizophrenic stereotype imposed on her by mono-cultural Anglo-Americans who cannot, and will not, understand a bi-cultural reality.

She accomplishes this integrity by the act of writing itself. This process constitutes an affirmation, and then definition, of that inter-cultural self and serves as her way of returning to the community those stories they have collectively and historically shared with her, recreating them now into new imaginary worlds. For Algarín, it is the job of the poet to "tell tales of the streets to the streets."[58] Whether Latinas define themselves as poets, novelists, essayists, or playwrights, most see themselves as writing for their people. As women writers, though, the spaces inhabited by their characters have tended not to be exclusively the streets, but rather those traditionally defined as female spaces: kitchens, bedrooms, hospitals, churches, schools, markets, fortune-teller parlors. This is not to say that Latina literature is reduced or restricted only to these places. There is, for example, almost an entire genre of Latina literature concerned with the writer's contact with nature or her immediate environment, whether that be the Southwest desert,[59] New York City,[60] or the Caribbean landscape.[61]

Latina writers have not only occupied new literary spaces, they have also created new genres. The majority of Latina literature has tended to be poetry, but recently they have developed a genre of their own, still to be defined and still emerging, which specifically articulates Latina experience. It draws on the Latina as storyteller and situates the speaking voice in a genre somewhere in between poetry and fiction, blurring the line between the short story and the novel, between conversation and literary discourse.[62]

Undoubtedly, this discourse is informed and articulated by popular culture and the oral tradition that resides within it, both in urban and rural settings. Wherever their community is likely to congregate—neighborhood cafés, factories, barrios, galleries, public poetry readings, street theater—Latinas find this oral tradition embedded in corridos, boleros, salsa, open-air theater, proverbs, cuentos, legends, and myths. In this context, popular culture and bilingualism together provide accessibility to the non-literate Latino public, as well as establishing cultural bonds with a literate Latino reading public. Drawing strongly on oral tradition and its Latin American roots, this literature is consequently both spoken and written. For Michael Taussig, oral tradition stems from the bonding of rurally based cultures, providing them with a language and a narrative for dealing with the violent process of modernization.[63] Oral tradition in

Latina writing, then, continues to provide a context for a narrative when its speakers are faced with the contradictions and inequities of "the American way of life."

Yet orality is not the only tradition on which Latina literature draws. Although the influence from an oral tradition is based solely on a Latin American heritage, a written tradition comes from both cultures. Many Latina writers had access to classics of U.S. literature, but the accessibility of Latin American literature occurred in two specific ways. Certain Latin American writers of international renown were always available as literary models (Neruda, Julia de Burgos, Sor Juana, Rulfo, Castellanos, Martí). But others, those more recently published and translated authors of the sixties whose international recognition coincided with the university education of Latina writers, put them in touch with an entire Latin American tradition. Since almost all of these writers were men, Latina authors would have to wait until the seventies and eighties to discover Latin American women writers.[64]

If it is possible to speak of a tradition in this current wave of Latino writing within the last twenty years, it is because of the existence of two other bodies of literature that "spoke their language" and articulated "minority" experiences of the U.S. One was the poetic trajectory of the first generation of the so-called Chicano Renaissance, which provided a cultural context for Latina work. The other was the discourse of U.S. women writers, most especially Black writers, which provided a female context. To this day, Latina writers may express a debt to Black women writers.[65]

As all of these processes of historical, political, artistic, cultural, literary, and feminist consciousness indicate, the Latina writer is a woman who, first and foremost, recognizes her historical context as a Latina in the U.S. in the conflictive and often threatening reality of the eighties. Her works, then, reveal a gamut of richness incorporating and comprising, acknowledging and transforming her interlingual reality, her intertextuality, and her message of uncompromising struggle into a discourse that is at once woman-affirming, life-affirming, and mestizaje-affirming.

NOTES

1   Etnairis Rivera, *Wydondequiera* (Río Piedras, P.R.: Editorial Puerto, 1974), 11. "Puerto Rico is a curve / toward me" (our translation). Unless otherwise specified, all translations are our own.

2   Sandra María Esteves, "From the Commonweath," cited in Margarite Fernández-Olmos, "From the Metropolis: Puerto Rican Women Poets and the Immi-

gration Experience," *Third Woman* 1, no. 2 (1982): 47 (And if our country is a woman).

3 Sylvia Gonzales, "I am Chicana," in *The Third Woman: Minority Women Writers of the United States*, ed. Dexter Fisher (Boston: Houghton Mifflin, 1980), 421.

4 Rosario Morales, *Getting Home Alive* (Ithaca, N.Y.: Firebrand Books, 1986), 138.

5 "I am standing, facing my destiny. / Standing next to my voices of silence, / next to the green waiting that roots / me and grows inside of me." Amelia del Castillo, "Cara al viento," *Third Woman* 1, no. 2 (1982): 28.

6 Alma Villanueva," Mother, May I?," cited in Marta Esther Sánchez, *Contemporary Chicana Poetry: A Critical Approach to an Emerging Literature* (Berkeley: University of California Press, 1985), 54–55.

7 Dexter Fisher's anthology, *The Third Woman: Minority Women Writers of the United States* (Boston: Houghton Mifflin, 1980), was the first example of the inclusion of Latinas though it contains only Chicanas. Gloria Anzaldúa and Cherríe Moraga's *This Bridge Called My Back* (Watertown, Mass.: Persephone Press, 1981) united writings by women of color who defined themselves as radical, but did not limit their inclusion only to Latinas. In the late seventies and early eighties Latino journals such as *Revista Chicano-Riqueña, De Colores,* and *La Palabra* began devoting special issues to women's literature. A special feminist edition of *Imagine: International Poetry Journal*, vol. 2, no. 1, was published during the summer of 1985. Journals of mainstream feminism such as *Calyx* devoted an issue to the writing of Native American and Latina women (vol. 8, no. 2) in the spring of 1984. *Heresies* devoted a special issue to racism in the Fall of 1982 (vol. 15). *Frontiers* had a special issue called "Chicanas in the National Landscape," vol. 5, no. 2 (Summer 1980). More recently, the journal *Connexions: An International Women's Quarterly* called their Fall 1986/Winter 1987 issue, no. 22, "Facets of Racism"; also, *For Alma Mater*, ed. Paula Treichler, Cheris Kramarae, and Beth Safford (Urbana and Chicago: University of Illinois Press, 1985), included two articles by Chicanas. Yet the only journal devoted exclusively to Latina literature is *Third Woman*, published by Chicano-Riqueño Studies at Indiana University. Because all this literature belongs to the dynamic, forceful processes of the present, any bibliographies, however useful, will need revision, for this is a literature that grows almost on a daily basis.

8 Michele Barrett, "Ideology and the cultural production of gender," in *Feminist Criticism and Social Change: Sex, Class and Race in Literature and Culture*, ed. Judith Newton and Deborah Rosenfelt (New York and London: Methuen, 1985), 65.

9 Paul Lauter, "Race and gender in the shaping of the American literary canon: A case study from the twenties," in *Feminist Criticism*, 24ff.

10 Annette Kolodny, "Dancing through the Minefield: Some Observations on the Theory, Practice and Politics of a Feminist Literary Criticism," *Feminist Studies* 6 (Spring 1980): 1–25 (esp. p. 8).

11 Lauter, "Race and Gender," 21.

12 Ibid., 37.

13 Eliana Rivero, in reference to Chicano literature in particular, calls for these new parameters because "Chicano reality has its own signifiers as well as its

particular development of minority culture, literature and art within the context of a majority society which does not speak its language. It does not share (nor understand) its past, and to be frank, is not overly enthusiastic about giving a place to a racial group which is ethnically and 'socially' different within its privileged space," "Escritura chicana: La mujer," *La Palabra* 2, no. 2 (Fall 1980): 3.

14   Joseph Sommers, "From the Critical Premise to the Product: Critical Modes and their Applications to a Chicano Literary Text," *The New Scholar* 6 (1977): 62.

15   By *Latina*, we mean a woman of Latin American origin or descent who is permanently residing in the United States. We are building upon Juan Bruce-Novoa's definition of *Chicano* elaborated in *Chicano Authors: Inquiry by Interview* (Austin: University of Texas Press, 1980), 3.

16   Alma Gómez, "By Word of Mouth," in *Cuentos: Stories by Latinas*, ed. Cherríe Moraga, Alma Gómez, and Mariana Romo-Carmona (New York: Kitchen Table Press, 1983), x; and Efraín Barradas and Rafael Rodríguez, *Herejes y mitificadores: Muestra de poesía puertorriqueña en los estados unidos* (Río Piedras: Huracán, 1980), 11.

17   Of course there are both Spanish departments (our own, for example) and English departments which sometimes teach Latina(o) literature. Yet for the most part it continues to remain marginalized.

18   Sommers, "From the Critical Premise," 53, and Margaret L. Andersen, "Changing the Curriculum in Higher Education," *Signs: Journal of Women and Culture in Society* 12, no. 2 (Winter 1987): 232, for a discussion of this phenomenon with reference to women's studies.

19   Jean Franco, "Trends and Priorities for Research on Latin American Literature," *Ideologies and Literature* 4, no. 16 (May-June 1983): 117.

20   For example, Octavio Ignacio Romano-V., ed. *Voices: Readings from El Grito, A Journal of Contemporary Mexican American Thought* (Berkeley: Quinto Sol, 1973); Arnulfo D. Trejo, ed., *The Chicanos As We See Ourselves* (Tucson: University of Arizona Press, 1979); Mario T. García, "Internal Colonialism: A Political Essay," *Revista Chicano-Riqueña* 6, no. 3 (1978). Luis Valdez' *Zoot Suit* is another example of a reversal of an Anglo-American account of the Zoot Suit Riots.

21   For example, Francesco Cordasco and Eugene Bucchioni, *The Puerto Rican Experience: A Sociological Sourcebook* (Totowa, N.J.: Littlefield, Adams and Company, 1973).

22   Eliana S. Rivero, "Hispanic Literature in the United States: Self-Image and Conflict," *Revista Chicano-Riqueña* 13, nos. 3–4 (Fall-Winter 1985): 173–92 (esp. p. 186).

23   The term "pan-hispanic" was coined by Bruce-Novoa in *Chicano Authors*, 8.

24   Catharine Belsey, "Constructing the subject: deconstructing the text," in *Feminist Criticism*, 63.

25   Literally the cross between two races, two cultures. Originally used exclusively in reference to the cross between Spaniards and Indians.

26   Testimony of Cherríe Moraga in "Desde la entraña del monstruo: Voces 'hispanas' en EE.UU.," in *La sartén por el mango*, ed. Patricia González and Eliana

Ortega (Río Piedras, P.R.: Huracán, 1984), 166. Moraga claims that the rapprochement with the Latin American women will occur when the latter is "willing to also say, 'we are people of *color*.'"

27 Juanita Ramos, ed., *Compañeras: Latina Lesbians* (New York: Latina Lesbian History Project, 1987).

28 Tey Diana Rebolledo, "The Maturing of Chicana Poetry: The Quiet Revolution of the 1980s," in *For Alma Mater: Theory and Practice in Feminist Scholarship*, ed. Paula Treichler, Cheris Kramarae, and Beth Stafford (Urbana: University of Illinois Press, 1985), 145.

29 Marilyn Schuster and Susan Van Dyne, "Stages of Curriculum Transformation," in *Women's Place in the Academy: Transforming the Liberal Arts Curriculum* (Totowa, N.J.: Rowman and Allanheld, 1985), 17.

30 Efraín Barradas, "Conciencia Femenina, Conciencia Social: La Voz Poética de Sandra María Esteves," *Third Woman* 1, no. 2 (1982): 31–34; "De lejos en sueños verla: Visión mítica de Puerto Rico en la poesía nuyorican," *Revista Chicano-Riqueña* 8, no. 4 (1979): 46–56; Margarite Fernández-Olmos, "From the Metropolis: Puerto Rican Women Poets and the Immigration Experience," *Third Woman* 1, no. 2 (1982): 40–51; Eliana Ortega, *La sartén por el mango*, 163–69. Luz María Umpierre's "De la Protesta a la Creación—Una Nueva Visión de la Mujer Puertorriqueña en la Poesía" (*Imagine: International Chicano Poetry Journal* 2, no. 1 [Summer 1985]: 134–42) deals with poets from the Island; also see her article, "La ansiedad de la influencia en Sandra María Esteves y Marjorie Agosín," in *Revista Chicano-Riqueña* 11, nos. 3–4 (1983), in a special issue on women edited by Evangelina Vigil entitled *Woman of Her Word: Hispanic Women Writers;* Edna Acosta-Belén, "Conversations with Nicholasa Mohr," *Revista Chicano-Riqueña* 7, no. 2 (1980): 35–42; Juan Flores, "Back Down these Mean Streets: Introducing Nicholasa Mohr and Louis Reyes Rivera," *Revista Chicano-Riqueña*, pp. 51–56 of the same issue; Julia Ortiz Griffin, "The Puerto Rican Woman in René Marqués' Drama," *Revista Chicano-Riqueña*, 11, nos. 3–4 (1983): 169–79. Although there are other studies on the Nuyorican poetic experience, these tend to group Nuyoricans as a whole without any distinction of gender. Critical studies specifically on women are few.

31 Andersen, "Changing the Curriculum," 235.

32 We may include in this category writers such as Rosario Ferré, Lucía Guerra, Sylvia Molloy, Alicia Partony, and Eliana Rivero, to name a few.

33 Marta Cotera has written: "Chicanas are in step with changes occurring all over the world concerning the status of women . . . [but are not] swayed by foreign ideologies," in *The Chicana Feminist* (Austin: Information Systems Development, 1977), 22.

34 Yolanda Mancilla, "Dream for *"Tía Cuca,"* Bearing Witness/Sobreviviendo, *Calyx: A Journal of Art and Literature by Women* 8, no. 2 (Spring 1984): 11.

35 Efraín Barradas and Rafael Rodríguez, *Herejes y mitificadores*, and Juan Bruce-Novoa, *Chicano Poetry: A Response to Chaos* (Austin: University of Texas Press, 1982).

36 César Leante, in an interview with Alejo Carpentier, in "Confesiones sencillos de un escritor barroco," *Homenaje a Alejo Carpentier* (New York: Las Américas Publishing Company, 1970), 13–31.

37   Ana Castillo, Class Lecture, Smith College, April 17, 1987. Also see Tey Diana Rebolledo, "Abuelitas: Mythology and Integration in Chicana Literature," *Revista Chicano-Riqueña* 11, nos. 3–4 (1983): 148–58, a special issue entitled *Woman of Her Word: Hispanic Women Write*, edited by Evangelina Vigil.

38   Lorna Dee Cervantes, *Emplumada* (Pittsburgh: University of Pittsburgh Press, 1981) for "a long line of eloquent illiterates"; Cherríe Moraga, "A Long Line of Vendidas," in *Loving in the War Years* (Boston: South End Press, 1983) and Aurora Levins Morales, "Immigrants," in *Getting Home Alive* (Ithaca, N.Y.: Firebrand Books, 1986).

39   Barbara Smith, "Toward a black feminist criticism," in *Feminist Criticism*, 15.

40   Marcela Trujillo, "Resources for the Chicana Feminist Scholar," in *For Alma Mater*, 393–94.

41   Carmen Tafolla, *To Split a Human: Mitos, Machos y la Mujer Chicana* (San Antonio: Mexican American Cultural Center, 1985), 34, 44.

42   Barrett, "Ideology and the cultural," 83.

43   Lauter, "Race and Gender," 33.

44   Belsey, "Constructing the subject," 46.

45   Margo Culley, ed., Introduction to *A Day at a Time: The Diary Literature of American Women from 1764 to the Present* (New York: The Feminist Press, 1985), 3.

46   Belsey, "Constructing the subject," 44.

47   Emile Benveniste, *Problems in General Linguistics* (Miami: University of Miami Press, 1971), cited in Belsey, "Constructing the subject," 47.

48   Lorna Dee Cervantes, "Poem for the Young White Man Who Asked Me How I, An Intelligent, Well-Read Person, Could Believe in the War Between Races," in *Emplumada* (Pittsburgh: University of Pittsburgh Press, 1981), 36.

49   Rosario Morales, *Getting Home Alive*, 100.

50   Interview with Cherríe Moraga, April 17, 1987.

51   Juan Bruce-Novoa, *Chicano Authors: Inquiry by Interview*, 29.

52   Efraín Barradas, *Herejes y mitificadores*, 28.

53   Tafolla, *To Split a Human*, 36.

54   Bernice Zamora, "Notes from a Chicana 'COED,'" *Caracol* 3 (1977):19, cited in Sánchez, *Contemporary Chicana Poetry* 232. The term *gabacho* refers to Anglos and Anglo culture, *guisa* means woman, and *movimiento* is movement.

55   Radio Production, "Inside the Monster," produced by Nicholasa Mohr, National Public Radio, 1981.

56   Miguel Algarín and Miguel Piñero, *Nuyorican Poetry: An Anthology of Puerto Rican Words and Feelings* (New York: William Morrow and Co., 1975), 129.

57   Tafolla, *To Split a Human*, back cover.

58   Algarín and Piñero, *Nuyorican Poetry*, 10.

59   Pat Mora, *Chants* (Houston: Arte Público Press, 1984, 1985).

60   Sandra María Esteves, *Yerbabuena* (Greenfield, N.Y.: Greenfield Review Press, 1980).

61   Aurora Levins Morales and Rosario Morales, *Getting Home Alive* (Ithaca, N.Y.: Firebrand Books, 1986).

62   Ibid.; Sandra Cisneros, *The House on Mango Street* (Houston: Arte Público Press, 1985); Denise Chávez, *The Last of the Menu Girls* (Houston: Arte Público Press, 1986).

63   Franco, "Trends and Priorities," 117.

64   There are also problems with a too-facile identification with Latin American women writers, as the editors of *Cuentos* have written: "The question remains . . . to what extent can most Latin American women writers be considered our literary legacy when so many, like their male counterparts, are at least functionally middle-class, ostensibly white, and write from a male-identified perspective" (p. viii).

65   The formation of Kitchen Table Women of Color Press attests to this coalition.

Part I. Chicanas

Heat and Rain

(Testimonio)

DENISE CHÁVEZ

My first childhood recollection is of heat. Perhaps because I was born in the middle of August in Southern New Mexico, I have always felt the burningly beautiful intensity of my dry, impenetrable land. Land not often relieved by the rain—that wet, cleansing, and blessed catharsis. I remember as a little girl sitting waist–deep in the cool, grassy water that had been channeled from the irrigation ditch behind our house. The heat, then the rain, and the water were my first friends.

My other friend was my imagination that invented an extended family of loving, congenial spirits who wandered with me nighttimes in my dreams—into the other worlds I inhabited as vividly and completely as I did my own waking existence as middle daughter in a family of three girls, one mother, Delfina Rede Faver Chávez, a teacher divorced by my father, E. E. "Chano" Chávez, one lawyer, long gone.

These friendships with spirits were real to me, and still are. The spirits were voices of people, people I'd known and not known, feelings I felt and couldn't at that time conceive of feeling. I had no way to explain my creative world to anyone, could not even explain it to myself. All I know is that my life was rich and deep and full of wonder.

I always felt advanced for my age, somehow different. I always thought I *thought* more than people my own age. My imagination was a friend at first, and later a lover, a guide, a spirit teacher.

I grew up in a house of women. That is why I often write about women, women who are without men. My father divorced us early on; he was a brilliant lawyer, but an alcoholic. My mother was incredibly intelligent, with a keen curiosity and love of life and people. Their minds were

27

compatible, their spirits and hearts were not. I grew up knowing separation as a quality of life—and this sorrow went hand in hand with extensions—for despite the fact my parents were apart, both families were an everpresent part of my life. So I grew up solitary in the midst of noise, a quality I didn't know then was essential to my work as a writer.

People always ask me how and when I started writing. The answer never varies. From an early age I kept diaries, some with locks, locks I kept losing or misplacing, others with no locks. I'm sure my mother read my diary. I'm positive my younger sister did.

DIARY
A Page a Day for 1958

New Year's Day, Wednesday January 1, 1958

1st Day—364 Days to Follow
Dear Diary,

Today is New Year and the old year is gone and the new one here. Today school starts. I can't wait to go.

Sunday June 15, 1958

166th Day—199 Days to Follow
Dear Diary,

Today I didn't go to Mass, I must tell the priest my sin. I'm not to happy about it.

Friday, August 15, 1958

227th Day—138 Days to Follow
Dear Diary,

Today is my birthday. I am ten in a few years I'll be twenty. Boy oh boy ten years old

Tuesday, November 11, 1958

315 Day—50 Days to Follow
Dear Diary,

School was fun, But I forgot to do my homework. I'm praying for daddy to come home, I hope so. He did. Thank god. Bless us all.

Thursday, November 20, 1958

324th Day—41 Days to Follow
Dear Diary,

I did not go to school today because we stayed home with Mama. She is heart sick (broken heart) She feels bad, I hope she gets well. I missed school but I loved to stay home. You know why! Don't you?

All wrong. I did go to school. drat.

Somehow, looking back on myself in these diary entries, I am aware of myself, even then, as an observer of life. Without my diaries, I don't think I'd ever have become a writer. I now see that 1958 was a hard year, the breakup of my parents' marriage, a devastating time for all of us. I see the order I began to put into my life, the need to account for, evaluate, assess. Time was of significance, my life of value. Religion was important then as spirituality is to me now. I wanted to grow up so badly, to be an adult, to understand. My life was rich then, I see that too, with much experience that was to feed me for years to come.

I see that I was not a good student, ever. I rarely did homework. I would study in bed, usually lying down, waking up the next morning, the light on, in my clothes, very hot and clammy, dry mouthed, Mother yelling for me to wake up, to find the History or Math book mashed into my face. I would race to school, then fly back to enter the latest news into my diary. Painful accounts were entered, then torn. Did *I* tear them, and if not me, who? My mother, my sister? Or that other girl, the me who wanted to be happy? I note with interest my early stream of consciousness technique (not a technique then), my disinterest in chronological time (critics take note), I see the roots of my still poor grammar and spelling, and observe the time I begin to sign my writing—Denise. The writing had become a statement for someone other than me. What I had to say, suddenly, to me "mattered."

I see also the many gaps between entries, and that too is of significance. I see that I wrote on sad, happy, elated, and depressed days. The regular days were entry–less. Writing was a gauge of my personal life. It was a record of my physical, spiritual, and emotional ups and downs. I enjoyed writing, always have, the actual physical movement of pen or pencil across a piece of paper. I enjoyed/enjoy the mind-eye-to-hand-acting-out-delineation of internalness. I practiced my handwriting constantly:

I see now that I was training myself unconsciously to "write" efficiently, quickly. A sort of "scales" for the writing self/hand. Rolling letters, moving them through space, limbering up mechanically so that later I could use my hand like a tool, limbered, unrestrained. I still find myself practicing the alphabet on random sheets of paper, testing letter style, still looking for a more effective fluid line. Much flight time on the white canvas of my constantly emerging movement toward my work as a writer. I didn't know it then. I didn't know it when I got a notebook and started copying other people's poems, songs. But this was later, because first there were books, books, and more books to read, like my favorite childhood book called *Poems of Childhood* by Eugene Field, with scary-wonderful poems like "Seein' Things."

I was a voracious reader. Anything. Everything. I went on binges. My mother would hide our books in the summertime so we would help her with the housework. My sister would lock herself in the bathroom with a book, heedless of my mother's cries. It never occurred to me to do that. Everyday my book would be missing, I'd find it, read awhile, then find it missing. It went on like that. I read fairy tales. Mysteries. Nancy Drew. You name it. Later on it was Ian Fleming's James Bond, D. H. Lawrence, Thomas Mann, Thomas Wolfe, Chekhov, Eugene O'Neill, Samuel Beckett. Now it's the *Enquirer*. I love the scandal sheets and movie mags and bowling and soap operas in the middle of the day, and so much of what everyone else considers pedestrian, sub-mainstream culture. Director John Waters calls Baltimore the Hairdo capital of the world. New Mexico/Texas was and is Character Capital of the Universe. Unbelievable stories, lives. I have always been a talker, friendly to strangers, and so invariably people tell me about their lives. It's a gift to listen to so many of these stories. The *Enquirer* has nothing over New Mexico/Texas or the world I see every day!

But this sense of wonder came early. I began to copy my favorite passages, poems. One of the earliest was a cowboy song. I loved the rhythm. Sang it to myself. Later on I copied Gibran and the Black poets, wrote angry poems to the nuns at Madonna High School, where I attended school for four years, poems they refused to publish in the *Mantle*, the school newspaper. Once, as a joke, I invented a quote for the "Quote of the Day" for World Literature class: "Christmas is the flowing of honey on a mound of cold, white snow." Mrs. Baker, lovely, frail, intelligent, and wispy-haired, loved it. I didn't know what the hell it meant. I was playing the rebellious know-it-all, making up my own poems and quotes. I didn't know writing was becoming a facile thing. Then it was just a joke. The other day I heard a writer say, "All those lies, writing all those lies—I love it!" I didn't say anything. For me, writing is no longer a facile joke, a prank to be played on a well-meaning and unsuspecting reader, nor is it a lie. I have said to writers I have taught: Don't lie. And to myself: You may lie in other things, but never in this. It's a sacred covenant I have with myself. Honesty. And no meanness. Sometimes it's been hard. Lies always surface, don't you know?

I never thought of lying in my writing. It would have been like hiding in the bathroom to read.

I could never lie to those voices, to those spirits, to those voices I hear clearly. Voices like my mother, who always spoke in Spanish, or my father, who mostly spoke in English. Mother grew up in West Texas, moved to New Mexico as a widow and met and married my father. My father, as a child, was punished for speaking Spanish in the school yard. He decided to beat the Anglos at their game. He went and got a law degree from Georgetown during the Depression. And he became, in his mind, more Anglo than those Anglos who had punished him. I remember my mother saying, "I never think of your father as Mexican." My mother was, though, in her heart and soul. She studied in Mexico for thirteen summers, was a student of Diego Rivera. She'd been widowed for nine years, all that time wearing black, when she met my father, just returned from the Big City. Both my parents were very intelligent, perceptive, sensitive people. My mother's grandparents were the first Spanish-speaking graduates of Sul Ross State College in West Texas. All of them became teachers. Both my grandfathers were miners, all-around men, carpenters, teamsters, fixer-uppers, workers with their hands. They used their brains and their hands to support their large families. The women were independent, creative, and did most of the child-rearing, alone. The Chávez men are painters now, artists with canvas and paint, or architects, builders of some kind. The Rede Family (my mother's clan) are educators, fighters for human rights, communicators, and believers in the equality of all people.

I grew up between and in the middle of two languages, Spanish and English, speaking my own as a defense. My mother always said I "made up words." Speaking Spanish to the Redes or English to the get-ahead Chávezes and Spanish to the traditional Chávezes and English to my Rede cousins was all taken in stride. We went back and forth, back and forth. My mother taught Spanish and she was always correcting, in any language. When I asked how to spell a word, she would tell me to sound out the syllables, and to find a dictionary. "There she goes again," I'd think, "teacher-ing me." I was lazy, still am. My English needs work and so does my Spanish. I can't spell, punctuate or understand the possessive. My multiplication is a mess and I can't tell time. I was absent the day we kids learned the 7, 8, and 9 multiplication tables. I have gaps—huge ones. But I've taught myself what little grammar I know, what math I know, and how to type. I can take any vacuum cleaner apart and fix it and my pen hand is very fast at the draw. I really write according to what I hear— sometimes English, sometimes Spanish, sometimes both. As a writer, I have tried to capture as clearly as I am able *voices*, intonation, inflection, mood, timbre, pitch. I write about characters, not treatises, about life, not make-believe worlds. If my characters don't work, I will go back and make them work. Without them, robust and in the living flesh, there is no story for me. Readers should stop looking for traditional stories, ABC. Writing, to me, is an assemblage of parts, a phrase here, an image there, part of a dialogue.

Suddenly it occurs to me that Jesusita Real, the not-so-mousy spinster in my play, *Novenas Narrativas*, should wear green tennis shoes, and so I add them to the script. When she finally does walk, it will be in comfort, with support from the ground up. I work with my characters in the way an actress or actor assumes a role, slowly, carefully, with attention to physical, emotional, and spiritual detail. I may read the material out loud, speak it into a tape recorder, play it back, rewrite it, and then tape it again. My years as a theatre person have helped me immensely. I have acted, directed, and written for the theatre. I have done props, hung lights, performed for all types of audiences, young, old, handicapped, drunk, aging, for prisoners, in Spanish and English. My work has always been for alternative groups, the people who never get much, for the poor, the forgotten. My writing as well is about the off-off Main street type of characters. My short stories are really scenes and I come from the tradition of the traveling *cuentista*. I believe stories should captivate, delight, move, inspire, and be downright funny, in a way. The "in a way" is what I try to do with all my heart. But always, I go back to the characters and their voices. I see them: flat feet, lagañas, lonjas, lumps, spider veins, and all. From the feet up and back down and around the other side. And I love them. Dearly. But I don't excuse them nor will I lie for them.

I write for you. And me. And Jesusita with the green tennies, spinster owner of Rael's Tiendita de Abarrotes, active member of the Third Order of St. Francis, and for the people: Anglo, Hispanic, Black, you name it: anybody out there who doesn't know Jesusita is alive, inside her little store, swatting flies, and wondering aloud about Prudencio Sifuentes, the only man who asked her to marry him.

I write for the viejitas at the Save-And-Gain in black scarves, for the tall blond man testing tomatoes, for the Vietnamese cashier, and for the hot dog man outside the electric door. For me, it is a joy to carry my bag full of stories.

Naturally I write about what I know, who I am. New Mexico. Texas. Chicanismo. Latinismo. Americanismo. Womanismo. Mujerotismo. Peopleismo. Worldismo. Peaceismo. Loveismo.

Writing has been my heat, my accounting, my trying to understand; and rain has been my prayer for peace, for love, and mercy. August in Southern New Mexico is very hot, for many, unbearable. It has been my blessing in this life of mine to share that heat. And to remember the rain.

Las Cruces, New Mexico
Summer 1987

"Nopalitos": The Making of Fiction

(Testimonio)

HELENA MARIA VIRAMONTES

Fiction is my jugular. For me it is a great consolation to know that what-ever miserable things happen in my lifetime, goodness will inevitably result because I will write about it. There is strength in this when none is left in the soul.

I was born and raised in the U.S., East L.A., Califas, to be more exact, on First Street not too far from Whittier Blvd., close enough to enable me to see the smoke from the Chicano Moratorium riots. I come from a family of eleven, six sisters and three brothers, but the family always extended its couch or floor to whomever stopped at our house with nowhere else to go. As a result, a variety of people came to live with us. Former boyfriends of my sisters who were thrown or pushed out of their own homes, friends who stayed the night but never left, relatives who crossed the border and stayed until enough was saved. Through all this I remember two things well: first, the late night kitchen meetings where everyone talked and laughed in low voices, played cards, talked of loneliness, plans for the future, of loves lost or won. I heard men cry, drunken stories, women laughing. It was fascinating to listen in the dark, peek into the moments of their lives. For me, it seemed like a dream to wake up at midnight and hear the voices and listen to the soft music, see the light under the door. This was adulthood and I yearned to one day be the one on the other side of that door.

Little did I realize that this is the stuff good fiction is made of: the stories, the fascination of the subject matter, capturing the moments and fleeing with them like a thief or lover. I began my apprenticeship without even knowing it.

The other thing I remember is my mother. Her relentless energy. She must have been tired a good part of her life and yet she had to keep going and going and going. I also remember her total kindness, the way a sad story made her cry, the way she always found room somehow in an already-crowded household for those with the sad stories. The nights she would stay up, a small black and white T.V. blaring, waiting for the girls to come home. The mornings she would get up, KWKW Spanish radio low, making the big stack of tortillas for the morning breakfast.

These two things, love of stories and love of my mother, or all that seemed female in our household, influenced me to such an extent that it became an unconscious part of me, so unconscious that I didn't realize it until just moments ago. In fact, the first story that I wrote, titled "Requiem for the Poor," opened with my mother awaking to make breakfast. To think: she was the first image in my mind, my heart, my hand. Naturally.

If my mother was the fiber that held a family together, it was my father who kept snapping it with his oppressive cruelty. With virtually no education, stressed with the responsibility of supporting such a large family, he worked as a hod carrier—a carrier of cement in construction. He drank, and was mean. Impatient, screaming a lot of the time, temper tantrums, we were often trembling in his presence. If my mother showed all that is good in being female, my father showed all that is bad in being male. I'm only now understanding the depth of this conclusion, and am making a serious effort to erase this black and white. See the good and bad in both sexes. That's the power of imagination, peeking beyond the fence of your personal reality and seeing the possibilities thereafter.

A basic problem for any writer is time. I lament the lack of time. As I pass my shelves of books, I think, these are books I will never read; or as my notebooks pile up, spilling over with plots, characters, great and moving sentences, I think, these are the words that will never find a story. Ideally, it would be bliss to manipulate the economic conditions of our lives and thus free our minds, our hands, to write. But there is no denying that this is a privilege limited to a certain sex, race, and class. The only bad thing about privilege, Virginia Woolf wrote (I'm paraphrasing from Tillie Olsen) was that not every one could have it.

How does one solve the problem of time? Fortunately, we mujeres are an inventive people. My mother, for example, faced the challenge of feeding eleven people every evening. Time and time again, I saw her cut four pork chops, add this and that and this, pour water, and miraculously feed all of us with a tasty guiso. Or the nopales she grew, cleaned, diced, scrambled with eggs, or meat, or chile, or really mixed with anything her budget could afford, and we had such a variety of tasty dishes!

I have never been able to match her nopales, but I have inherited her capacity for invention. I myself invent time by first conjuring up the voices and spirits of the women living under brutal repressive regimes. In the light of their reality, my struggles for a few hours of silence seem like such a petty problem. I am humbled, and no sooner do I think of their courage that I find my space on the kitchen table, my time long after midnight and before the start of the children's hectic morning. Because I want to do justice to their voices. To tell these women, in my own gentle way, that I will fight for them, that they provide me with my own source of humanity. That I love them, their children. Once seen in this perspective, the lack of sleep is more of an inconvenience than a sacrifice.

What little time we do invent we guard like our children. Interruption is a fact in our lives and is as common as pennies. Solely because we are women. A man who aspires to write is sanctioned by society. It is an acceptable and noble endeavor. As for us, writing is seen as a hobby we do after all our responsibilities are fulfilled. Nay, to write while the baby is crying is a crime punishable by guilt. Guilt is our Achilles' heel. Thus the work of the mujer suffers immensely, for the leisure of returning to her material, to rework it, polish it, is almost impossible. Because phones will ring, children will cry, or mothers will ask for favors. My mother, it seemed for a time, believed me to be half-baked for wanting desperately to write. It was inconceivable to her that I spent mornings scratching a sharpened pencil against paper. She would stand and look over my shoulder, try to read a paragraph or two, and seeing that I was simply wasting my time staring into space, she'd ask me to go get some tortillas, or could you vacuum the living room, maybe water the plants outside? After turning her away with a harsh no, guilt would engulf me like a blob, and although I hated myself for doing it, there I was, once again, holding a garden hose, watering her roses.

We must come to understand that stifling a woman's imagination is too costly a price to pay for servitude. The world would be void of any depth or true comprehension if we were not allowed to exercise our imaginations. We must challenge those beliefs which oppress us within our family, our culture, in addition to those in the dominant culture.

Family ties are fierce. Especially for mujeres. We are raised to care for. We are raised to stick together, for the family unit is our only source of safety. Outside our home there lies a dominant culture that is foreign to us, isolates us, and labels us illegal alien. But what may be seen as a nurturing, close unit, may also become suffocating, manipulative, and sadly victimizing. As we slowly examine our own existence in and out of these cultures, we are breaking stereotypes, reinventing traditions for our own daughters and sons.

What a courageous task! In the past, we have been labeled as the weaker sex, and it is logical to assume that we are of weaker minds as well. As women, we have learned to listen, rather than speak, causing us, historically, to join with others who maintain we have nothing to say. Only now we are discovering that we do. And those who do not seem interested in knowing our voices are just plain foolish. To limit their knowledge of people, places, cultures, and sexes is to live in a narrow, colorless world. It is not only a tragedy, but just plain silly, for only foolish people would not be interested in embracing such knowledge.

We can not, nor will we divorce ourselves from our families. But we need a change in their attitudes. If I am to succeed as a writer, I need my family to respect my time, my words, myself. This goes for my parents, brothers, sisters, my children, my husband. Respectability is a long and sometimes nasty struggle. But you'd be surprised at the progress one can make. Eventually, my mother proved to be very flexible. When I signed my first honorarium over to her, she discreetly placed it in her pocket. Later, as I spread my notebooks over the dining room table, she carried in a steaming cup of coffee, sweetened just the way I like it.

Now for some nopalitos.

My tio Rogelio was one of those who stayed for years. I became his consentida, he my best friend, until other interests developed in my life. He eventually moved and the distance between his house and mine became so far it took years to get together again. Recently, he visited me and was astonished to find that I spoke only in English. Straightforward, as has always been his manner, he asked me: "Why don't you speak Spanish anymore?"

Good question. What happened? I did as a child, I know only from others' recollection, but what happened? Somewhere along the educational system I lost it, and with it I lost a part of me. Yes, I can communicate all right now, but to feel that it is my own, to feel comfortable enough to write in it, that's what I am missing. As a result, I will not be a whole person until I reacquire this part of me. For you see, a good part of my upbringing was in Spanish. Spanish images, words, moods that I feel I must explore before they are buried for good.

Of course English is my language too. I'm entitled to it, though it is the one I have learned artificially. But having Spanish stolen from me is lingual censorship. A repression that reveals to me the power of the language itself.

Consequently, I do not feel comfortable in either language. In fact, I majored in English and acquired a degree to erase what Lorna Dee Cervantes calls "my excuse me tongue." However, my English is often awkward, and clumsy, and it is this awkwardness that I struggle so hard with. But isn't that what writing is all about? The struggle with the word for the perfect meaning? Sometimes my mistakes turn out to be my best writing. Sometimes I think in Spanish and translate. Sometimes I go through the dictionary and acquaint myself with words I wouldn't otherwise use in conversation. Sometimes I am thrilled by the language and play with its implications. And sometimes I hate it, not feeling comfortable.

And yet, I am amazed when people say one of my greatest strengths is my language. Funny, no? I was also recently informed that my book, *The Moths and Other Stories,* will be included as required reading in the English Department's qualifying exam for the Ph.D. program at University of Texas, Austin.

I still say that if my works were translated into Spanish, they would somehow feel better. More, more, what's the word? At home.

In my case, Faulkner was right; I became a short story writer because I was a failed poet. But when I began to write, I honestly went into it rather blindly. I never once thought of a potential audience. Perhaps just starting out, I didn't have the confidence to think that people would actually be interested in reading it. I wrote what was natural, personal to me. I showed my work to Chicanas mostly, and since they related to it, they became supportive and thrilled at what I was doing. And the more they were thrilled and supportive, the more I wrote.

By that time, I had discovered the Latin American writers: Borges, García Márquez, Rulfo, Yañez, to name a few. Their exploration with form and voice was a thrilling experiment in modern fiction, I felt, and was eager to try my hand at it. It was a rebellion against accepted rules that, in essence, reflected their politics as well. Like Faulkner, they sought to see what they could get away with, and, as a result, gave birth to such a rich texture of literature that it is a sheer celebration to read.

This is where I got my angst for form, technique. But my worldview was obviously a different one because I was a Chicana. Once I discovered the Black women writers—Walker, Morrison, Brooks, Shange, again to name a few—womanism as subject matter seemed sanctioned, illuminating, innovative, honest, the best in recent fiction that I've seen in a long time.

Subject matter and form. They met, became lovers, often quarrelled, but nonetheless, Helena Maria Viramontes was born.

As Chicanas, we must continue to have the courage to examine our lives. Sometimes, when I see all that goes on around me, I begin to question the importance of fiction and its value against the face of a starving child. Yet, we continue to write. Perhaps it is because we have such a strong belief in the power of the written word. It is a link which bonds us. Their starvation becomes mine, their death becomes mine. Our destiny is not embedded in cement. We can determine its destination. Some use the soapbox, others, weapons. I choose to write.

I am genuinely happy to be a part of a growing, nurturing group of writers, radical women of color who are not afraid to explore culture, politics, humanity, womanism, not afraid to sabotage the stereotypes with whatever words are necessary to get the job done.

Doña Josefa: Bloodpulse of Transition and Change

JANICE DEWEY

An analysis of Estela Portillo Trambley's Chicana drama, *The Day of the Swallows* (1971),[1] presents numerous ambiguities that surround the unifying theme of woman in relation to her psychocultural and physical environment. These ambiguities become clarified through the interpretation of the central character of Doña Josefa, the town high priestess of charity and love. A declaration is made for the theater-going public in general and the Chicano community in particular; any human being stifled in the natural unfolding of her/his life can either rebel or submit. Though the dramatic circumstances of the play are at best shocking and mystifying, Doña Josefa represents an explosive interruption, variance, and change in the midst of temporal and cultural uniformity. Her acts are apparently evil, her ultimate suicide the final unmasking, and yet the dialectical undercurrent of ritualized good behavior (as opposed to ritualized bad) works effectively to expose the central thesis of woman trapped against her own will.

This revisionist reading intends to more clearly define what critics, the public, and readers have found difficult: interpretation, categorization, and placement of this work within the trajectory of Chicano literature. It would appear that the poetic, magic, and lesbian elements of the play place it outside the mainstream of the agitprop and consciousness-engendering theater techniques that dominate Chicano drama. Rhetorically, Luis Leal asks: "Are we to say then that such works as Rudolfo Anaya's novel *Bless Me, Ultima*, Estela Portillo's drama, *The Day of the Swallows*, and others not dealing with social protest do not belong to chicano literature?"[2] Or, as stated more fully by Jorge Huerta:

> In discussing any Chicano art, we cannot ignore the burning question which has followed the Movimiento since its inception: What makes a work of art *Chicano?* Is *Day of the Swallows* a

39

Chicana play simply because it was written by a Chicana from El Paso? Even though there are no Chicano politics in her play, is it yet Chicano since it deals with Mexican or Chicano characters?[3]

Not dealing with *social protest* the critic states, or in the absence of *any* Chicano politics, yet, how can a woman's suicide in the face of an entire town's condemnation of her lesbian love not be considered a symbolic protest, a protest "staged" against both the violence that leads to her own death and the farce of the lie that she lived? Perhaps this is the culmination of theater for social protest: when the codes of both violence and a patriarchal value system that can entrap free expression of humanity are exploded in full view in the tragic self-drowning of a woman driven beyond the very limits of social acceptance. Politics and social protest challenge the use, manipulation, and negotiation of power; thus defined, most human behavior and its subsequent artistic rendering are inherently political. Portillo herself provides an important revelation for resolving this apparent dilemma vis à vis the "political" nature of her play, for she confesses in a 1980 interview:

> When my first book was rejected, someone told me to do fiction. I had just seen the movie *The Fox,* from the D. H. Lawrence story, and someone said, why don't you write something like that and make a million? I'm always thinking of a buck. So in a month and a half I wrote *The Day of the Swallows* and I put everything in. The plot is about lesbians; I knew nothing about them, but I was going to sell it. Well, it got published, it appeared in four anthologies, I get invited to talk about it, it gets analyzed to death, and it's a play I wrote in a very short time and for a terrible reason. I was just being mercenary.[4]

When Portillo exposes her own intentionality in *The Day of the Swallows* as one intrinsically linked to a driven need for economic survival (commented on more fully in this same interview), she curiously prescribes lesbian love as a selling point. The sensationalism of so-called "deviance" within dominant culture is keenly perceived by a woman whose own personal lifestyle and culture live restricted and often mute(d).[5] Portillo is quite conscious and astute when assessing the market, gaining publication and notoriety as a result. Yet intuitively, perhaps, she creates theater of tragedy[6] around a central character who integrates both a culture she admittedly knows nothing about with one she knows intimately. In the end, both lesbians and Chicanos live marginal and often repressed lives and create culture and community vivified by strong political conscious-ness.

Portillo's play cannot escape comparison with the work of Federico García Lorca. It is with his words that this work can perhaps best be defined:

> Theater is a school of sorrow and laughter and a free platform where men [sic] can criticize old or erroneous morals and explain with vivid examples the eternal norms of the heart and of the feelings of man [sic].[7]

Also, Lorca explains:

> Theater is the poetry that rises up from the book and becomes human. And on becoming so it speaks and yells, cries and despairs. Theater requires that the characters who appear in the scene wear a suit of poetry, and at the same time that they display their bones and blood.[8]

Lorca's concept of theater, then, is of intimate poetic truths, dramatically translated to teach, illuminate, and reveal the perpetual movement of life and its eternal questions. His theater attacks social conventions through poeticized imagery that often pushes the dramatic protagonist to a violent death as a result of sexual frustration. It is in this sense that a brief consideration of Lorca's last play, La casa de Bernarda Alba (1936)[9] (a defiant literary forebear), be made in order to illuminate the conceptualization of The Day of the Swallows.

Lorca's play sets up the territory of myth and psyche in much the same manner as Portillo's, thus striking interesting parallels. Here, a barren and stark white house, dominated and domineered by the central protagonist of Bernarda, creates the foundation for a drama about women incarcerated both physically and emotionally. The five sisters have been confined to black dresses for a rigorous and lengthy mourning period following the death of their father. All sisters participate in the ritualistic activity of embroidering sheets for a future wedding. The monstrous matriarch, Bernarda, forbids her daughters free interchange with men and imprisons them in this sterile environment without even access to conver-sation with would-be suitors. In contrast, Bernard's mother of 80, María Josefa, flashes intermittently across the stage, professing the need for expressed sexuality. She embodies the freedom represented by the chorus' refrain of Act II, "open up all the doors and windows you women who live in the pueblo" (p. 1487), and frequently expresses herself with words that image flowing water. It is the youngest daughter, Adela, who most yearns to break through the constraints upon her womanhood and sexuality. The playwright has not named Adela, or any of the other characters, without pointed symbolic intention. Adela becomes the embodiment of the Spanish verb "adelantarse" (to go ahead, to move forward) and drastically pushes forward against her mother's constant beating down of any emotional release.[10] The impoverished understanding of society based on tradition, on the dread of public opinion, and the inherent claustration of woman is exploded full force in the representation of Adela. In her inability to accept the restraint of the mourning period, she puts on a green dress (the lush fertility of evergreen nature) and continues forward to an inevitable death, punishment for her rebellious personality. A fateful discovery of her rendezvous with a sister's fiancé in the corral (where mares are locked up and the stallion runs free) results in her hanging suicide. Bernarda, upon insisting that her daughter died a virgin, asserts the final word of the play, which is also her very first: "¡Silencio!" The silence of hanging lifeless, the silence of woman unexpressed, and the silence of stagnation are but a few of the counterbeats of thought that spring forth from this shocking ending. As the play states directly, "To be born a woman is the greatest punishment" (p. 1486).

La casa de Bernarda Alba and The Day of the Swallows are compelling literary analogues. Lorca's play enlightens our perception and understanding of Portillo's and, perhaps, shapes the very writing of it.[11] To wit, The Day of the Swallows meets all of the Spanish poet's dramatic requisites: a need for protest and a poetry of self-expression, uninhibited by the codes of language and human behavior within societal and traditional norms. Ritual, naming ("Josefa"), tradition, symbols, virginity, silence, and suicide run parallel throughout the two plays. The Day of the Swallows opens on a symbolic level and continues to build in tension and mystery by means of a rich web of poetic imagery and ritualistic myth. Alysea, Doña Josefa's companion, hides a bloody knife as Clemencia arrives to deliver milk. Eventually, we learn that Doña Josefa has cut out a young boy's tongue with this knife after he has witnessed her lovemaking with Alysea. Thus, with the curtain's rising, the signs are presented for the audience's perception of a greater truth; the milk/nourishment/female source is delivered in the wake of a violent act against man, whose tongue/phallus/male source has been removed by the hand of a rebellious and crazed woman. The boy's words have been silenced; his ability to generate a conversation that could condemn Josefa has been cut off immediately prior to a milk delivery that symbolically reiterates female generative power.

All dialogue and dramatic development continue to trace symbolic meaning. Doña Josefa lives in a "thoroughly feminine" (p. 208) house of order and beauty. Besides performing charitable works for the town of Lago de San Lorenzo, she embroiders lace of her own intricate design. She worships light, the moon, her "magicians" (p. 221), and the swallows soon to arrive at her exquisite garden, seen through the "orb" (p. 208) of a tree in the French window. Her home, or center, is described with these traditionally mandalic images, alluding to the higher truth of transcendence or personal growth of the greatest kind—arrival and union. The images include complicated lace patterns that repeat endlessly and possibly converge on a central point, the orb of the tree, the lake that names the town and provides its most important ritual, the small tree house made to welcome the homeward-bound swallows, the garden of light. The yearly ritual feast of San Lorenzo, for which Doña Josefa has been chosen to lead, serves as the platform for her ire and personal critique of society's closed system. Each year the town's virgins bathe in the lake with the assurance of a future husband and the hope of a marriage "made in heaven" (p. 208). As the dramatist's notes indicate, "The tempo of life, unbroken, conditioned, flavors its heartbeat with dreams and myths. . . . No one dares ask for life" (p. 207). The dream, the myth, is a falsehood. Stagnation and stasis are bound up in tradition.[12] Ritual can signify a perpetual present, a group rather than an individual meaning. Anthropologist Victor Turner discusses rites of passage as characteristic of liminality, or ambiguous states of transition from one cultural realm into another:

> Liminal entities are neither here nor there; they are betwixt and between the positions assigned and arrayed by law, custom, convention, and ceremonial. As such, their ambiguous and indeterminate attributes are expressed by a rich variety of symbols . . . likened to death, to being in the womb, to invisibility, to darkness, to bisexuality, to the wilderness, and to an eclipse of the sun and the moon.[13]

These beings that exist in a liminal state may possess nothing, go naked, behave passively or humbly, and experience intense comradeship and egalitarianism.[14] Josefa dramatically recognizes the "betwixt and between" of the ritual feast of San Lorenzo, the passivity and even death of a life's course that offers no choice or variance in its direction toward "sacred marriage." She challenges the ritual definitions in her break with the cycle of predictable societal norms; she rebels in her love of women and in her refusal to accept allegiance to man as her ultimate responsibility and fulfillment. In the end, Josefa denies the town her leadership in this virginal rite of passage when she takes her own life. The truth she knows and compares to that of Santa Teresa cancels out the "truth" of the myth. As a young girl, she had refused to bathe in the lake and had chosen the moonlight as her lover, with whom she would bear the children of light. She had seen clarity, not the dream, and had accepted herself in unified oneness. Portillo herself elucidates this point most definitively when she writes:

> What is tradition to a man differs in varying degree from what is tradition to a woman. The traditions of men are closely woven to codes, ethics, or nationalistic mores. A woman listens to her heart. She relives the reconstruction of reflection and remembrance with clear intuition. Thus the tradition that most moves a woman is inherent evolution, the nesting instinct, the mating instinct, and the simple order in some survival pattern. A woman touches, senses, feels, and then says, "This I know." The circuit of that knowing usually is very personal, thus very universal.[15]

As a consequence of this denial of cultural and sexual socialization, Doña Josefa moves and speaks in opposition to men. Having rescued Alysea from prostitution, she takes her as her lover and refers to man's love as a "violence" (p. 220). "Men don't love, they take" (p. 227). Though her good deeds for all the townspeople are alluded to, her conversations reveal a personal vindictiveness toward male intentions. All male characters in the play, save the priest, are presented unidimensionally and in a negative light as users of women, as temporal providers, as deceivers. Paradoxically, the male characters provide equally intense portrayals of women, establishing a structural axis of contrast and tension. Eduardo, who has already discarded one lover and now courts Alysea, announces that "no one in their right mind turns down a marriage proposal" (p. 217). Thus, a woman who rejects marriage is crazy. Don Esquinas speaks of women as "stupid" (p. 232) and loves "the man's way" (p. 233) with secret liaisons. Young David watched the women lovers with "horror" (p. 241). In depicting such unilateral sexual opposition, the author sets up her central figure for the ultimate sacrifice. Though Josefa's character would seem ultimately ambiguous, given the contrast of her public and private selves and her violent silencing of the boy David, her dramatic function works consistently within a simplistic paradigm for social change; once the oppressor has been defined, one rebels openly or subversively. Doña Josefa's violent act and subsequent suicide are not so much admissions of guilt and human frailty as they are the dramatic climax within the societal set-up; rather than suffer the revelations of being a criminal and "degenerate pervert" in a structure designed in opposition to her innermost being, she destroys herself. She is the final sacrificial lamb at the doorstep of aborted change because she is isolated and alone in her attempt to combat the myth of stereotypical lives.

The theme of sacrifice is quite common in Chicano theater and literature, as well as in Portillo's own works. In her story "The Burning," a woman healer, believed to be a witch, is burned at the stake while already dying of a high fever. In another story, "The Apple Trees," a woman commits suicide after transforming herself into a power-hungry capitalist, unsuitable to her family. Josefa's suicide can best be analyzed within this framework of sacrifice, with close attention given to the signs pointing the way. Josefa criticized Alysea for her plans to run off with the untrustworthy Eduardo, a man whose God and life are "out in the open" (p. 216), in the free and green. She warns: "You are like all the rest. You insist on being a useless, empty sacrifice!" (p. 235). In like fashion, the doña is repelled by the entreatment of the virgins to marriage; they sacrifice themselves rather than live freely and openly. They have no other choice, just as Josefa does not in the final scenes. As a child, she had been terrorized by a group of young boys who had killed numerous swallows for fun. As in a ritual sacrifice, a bird's throat was cut over a pinned-down Josefa, allowing the blood to run into her mouth: a bird killed at the hands of the powerful. This incident, and the final scene, give title to the play. The swallows have been sacrificed and yet they return with the perpetual motion of the cycles and seasons.[16]

Just as in the theater of García Lorca, the human condition is exaggerated through a poetic imagery that often cuts at the very bloodpulse of a given emotion or response. Josefa, without guilt, dressed in white and with her hair loose, drowns herself in the lake of cyclical ritual. She has silenced the world of reprimand by removing a tongue and removing herself:

> Alysea: His eyes told me. You and I were all the terror in the
> world.
> Josefa: No. The terror is in the world out there. Don't say
> that! (P. 235)

As in Aztec thought, this sacrifice contributes to the movement of the universe. Blood has been shed. The final metaphor bursts wide open in its revolution against the norm with its rebellious peace. A woman in a cultural strait jacket can become a monster; a human being can, too. A woman in a societal strait jacket can take her own life; a human being can, too. The metaphor is one for change, for dramatic change, in a world programmed for conflict between the sexes.

NOTES

1   Estela Portillo, *The Day of the Swallows*, in *Contemporary Chicano Theater*, ed. Roberto J. Garza (Notre Dame: University of Notre Dame Press, 1976). All quotations from this play, cited by page number, are found in the main body of the text.

2   Luis Leal in *The Identification and Analysis of Chicano Literature*, ed. Francisco Jiménez (New York: Bilingual Press, 1979), 3.

3   Jorge Huerta, "Where Are Our Chicano Playwrights?" *Revista Chicano-Riqueña* 3, no. 4 (1975): 35. Arthur Ramírez, in "Estela Portillo: The Dialectic of Oppression and Liberation," *Revista Chicano-Riqueña* 8, no. 3 (Summer 1980): 113 n.3, makes a similar point: "far from being devoid of politics, *The Day of the Swallows* is highly charged politically—with the particular ideology of a Chicana feminist." This article also corroborates the portrayal of Josefa as a "liberating" representation.

4   Juan Bruce-Novoa, *Chicano Authors: Inquiry by Interview* (Austin: University of Texas Press, 1980), 170.

5   I admit to being upset when I first discovered Portillo's revelation. As a lesbian, I am dismayed, yet hardly mystified, by the sensationalizing of literature and art (through the metaphor of lesbianism) for the sake of selling to an insatiable, voyeuristic, and homophobic public. But how many artists, filmmakers, and writers dare confess their intentions so honestly? As a Chicana writer, Portillo found herself unrecognized and unpublished; as a skilled woman with a family to hold together, she found herself without the means for economic sufficiency. The more I ruminated on my discovery, the more the issue became completely clear. Overshadowed by dominant, partial, and repressive cultural values, all women, women of color, lesbians, *are displaced and marginalized,* and Portillo knows this both personally and politically. She recognized the portrayal of a lesbian character as the lightning rod for her story. In the end, I found her highly symbolic representations to be subversive.

6   Refer to Alfonso Rodríguez' "Tragic Vision in Estela Portillo's *The Day of the Swallows*," *De Colores: Journal of Chicano Expression and Thought* 5, no. 1–2 (1980): 152–58, for a full analysis of this play as classical tragedy.

7   Federico García Lorca, "Charla sobre el teatro," in *Obras Completas*, (Madrid: Aguilar, 1967), 150. "El teatro es una escuela de llanto y risa y una tribuna libre donde los hombres pueden poner en evidencia morales viejas o equívocas y explicar con ejemplos vivos normas eternas del corazón y del sentimiento del hombre." All translations found in the text are mine.

8   García Lorca, "Conversaciones literarias," in *Obras Completas*, 1810. "El teatro es la poesía que se levanta del libro y se hace humana. Y al hacerse, habla y grita, llora y se desespera. El teatro necesita que los personajes que aparezcan en la escena lleven un traje de poesía y al mismo tiempo que se les vean los huesos, la sangre."

9   Garcia Lorca, *La casa de Bernarda Alba*, in *Obras Completas*. Quotations from this play, cited by page number, are found in the main body of the text.

10   Jean Smoot's documentation of usage of this name/verb in *A Comparison of*

Plays by John Millington Synge and Federico García Lorca: The Poets and Time (Madrid: José Porrúa Turanzas, 1978), 155–56.

11   Estela Portillo's literary knowledge and breadth of reading is extensive. Though she does not specify Lorca within the litany of names she gives Bruce-Novoa in her interview (*Chicano Authors: Inquiry by Interview*, 168), it would seem probable that she knows Lorca's work well.

12   Olivia Castellano, "Of Clarity and the Moon: A Study of Two Women in Rebellion," in *De Colores: Journal of Emerging Raza Philosophies* 3, no. 3 (1977): 25–31, for her analysis of ritual, stasis, myth, and Josefa as a figure of rebellion.

13   Victor Turner, *The Ritual Process* (Chicago: University of Chicago Press, 1969), 95.

14   Ibid.

15   Portillo, in the introduction to *Chicanas en la literatura y el arte*, ed. Herminio Ríos and Octavio Romano (Berkeley: Quinto Sol, 1974), 5.

16   Portillo could be alluding indirectly to the Greek myth of Philomela. Here also swallows, cut-out tongues, and victimized, sacrificial women are configured. Consult Robert Graves, *The Greek Myths: I* (Harmondsworth, Middlesex, England: Penguin Books, 1955), 165–68, and Edith Hamilton, *Mythology: Timeless Tales of Gods and Heroes* (New York: Little, Brown and Company, 1953), 270–71.

"A Deep Racial Memory of Love": The Chicana Feminism of Cherríe Moraga

NANCY SAPORTA STERNBACH

One of the most pressing and current feminist debates in the U.S. is the long-standing complaint that U.S. Third World women have lodged in regard to the continued racism within Anglo-American feminist circles; the accusations tend to focus on the latter's failure to acknowledge, take into account, or address the issues of women of color. Even the most well-intentioned feminists find themselves being asked about, and thus responding to, the questionability of women's liberation when an entire population is oppressed. During the seventies, a new genre of Chicana poetry emerged that began to address some of those issues; in them, the Chicana speaker rails against the Anglo-American women's liberationist for her condescension, her lack of sensitivity, and her choosing of the agenda for all women. Such is the context for Marcela Lucero's poem, "No More Cookies, Please":

> WASP liberationist
> you invited me
> token minority
> but your abortion idealogy
> failed to integrate me.
> Over cookies and tea
> you sidled up to me and said
> 'Sisterhood is powerful.'[1]

Certainly Chicanas were not alone in their evaluation of the Anglo-American feminist movement. In Black activist and academic circles, to mention only a few, open debates with some of the most widely respected feminist theorists in the Anglo-American world took place; again, the accusations focused on white women having co-opted, generalized, condescended to, or ignored the perspective of women of color. These debates were public, as we can appreciate from Audre Lorde's "Open Letter to Mary Daly" and Barbara Smith's "Towards a black feminist criticism,"[2] and served as a springboard to openly raising the questioning that remains controversial today. Because of these and many other initiatives, some Anglo-American feminists began to appreciate that their presumptuousness about the "liberation" of "minority women" was actually preventing any meaningful dialogue from taking place between white and Third World women. Likewise we learned that our own problematized definition of liberation was not a model to be imposed on others. Nothing could be clearer than Chicana poet Bernice Zamora's recent affirmation: "I'm not a feminist because I wish not to imitate the North American white woman."[3]

Those of us who are bilingual (and many of us who are not) have noticed one of the few Spanish words that fully and completely integrates itself into everyday English is "machismo." More dramatically, we have begun to hear a feminine form, *macha*, a tough, patriarchally-defined woman who is not necessarily of Latina heritage. We are familiar, too, with the complaints of Anglo-American women traveling in Latin American countries, about what they have called "the rampant machismo," and their testimonies that read like diatribes against a culture they claim to love. They wonder aloud how their Latin American counterparts can tolerate it. Likewise, we hear the defenses of these cultures; machismo is just as prevalent in the U.S., but with greater degrees of subtleties; a far higher percentage of women are doctors and lawyers in Latin America than in the U.S., a fact that has been true for most of the century and is not simply the result of the liberation movements of the seventies. There is a respect for the older woman in the Latin American culture that the U.S. would do well to learn and practice as well.[4]

A further complication of the question was incorporated into a Chicana's response to the machismo from which she personally suffered. Such has been the case in poems like "Machismo Is Part of Our Culture":

> Hey Chicano bossman
> don't tell me that machismo is part of our culture
> if you sleep
> and marry W.A.S.P.
>> You constantly remind me,
>> me, your Chicana employee

that machi-machi-machismo
is part of our culture.
   I'm conditioned, you say,
to bearing machismo
which you only learned
day before yesterday.
   At home you're no patrón
   your liberated gabacha
   has gotcha where
   she wants ya,
   y a mi me ves cara
   de steppin' stone.
Your culture emanates
   from Raza poster on your walls
   from bulletin boards in the halls
   and from the batos who hang out at the barrio bar.
Chicanismo through osmosis
acquired in good doses
remind you
to remind me
that machi-machi-machismo
is part of our culture.[5]

In Lorna Dee Cervantes' poem, "Para un revolucionario," the speaker must remind her "carnal" that she, too, is Raza and would like to share in the dream of the revolution that, up until that time, he had only offered to his *hermanos:*

Pero your voice is lost to me, *carnal,*
in the wail of *tus hijos*
in the clatter of dishes
and the pucker of beans on the stove.
Your conversations come to me
de la sala where you sit,
spreading your dream to brothers,
where you spread that dream like damp clover
for them to trod upon,
when I stand here reaching
para ti con manos bronces that spring
from *mi espíritu*
(for I too am Raza).[6]

We also learned that sexuality and its free choice and practice—a major component of white feminism—was simply not a unilateral agenda for women of color, or not always prioritized as it was with white feminists. Rather, we began to see that it had to be viewed concurrently with other issues such as class, ethnicity, cultural norms, traditions, and the paramount position of the family. This issue alone resulted in difficult lessons for white women who had not yet begun to perceive the complexities of being a Latina woman in the U.S., let alone a Latina feminist.

For all of these reasons, Cherríe Moraga's *Loving in the War Years: Lo que nunca pasó por sus labios* is a timely and important work.[7] It is a compendium of nearly a decade of Moraga's works that includes short fiction, poetry, and testimonial essay. Two of those essays, whose length comprise the majority of that book, contain the essence of Moraga's thinking, incorporating dreams, journal entries, and poetry as part of her testimonial discourse. One of the essays in particular, a work she has entitled "A Long Line of Vendidas," addresses some of the issues I have just mentioned and will be the focus of this essay.

The naming of this essay (a title appropriated, whose meaning is then reassigned, an ironic and contemporary use of the term "vendida") not only connects Moraga to a mestiza Chicana past but also questions, reevaluates, and finally takes issue with it. As we shall see, the customary uses of the *vendida* myth are restructured in Moraga's analysis in order to forge a reevaluation of the Malinche legend from which it derives.

The entire collection begins with the words: "Este libro covers a span of seven years." From the outset, the speaker prepares the reader for the bilingual text that ensues: the trajectory of the light-skinned Chicana whose paternal Anglo surname[8] helps her pass for white in a culture that demands conformity from her. Submerged into this dominant culture, alien to her maternal Chicana heritage, Moraga uses the act of writing as a process of *concientización* in order to reclaim her Chicanismo. The writer's relationship with her text, as a medium by which to define and articulate herself, parallels a process of withdrawal and then renewal; that is, her separation from both family and culture lasts until she is eventually led back to these heritages as the *política* (radical political woman) of the last essay whose feminist, lesbian consciousness offers us a theoretical basis for some of the above-mentioned issues.

Her purpose, she tells us in the introduction, is not merely artistic or literary, but rather political "because we are losing ourselves to the gavacho" (p. iii). In this sense, the book itself becomes a kind of sacrificial offering, thereby aligning it with other Latin American testimonial texts whose purposes are to counteract or give voice to a certain historical circumstance by the act of writing or converting oneself into what René

Jara has called, "testigo, actor y juez."[9] That which Moraga witnesses, acts upon, and judges is the confluence of the two social movements that inform her discourse: the women's movement and the Chicano movement.

In an act that places her within her historic and literary moment, Cherríe Moraga (like so many Chicana/o writers) draws upon, conjures, reinvents, and reinterprets Mexican myth and pre-Hispanic heritage. Like other Chicana writers of her generation (and certain Mexican writers of the previous one), Moraga begins her own analysis by a contemporary Chicana feminist application of the Malinche myth and its personal significance to her. While Moraga is not original in her desire to reassess Malinche, her view of the myth does offer a sharp departure from contemporary Chicana re-evaluations. In both literature and criticism, Malinche's mythical presence has affirmed the fact that neither Mexicans or Chicanos (although for different reasons in each case) have made their peace with her. When Chicana writers began their re-assessment, almost all of them spoke in counterpoint to Octavio Paz' landmark essay, "Los hijos de la Malinche," calling themselves instead "las hijas de la Malinche."

Paz' work underscores the need for Mexicans to examine their history in order to elucidate answers to their questions of identity. Paz sees Malinche as the ultimate Mother figure, but neither the Great Mother embodied in the female deities of the Aztec empire nor the Virgin Mother as represented by Guadalupe. Rather, she is the mythical, even metaphorical mother, her flesh serving as a symbol of the Conquest, the rape of Mexico.[10]

The well-known story is as follows: Malinche's mother, in an act of respect or fear toward her new husband, sold her daughter into slavery so that the son born of the new marriage would inherit both the title and the crown due the young Malintzín Tenepal (Malinche). When Hernán Cortés arrived in Tabasco, Malintzín was among the group of young women presented to him. Because Malinche grew up in the Valley of Mexico, she spoke Nahuatl; her residence with the Tabasco Indians made her bilingual. Soon thereafter she also learned Spanish and with this, the Spaniards renamed her doña Marina. Thus, by the time she set off with Cortés (actually to return home), she had already been offered twice as an object of exchange by the weaker of two parties in order to assuage any possible violence by the stronger.

This act, inspiring countless poems by both Mexican and Chicana writers, has offered as many points of view. Perhaps because Malinche is associated with the Aztec past, mestizaje, and violence of the Conquest, she may also be read as a metaphor for the silencing of the Indian voice that encased this act. Thus, in Rosario Castellanos' poem "La Malinche," for example, the poet puts words into Malinche's mouth, making her the speaker who now protests her use as an object of exchange, a currency traded for coffee beans, a colonized object who berates the woman responsible for the transaction—her mother. Although sympathetic to her plight, by such a characterization Castellanos simultaneously allows the reader to imagine Malinche's voice while still casting her as a victim.[11] Thus, the victimization of Malinche does not represent a contrary view to many male writers of her generation.[12]

Chicana poet Lucha Corpi also writes about her as a victim in her series, "Marina Poems." In the one entitled "Marina Mother," the speaker sums up Malinche's dilemma by addressing herself to Malinche's mother:

> Tú no la querías ya y él la negaba
> y aquel que cuando niño ¡mamá! le gritaba
> cuando creció le puso por nombre "la chingada."[13]

If these poets seem to indicate a Malinche vindication (and they are seconded by what can now be called a Chicana tradition of writers, critics, and historians such as Norma Alarcón, Cordelia Candelaria, Adelaida del Castillo, and Marcela Lucero-Trujillo),[14] others have written about how painful it is to be Malinche or her daughter ("como duele ser Malinche"),[15] or how they long for her to redeem them, or to finally speak in her own voice, as in Sylvia Gonzales' "I Am Chicana":

> I am Chicana
> Waiting for the return
> of la Malinche,
> to negate her guilt,
> and cleanse her flesh
> of a confused Mexican wrath
> which seeks reason
> to the displaced power of Indian deities.
> I am Chicana
> Waiting for the coming of a Malinche
> to sacrifice herself
> on an Aztec altar
> and Catholic cross
> in redemption of all her forsaken daughters.[16]

In a later Chicana rendition of Malinche, the speaker is Malinche herself, Malinche the feminist, Malinche who addresses herself to Cortés after his refusal to marry her, even after she bears his child:

Huhn–y para eso te di
mi sangre y mi pueblo!
Sí, ya lo veo, gringo desabrido,
tanto así me quieres
que me casarás con tu subordinado Don Juan,
sin más ni más
como si fuera yo
un kilo de carne
—pos ni que fueras mi padre
pa' venderme a tu antojo
güero infeliz . . .

!!!

Etcétera
etcétera.[17]

For Moraga, then, beginning to write, that is, an articulation of her Chicana identity, must include a re-evaluation of the problematic "role-model" Malintzín, the "traitor" and "chingada" she was taught to hate, mistrust, and never, under any circumstances, emulate. Even the Chicana who is unaware of Malinche's historical role "suffers under her name," Moraga claims. By underscoring the inherent contradiction in Malinche's dilemma (and, by association, all Mexican and Chicana women's), Moraga also confronts her own problem and resultant pain: the daughter betrayed by a mother who showed preference for her male children. What makes Moraga's assessment different is that in this case the daughter, in turn, is accused of betraying her race by choosing the sex of her mother as the object of her love. On the one hand, the importance of family and the closeness and attachment of the mother/daughter relationship is "paramount and essential in our lives" because the daughter can always be relied upon to "remain faithful a la madre" (p. 139). But the converse is not always the case; while the fidelity of the daughter is expected, the mother, who is also socialized by the culture, does not always reciprocate. It is here that Moraga parts company with other Chicana writers.

While other writers focus on Malinche herself as if they were her actual daughters, Moraga prefers to direct her analysis toward Malinche's mother, likening her to her own. A case in point is that, for both Malinche and Moraga, brothers were their mothers' choice. In order to show her "respect [for] her mother" (p. 90), the young Moraga was required not only to wait on her adolescent brother and his friends, but also to do so graciously.

The legacy of Malinche also lingers for any woman with the audacity to consider her own needs before those of the men of her family. By placing herself (or any woman, including her daughter) first, she is accused of being a traitor to her race (p. 103). By fulfilling her daughter's desire and need for love, the mother is also labeled la chingada. Her "Mexican wifely duty" means that sons are favored, husbands revered. "Traitor begets traitor," Moraga warns: like mother, like daughter. Malinche's mother, then, was the first traitor (mother) who begot the second one (daughter).

While Moraga stresses the daughter's inevitable pain with the discovery of this truth, she equates that pain with Malinche's: "What I wanted from my mother was impossible" (p. 103). In this respect, she focuses on Malinche's relationship with her mother: a daughter betrayed. All of these factors contribute to the cultural messages the young Chicana learns about herself and ultimately internalizes: that is, the "inherent unreliability of women" and female "natural propensity for treachery" (pp. 99–101).

Moraga continues the Malinche analogy by stressing her own identity as the product of a bicultural relationship: the daughter of a white father and a brown mother. "To be a woman," a brown woman, and a Chicana entailed reclaiming the "race of my mother." It meant loving the Chicana in herself and in other women; it meant departing from her mother and Malinche's model and "embrac[ing] no white man" (p. 94). It meant finally returning to the race of her mother through her love for other women— her Chicana lesbianism. Although Moraga acknowledges that her mother may be a "modern-day Chicana Malinche" (p. 117) by marrying a white man, she herself, the "half-breed Chicana," in a departure from both these predecessors and a transgression of all standards and norms, chooses a sexuality "which excludes all men, and therefore, most dangerously Chicano men" (p. 117). It is an act that labels her as the worst traitor of all, a "malinchista," one who is swayed by foreign influences. Her conclusion, paradoxically, brings her back to her people, the people of her mother: "I come from a long line of vendidas" (p. 117), she confesses, although she is obviously giving a new and perhaps reclaimed meaning, if such a thing is possible, to the word vendida.

In this new vocabulary, vendida refers to how Moraga is perceived rather than how she perceives herself. Similarly, it allows its author to poke fun at such labels. The term, like "bruja" and "loca," used specifically to trivialize women's experience, can now be seen as an act of female empowerment. Such appears to be the case for Moraga. In order to avoid being classified in this manner, she must be servile to one man and she must denounce her sexual love for women. In order to be the socially accepted Chicana, even if she is a politically active radical, she must not question the foundational basis of her loyalty and commitment to *la causa*, a commitment that, in Moraga's view, also entails an unswerving hetero-sexuality, a sexual loyalty to the Chicano male (p. 105).

Moraga reports that the current debate among Chicana women fo-cuses on how to "get their men right" (p. 105) rather than on questioning the premises of what Adrienne Rich has called "compulsory heterosex-uality."[18] The Chicana feminist who critiques sexism in the Chicano com-munity finds herself in a personal, political, and racial bind. She will be called *vendida* if she finds the "male-defined and often anti-feminist" values of the Chicano community difficult to accept. She will be accused of selling out to white women, of abandoning her race, of having absorbed the struggle of the middle class, of being malinchista, "puta," or "jota" (p. 98), even if she is heterosexual; it is greatly exacerbated if she is not. Thus, her role is not only the gender-neutral one of joining her man in earning a living and struggling against racism, but is also the gender-specific one as cultural nurturer, responsible, among other tasks, for the socialization of children. If she then cares to "challenge sexism," she will undergo this particular struggle single-handedly because this juggling act will also require that she "retain . . . her femininity so as not to offend or threaten *her man*" (p. 107). In this sense, Moraga sees her in the same light as the "Black Super-woman," the myth that only black women themselves were able to dispel.

In order to be a Chicana feminist, then, it is not enough for Moraga to examine the lost pages of history in order to reclaim female heroes, though this is one of its essential ingredients. Too often, these female luminaries are presented in relation to their men instead of in their own right. Calling this the "alongside-our-man-knee-jerk-phenomenon,"[19] Moraga asserts that the most valuable work being done in Chicana scholarship is that which puts "the female first, even when it means criticizing el hombre" (p. 107). She finally concludes that learning to do a self-study of one's culture, learning to read it critically, is not analagous to betrayal of that culture (p. 108).

In that vein, she takes issue with Chicana historians, guilty of the "knee-jerk phenomenon," who have attempted to trivialize the white women's movement as having nothing to offer them. Perhaps, because it was precisely within this movement that Moraga herself sought refuge and found it, she is particularly sensitive to this charge. Although her essay does not reveal this personal information, and the entire book could hardly be read as an apology to white feminism, it does contain a list of activities in which feminist women of color have been working at the grass-roots level for a decade: sterilization abuse, battered women's shelters, rape crisis centers, health care, and more (p. 106). Thus, she is quick to note that the use of white male theoreticians, such as Marx and Engels, is perfectly acceptable within the Chicano community but, paradoxically, the use of white female theoreticians is not, either within the Chicana or Chicano community. "It is far easier for the Chicana to criticize white women who . . . could never be familia, than to take issue with or complain . . . to a brother, uncle, father" (pp. 106–7).

The heterosexual Chicana who criticizes her male counterpart or relatives will jeopardize her chances of receiving male approval, be it through her son or her lover: an approval necessary to being a *política*, an approval that allows access to, or a taste of, male privilege, an approval that will procure her a husband. She is what Evangelina Enríquez and Alfredo Mirandé have identified as the "contemporary vendida."[20] This situation is further exacerbated if she is not heterosexual, although these authors do not discuss this point. Moraga explains that only the woman intent on the approval can be affected by the disapproval (p. 103). The lesbian, on the other hand, not subject to male sanctions and out of his control, will often serve as an easy scapegoat; weaknesses in the movement can be blamed on her, the model she sets for other women being a dangerous example. Her decision to take control of her own sexuality, as well as her independence, likens her to the Malinche model we discussed earlier. She is a "traitor" who "succumbs" to the foreign influences that have corrupted her people (p. 113).

In a study of the cultural stereotypes typically available to Chicana women, Shirlene Soto, for example, has noted that the figures most often used—Malinche, La Llorona and the Virgin of Guadalupe—have historically been models to control women, a point with which Moraga concurs. Soto, like Enríquez and Mirandé, also fails to address the issue of how much more poignant and true all those statements are when there is a clear sexual rejection of the male, as in Moraga's case. Nevertheless, sexual rejection does not necessarily signify a cultural one.

Viewed as an agent of the Anglos, the Chicana lesbian is seen as an aberration, someone who has unfortunately caught *his* disease. For these reasons, perhaps, Moraga believes that control of and over women cannot be based or blamed entirely on these so-called inherited cultural stereotypes but rather on the institution of obligatory heterosexuality. Nowhere in print had any Chicano or Chicana addressed lesbianism or homosexuality in their theoretical analyses of liberation. For this, Moraga would have to turn to the Black feminists, the same women, she asserts, who had served as role models for the Chicana feminist movement in its formation. "If any direct 'borrowing' was done, it was from Black feminists" (p. 132) and not from the white feminists normally blamed for infiltrating the Chicana feminist movement. Until she had this example, then, her sexuality had isolated and estranged her from her race: "It seemed to me to be a Chicana lesbian put me far beyond the hope of salvation" (p. 125). Yet she recognizes now that because one aspect of a culture is oppressive, it does not mean "throwing out the entire business of racial/ethnic culture" that is essential to identity (p. 127).

Such a questioning brings us to the ambiguous title and subtitle of her book, *Loving in the War Years: Lo que nunca pasó por sus labios*. By choosing to represent the book bilingually, she again likens herself to Malinche, her bilingual and trilingual forebear. "Lo que nunca pasó por sus labios" suggests that a silence is about to be broken, though the multiple possibilities of "sus" (her, his, their, your) do not reveal exactly who will break it: Moraga? Malinche? Chicana lesbians? All of them? In this way, her essay approximates the titles of Latin American women's testimonial discourse: "Let me speak!" "They Won't Take Me Alive," "Tales of Disappearance and Survival." All of these indicate a strength, a fortitude, and a resolve to break silences and assert one's voice. In the case of so many of Moraga's Latin American counterparts, a lack of education has impeded their single-handed publishing of their own testimonies; thus, many will contain a "co-producer" to actually write their discourse. For Moraga, the education is not a problem; in her case, bilingualism is the impediment.

Having learned what has mockingly been called "kitchen Spanish" or "Spanglish," yet also needing to be fluent in English in order to operate within the dominant culture and obtain the education that her mother encouraged her to pursue, Moraga confesses to her anglicization; it was a means to achieve her much-desired independence. In this sense, there is also a linkage; her reacquaintance with her Chicano roots required a return to Spanish, required a knowledge of it, implied an attitude on the part of the speaker who refused to be humiliated any longer by her bilingualism/biculturalism with such terms as "nolingual."[21]

When Moraga discovers a bicultural group whose most comfortable language is what I prefer to call "bilingual" (bilingual as a noun as well as an adjective), she finally is in a position of not feeling shame for "shabby" English or "incorrect" Spanish. Having come from a home where English was spoken, Moraga acknowledges that this claim on, and longing for, her Spanish "mothertongue" had no rational explanation. After all, she did not have her language stripped from her, as had so many children of the Southwest. Here, it is more appropriate to consider it the ancient language of her heart. In this sense, language is not simply a means of communicating ideas, passions, feelings, and theories, but is also symbolic, representing, among other emotions, love for one's culture. As it becomes a touch-stone for that culture, especially in circumstances of exile, one must also relearn its nuances as one learns to accept the entirety of one's culture, both its positive and its negative. "I know this language in my bones . . . and then it escapes me" (p. 141). Humiliated and mortified, Moraga must call the Berlitz language school in New York City in order to return to her Spanish, to her love of her mothertongue, to a love for her mother, to her love for her culture, to her love for her raza, to her "deep racial memory of love." "I am a different woman in Spanish. A different kind of passion. I think, *soy mujer en español*. No macha. Pero mujer. Soy Chicana—open to all kinds of attack" (p. 142). One of these attacks, no doubt, is the accusa-tion that she does not belong and does not speak the language of her mother, even if she feels it in her bones. She articulates the contradiction she faces with one of her journal entries after the Berlitz episode: *"Paying for culture. When I was born between the legs of the best teacher I could have had"* (p. 141). The painful journey she embarks upon in order to discover this truth allows her a return to her mother, to her people, to "la mujer mestiza," to a new awareness of what it means to be Malinche's daughter.

NOTES

1   Marcelo Christine Lucero-Trujillo, "No More Cookies, Please," in *The Third Woman: Minority Women Writers of the United States*, ed. Dexter Fisher (Boston: Houghton Mifflin, 1980), 402–3.

2   Lorde's "Open Letter to Mary Daly," in *Sister Outsider*, in which she dis-cusses the "history of white women who are unable to hear Black women's words, or to maintain dialogue with us" (Trumansburg, N.Y.: The Crossing Press, 1984), 66, and Smith's not knowing "where to begin," in "Toward a black feminist criticism," in *Feminist Criticism and Social Change: Sex, Class and Race in Literature and Culture*, ed. Judith Newton and Deborah Rosenfelt (New York, London: Methuen, 1986), 3.

3   Parul Desai, "Interview with Bernice Zamora, a Chicana Poet," *Imagine: International Chicano Poetry Journal* 2, no. 1 (Summer 1985): 29.

4   Oliva Espín, "Cultural and Historical Influences on Sexuality in His-panic/Latin women: Implications for Psychotherapy," in *Pleasure and Danger: Ex-ploring Female Sexuality*, ed. Carol Vance (Boston: Routledge and Kegan Paul, 1984), 155.

5   Marcela Christine Lucero-Trujillo, "Machismo is Part of Our Culture," in *The Third Woman*, 401–2. The fact that the same author exemplifies both positions, that is, the turning away from both the Anglo-American feminist and the Chicano macho, indicates her articulation of a new voice that will incorporate a feminism specific and appropriate to her Chicana reality.

6   Lorna Dee Cervantes, "Para un revolucionario," in *The Third Woman*, 381–83 (for you with bronze hands).

7   Cherríe Moraga, "A Long Line of Vendidas," in *Loving in the War Years: Lo que nunca pasó por sus labios* (Boston: South End Press, 1983). All subsequent passages will be from this edition and the page numbers will be contained within parentheses after each passage.

8   Moraga offers no example of what this surname was but leads us to imagine that in discovering her Chicana roots, she also molts the paternal name in favor of the maternal one.

9   René Jara, "Testimonio y literatura," in *Testimonio y Literatura: Monographic Series of the Society for the Study of Contemporary Hispanic and Lusophone Revolutionary Literatures*, no. 3, ed. René Jara and Hernán Vidal (Minneapolis: Institute for the Study of Ideologies and Literature, 1986), 1.

10   Octavio Paz, "Los hijos de la Malinche," in *El laberinto de la soledad* (México: Fondo de Cultura Económica, 1973), 59–80.

11   Rosario Castellanos, "La Malinche," in *Poesía no eres tú* (México: Fondo de Cultura Económica, 1972), 295–97.

12   Most notable are the views of Carlos Fuentes and Octavio Paz.

13   Lucha Corpi, "Marina Madre," in *Palabras de Mediodía/Noon Words*, trans. Catherine Rodríguez-Nieto (Berkeley: El Fuego de Aztlán Publications, 1980), 119. I prefer my own translation of these verses: "You no longer loved her and your husband denied her / When the child that used to call her 'Mamá' / grew up, he called her 'whore.' "

14   Norma Alcarcón, "Chicana's Feminist Literature: A Re-Vision through Malintzín/or Malinche: Putting Flesh Back on the Object," in *This Bridge Called My Back: Writings by Radical Women of Color*, 2d ed, ed. Cherríe Moraga and Gloria Anzaldúa (New York: Kitchen Table Women of Color Press, 1983), 182–90; Aledaida del Castillo, "Malintzín Tenepal: A Preliminary Look into a New Perspective," in *Essays on La Mujer*, part 1, ed. Rosaura Sánchez (Los Angeles: UCLA Chicano Studies Center Publications, 1977), 124–49; Marcela Christine Lucero-Trujillo, "The Dilemma of the Modern Chicana Artist and Critic," in *The Third Woman*, 324–31; Cordelia Candelaria, "La Malinche: Feminist Prototype," *Frontiers* 5, no. 2 (1980); Rachel Phillips, "Marina/Malinche: Masks and Shadows," in *Women in Hispanic Literature: Icons and Fallen Idols*, ed. Beth Miller (Berkeley: University of California Press, 1983), 97–114; Shirlene Soto, "Tres modelos culturales: La Virgen de Guadalupe, la Malinche y la Llorona," *fem*, 10, no. 48 (Octubre-Noviembre 1986): 13–16.

15   These exact words appear in two early Chicana poems, "Como duele," by Lorenza Calvillo Schmidt, and an untitled poem by Adaljiza Sosa Riddell, both in *Chicanas en la literatura y el arte*, ed. Herminio Ríos-C. and Octavio Romano–V. (Berkeley: Quinto Sol, 1973).

16   Sylvia Gonzales, "I Am Chicana," in *The Third Woman*, 422.

17   Angela de Hoyos, "La Malinche a Cortez y Vice Versa (o sea, 'El Amor No Perdona, Ni Siquiera Por Amor')," in *Woman, Woman* (Houston: Arte Público Press, 1985), 54. (Hmph, and that's why I gave you / my blood and my people! / Yes, now I

see it, you uncouth gringo / you love me so much / that you'll marry me off to your subordinate, Don Juan / without a second thought / as if I were a piece of meat / Well, even if you were my father / to go selling me at your whim / you stupid gringo . . . / !!! / Etcetera / Etcetera).

18 Adrienne Rich, "Cumpulsory Heterosexuality and Lesbian Existence," in *Women: Sex and Sexuality,* ed. Catharine R. Stimpson and Ethel Spector Person (Chicago and London: University of Chicago Press, 1980), 62–91.

19 Cherríe Moraga is perhaps one of the best known Chicana writers outside the Chicana community. She is widely anthologized and the one who most white women quote as a representative Chicana voice. The "alongside-our-man-knee-jerk-phenomenon" appears in Cheris Kramarae and Paula A. Treichler's *A Feminist Dictionary* (Boston: Pandora Press, 1985), 41. On the other hand, she is hardly ever anthologized by Chicano critics, which may have been one of the reasons for an essay such as this one. The Mexican feminist magazine, *fem.,* however, has regularly published her poetry. See their issue on Chicanas (10, no. 48 [Octubre-Noviembre 1986]).

20 Evangelina Enríquez and Alfredo Mirandé, "Liberation, Chicana Style: Colonial Roots of Feministas Chicanas," *De Colores: A Bilingual Quarterly Journal of Chicano Expression and Thought* 4, no. 3 (1978): 15.

21 Juan Bruce-Novoa, "Una cuestión de identidad: ¿Qué significa un nombre?" in *Imagenes e identidades: El puertorriqueño en la literatura,* ed. Asela Rodríguez de Laguna (Río Piedras, P.R.: Huracán, 1985), 283–88.

Sandra Cisneros'
The House on Mango Street:
Community-Oriented Introspection and the Demystification of Patriarchal Violence

ELLEN MCCRACKEN

Introspection has achieved a privileged status in bourgeois literary production, corresponding to the ideological emphasis on individualism under capitalism, precisely as the personal and political power of many real individuals has steadily deteriorated. In forms as diverse as European Romantic poetry, late nineteenth-century Modernismo in Latin America, the poetry of the Mexican Contemporáneos of the 1930s, the early twentieth-century modernistic prose of a Proust, the French *nouveau roman,* and other avant-garde texts that take pride in an exclusionary hermeticism, the self is frequently accorded exaggerated importance in stark contrast to the actual position of the individual in the writer's historical moment. Critical readers of these texts are, of course, often able to compensate for the writer's omissions, positioning the introspective search within the historical dimension and drawing the text into the very socio-political realm that the writer has tried to avoid. Nonetheless, many of us, at one time or another, are drawn into the glorified individualism of these texts, experiencing voyeuristic and sometimes identificatory pleasure as witnesses of another's search for the self, or congratulating ourselves on the mental acuity we possess to decode such a difficult and avant-garde text.

Literary critics have awarded many of these texts canonical status. As Terry Eagleton has argued, theorists, critics, and teachers are "custodians of a discourse" and select certain texts for inclusion in the canon that are "more amenable to this discourse than others."[1] Based on power, Eagleton suggests metaphorically, literary criticism sometimes tolerates regional dialects of the discourse but not those that sound like another language altogether: "To be on the inside of the discourse itself is to be blind to this power, for what is more natural and non-dominative than to speak one's own tongue?" (203).

The discourse of power to which Eagleton refers here is linked to ideology as well. The regional dialects of criticism that are accepted must be compatible, ideologically as well as semantically, with the dominant discourse. Criticism, for example, that questions the canonical status of the introspective texts mentioned above, or suggests admission to the canon of texts that depart from such individualistic notions of the self, is often labeled pejoratively or excluded from academic institutions and publication avenues.

We can extend Eagleton's metaphor to literary texts as well. How does a book attain the wide exposure that admission to the canon facilitates if it is four times marginalized by its ideology, its language, and its writer's ethnicity and gender? What elements of a text can prevent it from being accepted as a "regional dialect" of the dominant discourse; at what point does it become "another language altogether" (to use Eagleton's analogy), incompatible with canonical discourse?

The specific example to which I refer, Sandra Cisneros' *The House on Mango Street,* was published by a small regional press in 1984 and reprinted in a second edition of 3,000 in 1985.[2] Difficult to find in most libraries and bookstores, it is well known among Chicano critics and scholars, but virtually unheard of in larger academic and critical circles. In May 1985 it won the Before Columbus Foundation's American Book Award,[3] but this prize has not greatly increased the volume's national visibility. Cisneros' book has not been excluded from the canon solely because of its publishing circumstances: major publishing houses are quick to capitalize on a Richard Rodríguez whose widely distributed and reviewed *Hunger of Memory* (1982) does not depart ideologically and semantically from the dominant discourse. They are even willing to market an Anglo writer as a Chicano, as occurred in 1983 with Danny Santiago's *Famous All Over Town.* Rather, Cisneros' text is likely to continue to be excluded from the canon because it "speaks another language altogether," one to which the critics of the literary establishment "remain blind."

Besides the double marginalization that stems from gender and ethnicity, Cisneros transgresses the dominant discourse of canonical standards ideologically and linguistically. In bold contrast to the individualistic introspection of many canonical texts, Cisneros writes a modified autobiographical novel, or *Bildungsroman,* that roots the individual self in the broader socio-political reality of the Chicano community. As we will see, the story of individual development is oriented outwardly here, away from the bourgeois individualism of many standard texts. Cisneros' language also contributes to the text's otherness. In opposition to the complex, hermetic language of many canonical works, *The House on Mango Street* recuperates the simplicity of children's speech, paralleling the autobiographical protagonist's chronological age in the book. Although making the text accessible to people with a wider range of reading abilities, such simple and well-crafted prose is not currently in canonical vogue.

The volume falls between traditional genre distinctions as well. Containing a group of 44 short and interrelated stories, the book has been classified as a novel by some because, as occurs in Tomas Rivera's . . . *y no se lo tragó la tierra*, there is character and plot development throughout the episodes. I prefer to classify Cisneros' text as a collection, a hybrid genre midway between the novel and the short story. Like Sherwood Anderson's *Winesburg, Ohio*, Pedro Juan Soto's *Spiks*, Gloria Naylor's *The Women of Brewster Place*, and Rivera's text,[4] Cisneros' collection represents the writer's attempt to achieve both the intensity of the short story and the discursive length of the novel within a single volume. Unlike the chapters of most novels, each story in the collection could stand on its own if it were to be excerpted but each attains additional important meaning when interacting with the other stories in the volume. A number of structural and thematic elements link the stories of each collection together. Whereas in *Winesburg, Ohio*, one important structuring element is the town itself, in *The House on Mango Street* and . . . *y no se lo tragó la tierra* the image of the house is a central unifying motif.

On the surface the compelling desire for a house of one's own appears individualistic rather than community oriented, but Cisneros socializes the motif of the house, showing it to be a basic human need left unsatisfied for many of the minority population under capitalism. It is precisely the lack of housing stability that motivates the image's centrality in works by writers like Cisneros and Rivera. For the migrant worker who has moved continuously because of job exigencies and who, like many others in the Chicano community, has been deprived of an adequate place to live because of the inequities of income distribution in U.S. society, the desire for a house is not a sign of individualistic acquisitiveness but rather represents the satisfaction of a basic human need. Cisneros begins her narrative with a description of the housing conditions the protagonist's family has experienced:

> We didn't always live on Mango Street. Before that we
> lived on Loomis on the third floor and before that we lived on

Keeler. Before Keeler it was Paulina, and before that I can't
remember. But what I remember most is moving a lot . . .
    We had to leave the flat on Loomis quick. The water pipes
broke and the landlord wouldn't fix them because the house
was too old. . . . We were using the washroom next door and
carrying water over in empty milk gallons. (P. 7)

Cisneros has socialized the motif of a house of one's own by showing
its motivating roots to be the inadequate housing conditions in which she
and others in her community lived. We learn that Esperanza, the protagonist Cisneros creates, was subjected to humiliation by her teachers because of her family's living conditions. "You live *there?*" a nun from her
school had remarked when seeing Esperanza playing in front of the flat on
Loomis. "*There.* I had to look where she pointed—the third floor, the paint
peeling, wooden bars Papa had nailed on the windows so we wouldn't fall
out. You live *there?* The way she said it made me feel like nothing . . ."
(p. 9). Later, after the move to the house on Mango Street that is better but
still unsatisfactory, the Sister Superior at her school responds to Esperanza's request to eat lunch in the cafeteria rather than returning home
by apparently humiliating the child deliberately: "You don't live far, she
says . . . I bet I can see your house from my window. Which one? . . .
That one? she said pointing to a row of ugly 3-flats, the ones even the
raggedy men are ashamed to go into. Yes, I nodded even though I knew
that wasn't my house and started to cry . . ." (p. 43). The Sister Superior is
revealing her own prejudices; in effect, she is telling the child, "All you
Mexicans must live in such buildings." It is in response to humiliations
such as these that the autobiographical protagonist expresses her need for
a house of her own. Rather than the mere desire to possess private
property, Esperanza's wish for a house represents a positive objectification of the self, the chance to redress humiliation and establish a dignified
sense of her own personhood.

Cisneros links this positive objectification that a house of one's own
can provide to the process of artistic creation. Early on, the protagonist
remarks that the dream of a white house "with trees around it, a great big
yard and grass growing without a fence" (p. 8) structured the bedtime
stories her mother told them. This early connection of the ideal house to
fiction is developed throughout the collection, especially in the final two
stories. In "A House of My Own," the protagonist remarks that the desired house would contain "my books and stories" and that such a house is
as necessary to the writing process as paper: "Only a house quiet as snow,
a space for myself to go, clean as paper before the poem" (p. 100). In
"Mango Says Goodbye Sometimes," the Mango Street house, which falls

short of the ideal dream house, becomes a symbol of the writer's attainment of her identity through artistic creation. Admitting that she both belonged and did not belong to the "sad red house" on Mango Street, the protagonist comes to terms with the ethnic consciousness that this house represents through the process of fictive creation: "I put it down on paper and then the ghost does not ache so much. I write it down and Mango says goodbye sometimes. She does not hold me with both arms. She sets me free" (p. 101). She is released materially to find a more suitable dwelling that will facilitate her writing; psychologically, she alleviates the ethnic anguish that she has heretofore attempted to repress. It is important, however, that she view her departure from the Mango Street house to enable her artistic production in social rather than isolationist terms: "They will know I have gone away to come back. For the ones I left behind. For the ones who cannot get out" (p. 102).

Unlike many introspective writers, then, Cisneros links both the process of artistic creation and the dream of a house that will enable this art to social rather than individualistic issues. In "Bums in the Attic," we learn that the protagonist dreams of a house on a hill similar to those where her father works as a gardener. Unlike those who own such houses now, Esperanza assures us that, were she to obtain such a house, she would not forget the people who live below: "One day I'll own my own house, but I won't forget who I am or where I came from. Passing bums will ask, Can I come in? I'll offer them the attic, ask them to stay, because I know how it is to be without a house" (p. 81). She conceives of a house as communal rather than private property; such sharing runs counter to the dominant ideological discourse that strongly affects consciousness in capitalist societies. Cisneros' social motifs undermine rather than support the widespread messages of individualized consumption that facilitate sales of goods and services under consumer capitalism.

Another important reason why Cisneros's text has not been accepted as part of the dominant canonical discourse is its demystificatory presentation of women's issues, especially the problems low-income Chicana women face. Dedicated "A las Mujeres/To the Women" (p. 3), *The House on Mango Street* presents clusters of women characters through the sometimes naive and sometimes wise vision of the adolescent protagonist. There are positive and negative female role models and, in addition, several key incidents that focus the reader's attention on the contradictions of patriarchal social organization. Few mainstream critics consider these the vital, universal issues that constitute great art. When representatives of the critical establishment do accord a text such as Cisneros' a reading, it is often performed with disinterest and defense mechanisms well in place.

Neither does *The House on Mango Street* lend itself to an exoticized reading of the life of Chicana women that sometimes enables a text's canonical acceptance. In "The Family of Little Feet," for example, Esperanza and her friends dress up in cast-off high heels they have been given and play at being adult women. At first revelling in the male attention they receive from the strangers who see them, the girls are ultimately disillusioned after a drunken bum attempts to purchase a kiss for a dollar. While capturing the fleeting sense of self-value that the attention of male surveyors affords women, Cisneros also critically portrays here the danger of competitive feelings among women when one girl's cousins pretend not to see Esperanza and her friends as they walk by. Also portrayed is the corner grocer's attempt to control female sexuality by threatening to call the police to stop the girls from wearing the heels. Cisneros proscribes a romantic or exotic reading of the dress-up episode, focusing instead on the girls' discovery of the threatening nature of male sexual power that is frequently disguised as desirable male attention and positive validation of women, though what is, in fact, sexual reification.

Scenes of patriarchal and sexual violence in the collection also prevent a romantic reading of women's issues in this Chicano community. We see a woman whose husband locks her in the house, a daughter brutally beaten by her father, and Esperanza's own sexual initiation through rape. Like the threatening corner grocer in "The Family of Little Feet," the men in these stories control or appropriate female sexuality by adopting one or another form of violence as if it were their innate right. One young woman, Rafaela, "gets locked indoors because her husband is afraid [she] will run away since she is too beautiful to look at" (p. 76). Esperanza and her friends send papaya and coconut juice up to the woman in a paper bag on a clothesline she has lowered; metonymically, Cisneros suggests that the sweet drinks represent the island the woman has left and the dance hall down the street as well, where other women are ostensibly more in control of their own sexual expression and are allowed to open their homes with keys. The young yet wise narrator, however, recognizes that "always there is someone offering sweeter drinks, someone promising to keep [women] on a silver string" (p. 76).

The cycle of stories about Esperanza's friend Sally shows this patriarchal violence in its more overt stages. Like Rafaela, the young teenager Sally is frequently forced to stay in the house because "her father says to be this beautiful is trouble" (p. 77). But even worse, we learn later that Sally's father beats her. Appearing at school with bruises and scars, Sally tells Esperanza that her father sometimes hits her with his hands "just like a dog . . . as if I was an animal. He thinks I'm going to run away like his sisters who made the family ashamed. Just because I'm a daughter . . ."

(p. 85). In "Linoleum Roses," a later story in the Sally cycle, we learn that she escapes her father's brutality by marrying a marshmallow salesman "in another state where it's legal to get married before eighth grade" (p. 95). In effect, her father's violent attempts to control her sexuality— here a case of child abuse—cause Sally to exchange one repressive patriarchal prison for another. Dependent on her husband for money, she is forbidden to talk on the telephone, look out the window, or have her friends visit. In one of his fits of anger, her husband kicks the door in. Where Rafaela's husband imprisons her with a key, Sally's locks her in with psychological force: "[Sally] sits home because she is afraid to go outside without his permission" (p. 95).

A role model for Esperanza, Sally has symbolized the process of sexual initiation for her younger friend. Two stories in the cycle reveal Esperanza's growing awareness of the link between sex, male power, and violence in patriarchal society. In "The Monkey Garden," Esperanza perceives her friend Sally to be in danger when the older girl agrees to "kiss" a group of boys so that they will return her car keys; ". . . they're making her kiss them" (p. 90), Esperanza reports to the mother of one of the boys. When the mother shows no concern, Esperanza undertakes Sally's defense herself: "Sally needed to be saved. I took three big sticks and a brick and figured this was enough" (p. 90). Sally and the boys tell her to go home and Esperanza feels stupid and ashamed. In postlapsarian anguish, she runs to the other end of the garden and, in what seems to be an especially severe form of self-punishment for this young girl, tries to make herself die by willing her heart to stop beating.

In "Red Clowns," the story that follows, Esperanza's first suspicions of the patriarchy's joining of male power, violence, and sex are confirmed beyond a doubt. She had previously used appellation throughout the first story in the Sally cycle to ask her friend to teach her how to dress and apply makeup. Now the appellation to Sally is one of severe disillusionment after Esperanza has been sexually assaulted in an amusement park while waiting for Sally to return from her own sexual liaison:

> Sally, you lied. It wasn't like you said at all . . . Why didn't you hear me when I called? Why didn't you tell them to leave me alone? The one who grabbed me by the arm, he wouldn't let me go. He said I love you, Spanish girl, I love you, and pressed his sour mouth to mine . . . I couldn't make them go away. I couldn't do anything but cry . . . Please don't make me tell it all. (P. 93)

This scene extends the male violence toward Esperanza, begun on her first day of work, when an apparently nice old man "grabs [her] face with both hands and kisses [her] hard on the mouth and doesn't let go" (p. 52). Together with other instances of male violence in the collection—Rafaela's imprisonment, Sally's beatings, and the details of Minerva's life, another young married woman whose husband beats her and throws a rock through the window—these episodes form a continuum in which sex, patriarchal power, and violence are linked. Earlier, Cisneros had developed this connection in the poem "South Sangamon," in which similar elements of male violence predominate: "he punched her belly," "his drunk cussing," "the whole door shakes/like his big foot meant to break it," and "just then/the big rock comes in."[5] *The House on Mango Street* presents this continuum critically, offering an unromanticized, inside view of Esperanza's violent sexual initiation and its links to the oppression of other women in the Chicano community.

Cisneros does not merely delineate women's victimization in this collection, however. Several positive female role models help to guide Esperanza's development. Minerva, for example, although a victim of her husband's violence, makes time to write poetry. "But when the kids are asleep after she's fed them their pancake dinner, she writes poems on little pieces of paper that she folds over and over and holds in her hands a long time, little pieces of paper that smell like a dime. She lets me read her poems. I let her read mine" (p. 80). Minerva's artistic production is reminiscent of Dr. Reefy in *Winesburg, Ohio*'s "Paper Pills," who scribbles words of wisdom on scraps of paper he crumples up, finally sharing them with a patient. It is also similar to the character of Rosendo in Soto's *Spiks*, a barrio artist who can only find space to paint an idyllic scene on the crumbling wall of his tenement bathroom and whose wife, acutely aware of the pressing economic needs of their young children, cannot afford the luxury of appreciating this non-revenue-producing art. Like Dr. Reefy, but unlike Rosendo, Minerva succeeds in communicating through her art; exchanging poems with Esperanza, she contributes to the latter's artistic development while at the same time offering a lesson in women's domestic oppression and how to begin transcending it.

Also supportive of Esperanza's artistic creativity is her invalid aunt, Guadalupe: "She listened to every book, every poem I read her. One day I read her one of my own . . . That's nice. That's very good, she said in her tired voice. You just remember to keep writing, Esperanza. You must keep writing. It will keep you free . . ." (p. 56). Although the aunt lives in squalid, poor surroundings and is dying from a disease that has disfigured her once-beautiful body, she listens to the girl's stories and poems and encourages Esperanza's artisic talent. The story, "Three Sisters," recounts the wake held for the baby sister of Esperanza's friends Lucy and Rachel and is also the theme of Cisneros' earlier poem, "Velorio," in the collection entitled *Bad Boys*. Expanding upon "Velorio," however, this story introduces the figures of "the aunts, the three sisters, *las comadres*," visitors at the *velorio* who encourage Esperanza to see her artistic production in relation to the community: "When you leave you must remember always to come back . . . for the others. A circle, you understand? You will always be Esperanza. You will always be Mango Street. . . . You can't forget who you are" (p. 98). Although Esperanza doesn't understand the women's message completely, the seeds of her socially conscious art have been planted here through the directives these women give her at the baby's wake.

Alicia, another positive role model who appears in "Alicia Who Sees Mice" and "Alicia and I Talking on Edna's Steps," also counsels Esperanza to value Mango Street and return there one day to contribute to its improvement: "Like it or not you are Mango Street and one day you'll come back too." To Esperanza's reply, "Not me. Not until somebody makes it better," Alicia wryly comments "Who's going to do it? The mayor?" (p. 99). Alicia had previously appeared in the collection as a university student who takes "two trains and a bus [to the campus] because she doesn't want to spend her whole life in a factory or behind a rolling pin" (p. 32). Rebelling against her father's expectations of her, that "a woman's place is sleeping so she can wake up early . . . and make the lunchbox tortillas," Alicia "studies all night and sees the mice, the ones her father says do not exist" (p. 32). Fighting what the patriarchy expects of her, Alicia at the same time represents a clearsighted, non-mystified vision of the barrio. As a role-model and advice-giver to Esperanza, she embodies both the antipatriarchal themes and the social obligation to return to one's ethnic community that are so central to Cisneros' text.

Cisneros touches on several other important women's issues in this volume, including media images of ideal female beauty, the reifying stare of male surveyors of women, and sex roles within the family. In an effort to counter the sexual division of labor in the home, for example, Esperanza refuses one instance of women's work: "I have begun my own quiet war. Simple. Sure. I am the one who leaves the table like a man, without pulling back the chair or picking up the plate" (p. 82). Although this gesture calls critical attention to gender inequities in the family, Cisneros avoids the issue of who, in fact, will end up performing the household labor that Esperanza refuses here. This important and symbolic, yet somewhat adolescent gesture merely touches on the surface of the problem and is likely, in fact, to increase the work for another woman in Esperanza's household.

The majority of stories in *The House on Mango Street*, however, face important social issues head-on. The volume's simple, poetic language, with its insistence that the individual develops within a social community rather than in isolation, distances it from many accepted canonical texts.[6] Its deceptively simple, childlike prose and its emphasis on the unromanticized, non-mainstream issues of patriarchal violence and ethnic poverty, however, should serve precisely to accord it canonical status. We must work toward a broader understanding among literary critics of the importance of such issues to art in order to attain a richer, more diverse canon and to avoid the undervaluation and oversight of such valuable texts as *The House on Mango Street*.

NOTES

1 Terry Eagleton, *Literary Theory: An Introduction* (Minneapolis: University of Minnesota Press, 1983), 201 and passim.

2 Sandra Cisneros, *The House on Mango Street* (Houston: Arte Público Press, 1985). Subsequent references will be to this edition and will appear in the text. For the figures on the press run see Pedro Gutiérrez-Revuelta, "Género e ideología en el libro de Sandra Cisneros: *The House on Mango Street*," *Crítica* 1, no. 3 (1986): 48–59.

3 Gutiérrez-Revuelta, "Género e ideología," 48. This critic also cites nine articles that have appeared to date on Cisneros' text. They consist primarily of reviews in Texas newspapers and articles in Chicano journals. See also Erlinda González-Berry and Tey Diana Rebolledo's "Growing up Chicano: Tomás Rivera and Sandra Cisneros," *Revista Chicano-Riqueña* 13 (1985): 109–19.

4 Sherwood Anderson, *Winesburg, Ohio* (New York: Viking Press, 1964, rpt. 1970); Pedro Juan Soto, *Spiks*, trans. Victoria Ortiz (New York: Monthly Review Press, 1973); Gloria Naylor, *The Women of Brewster Place* (New York: Penguin Books, 1983); and Tomás Rivera, *. . . y no se lo tragó la tierra/And the Earth Did Not Part* (Berkeley: Quinto Sol, 1971). Among the many specific comparisons that might be made, Naylor's "Cora Lee" has much in common with Cisneros' "There Was an Old Woman She Had So Many Children She Didn't Know What to Do."

5 Sandra Cisneros, *Bad Boys* (San Jose, Calif.: Mango Publications, 1980).

6 Other critics have argued that Esperanza's departure from Mango Street is individualistic and escapist, and that the desire for a house of her own away from the barrio represents a belief in the American Dream. See Gutiérrez-Revuelta, "Género e ideología," 52–55 and Juan Rodríguez, "*The House on Mango Street* by Sandra Cisneros," *Austin Chronicle*, 10 Aug. 1984 (cited in Gutiérrez-Revuelta, p. 52). I find that the text itself supports the opposite view, as does the author's choice of employment. Cisneros has returned to a Chicago barrio, teaching creative writing at an alternative high school for drop-outs. See "About Sandra Cisneros," *The House on Mango Street*, 103.

Deconstructing the Dominant Patriarchal Text: Cecile Pineda's Narratives

JUAN BRUCE-NOVOA

Cecile Pineda, a California writer from the San Francisco Bay area, worked for a number of years in experimental theatre. From 1969 to 1981 she directed her own troupe, Theatre of Man, staging a wide range of dramas, including several of her original pieces. She was invited to Poland by the Kosciuszko Foundation in 1977 to view the work of renowned Polish directors; on this trip she also conducted workshops with her own, less traditional approach. She came to know the internationally acclaimed director Jerzy Grotowski and served as his interpreter during some of his visits in California. But her activities went unnoticed by Chicano or Latino critics, even those most active in drama. It was not until she published her first novel, *Face* (1985), that she gained our attention, and I began to mention her as a leading Chicana novelist. Yet even now, after the extraordinary success of *Face* and a second novel, *Frieze* (1986), Pineda remains, for the most part, ignored by Chicano criticism. As in the case of another accomplished Chicana author, Sheila Ortiz Taylor, the silence on the part of the Chicano literary establishment may be attributed to the lack of obvious ethnic identification of the characters or settings in the novels or of the author herself in the publisher's book promotion. Pineda's family heritage, however, qualifies her as a Chicana—a person of Mexican descent living permanently in the United States—and if Chicano criticism is to offer an accurate depiction of the entire field of writing, then it must account for such authors.[1] At the same time, Pineda exemplifies the noteworthy trend among Chicano authors toward addressing a wider audience, an attitude that places her closer to the position of Latin American women writers residing in the United States.

Unlike most Chicano authors, male or female, who ensure ethnic specificity by focusing on subjects and locales familiar to readers of their own group, Pineda prefers to inscribe the readers' position at a distance from her characters, the situation, and the action. Although *Face* takes place in our own time, distance is achieved by setting it first, in Brazil, and second, in the uniquely Latin American poverty zone of the makeshift shacks that ring metropolitan areas. The character suffers an incredible accident: defacement, quite literally, and then must reconstruct his face by himself. In addition, the blatant use of the surname "Cara" (Portuguese for face) for the protagonist creates an openly allegorical tone that gives one the sense of having to read through the presented events to another hidden and thus distanced set of alluded actions. These admittedly schematic devices place the plot far from the readers. In *Frieze,* Pineda repeats the strategy by placing the action in India and Java around the year A.D. 800. In this case, the protagonist/narrator was one of the elite tradesmen, a sculptor in the religious tradition; among these artisans, he distinguished himself by a talent for innovation, thus rising above the others to the position of artist. Pineda informs us from the beginning that the narrator is now blind. Thus she creates both a figure and a situation that are archetypal: the blind artist in the act of recalling and narrating the past. The narration assumes the quality of divinely inspired words used to tell an allegorically primal tale. Once again the readers are distanced, not only through the facts but also through the utilization of traditional, literary mediators.

In addition, Pineda further distances readers by apparently employing the perspective of the traditional omniscient narrator and author. *Face* begins with the report of a plastic surgeon read to the "Twenty-fifth Annual Meeting of Plastic and Reconstructive Surgery, Rio de Janeiro, Brazil, June 1975."[2] The narrative act is contextualized within the rarified limits of a closed meeting of an elite group whose function is, after all, to redesign appearances in order to change our visual impression or "reading" of them. A spokesman not only for, but simultaneously to, this group assumes the position of primal narrative voice, mediating between readers and protagonist by assuming the rhetorical role of subject, the "I," who at the start speaks about the object "he." The spokesman's position seems omniscient in that he has the knowledge and authority to summarize the plot in four short paragraphs. He then goes on to provoke the rest of the narrative by asking a further question about the content of the text, thus channeling readers' attention to the mystery of the later chapters: "You may ask what this man was doing all this time he was hiding . . ." (p. 4). The context gives one to understand that the speaker has posed the question rhetorically because he seems already to know the facts, which he will surely proceed to reveal.

Although readers are led forward by the desire to discover what has happened, they are not designated in the roles of judge or participant in the action but rather are inscribed into the role of passive listeners to an informed, highly authoritative narrator—who, despite an unimposing tone, has initiated the encounter with the text by assuming a didactic position. His is the "Prologue" with all the preemptive, logocentric possibilities of a "pro-logos": an a priori discourse, or its surrogate, claiming to constitute the regulating principle in the universe to be entered. Although individual readers may interpret meaning according to their own perception of the text (limited as they are in the capacity to transcend the singularity of their particular vision), the Prologist's discourse seems to constitute a preemptive allusion to "a meaning" not open to dispute in the realm of the text's ultimate existence.

In *Frieze*, the use of first-person narration does little to bridge distance because the tone is one of contemplative recall, far from conversational, and because of the archetypal nature of the narrator as explained above. In addition, the aged narrator/protagonist, once a master sculptor in India, then considered a First World zone, now resides in "a boarded-up backwater" in Java.[3] Added to this is his condition of having been blinded and relegated to near-immobility. His narrative has the quality of a soliloquy, but not a baroque, self-conscious one addressed to the audience; the context of ancient sacredness, as well as a series of monological indicators, lends it a classic hermeticism that readers are permitted to violate only through the accepted channel of overheard thoughts.

Pineda herself penned an "Author's Preface" for *Frieze*, directly assuming the role of logocentric spokesperson. In it, she explains her interest in the material, defines its historical significance, and even dictates within what terms she would like us to read the novel: a blinded sculptor's story about a ninth-century Javanese temple, constructed at the cost of the existence of the government it was meant to glorify and of the well-being of the native population. It is to be read as an allegory of our own country in the present: "The reader may perceive a nagging parallel between that ancient world and his own," Pineda states, and then proceeds to narrow the points of comparison by adding, "with one exception: it will be the rare curiosity seeker who one thousand years hence makes a tourist pilgrimage to a line of missile silos, guidebook in hand" (p. x). A previous juxtaposition of two epigraphs serves the same purpose:

> The great pagoda is raised. The country lies ruined.—Burmese Saying

For the fifth consecutive year, in the face of the highest child-poverty rate in eighteen years, our national leaders have targeted poor children and families again for billions in new budget cuts. . . . [Meanwhile] (sic.) an escalating arms race and nuclear proliferation not only hold hostage the future we hold in trust for our children, but also steal the present from millions of the world's children whose principal daily enemy is relentless poverty and the hunger and disease it breeds.— Marian Wright Edelman quoted in *The Barnard Reporter* (P. vi)

Once again, the prologist speaks with the authority of transcendent omniscience, bracketing the field of signification for the readers in order to guide them to an ultimate and thus "true" allegorical level of meaning.

This combination of rhetorical and thematic distance, authoritative stance, and allegorically didactic purpose gives Pineda's prose her characteristic quality of sacred proverb. Readers are led to experience the reading as a lesson from which they can learn, and perhaps utilize, in their own situation. The lesson in both novels involves a self-realization through physical mortification, worldly renunciation, and discipline, allowing us to validly categorize it as a form of asceticism.[4] Furthermore, since in the foreground of both novels is a creative, artistic project—the sculpting of a representation of a previously existent presence (presentation) of centralizing significance, now absent and thus in need of invocation—I would venture to call Pineda's a lesson in aesthetic asceticism. Her novels are about life as a creative act, one that is a part of an ascetic purification ritual.

In each novel the protagonist will be forced to leave the security of his professional setting, with its defined process of advancement and rewards, as well as the habitual space of intimacy that has sustained him. Torn from familiar surroundings, he must travel into a hinterland where he must practice his learned skill on a difficult project of artistic construction he never even dreamed of having to achieve, while simultaneously coping with being abandoned by loved ones, thrust far from the protection and security of his craft guild, and reduced to hunger and the fear of violence. Although each, in a different manner, has recourse to an authoritative text to guide him in his task, both are outsiders, nonmembers of the inner circle who have proprietory rights to the text.[5] Yet despite the odds, the protagonists succeed far beyond expectations. Neither achieves wealth, fame, or the social position he had envisioned, and both lose the woman they most desire. But they also realize a personal inner balance, a sense of place within society and of individual achievement.

The course of life on which they originally found themselves certainly would not have provided this.

True, this analytically reductive comparison glosses over the differences. Cara is a poor barber, a marginated proletarian from the slums of a contemporary Brazilian metropolis; Gopal is a master sculptor, an elite member of a small, privileged class in the center of religious/political activity in eighth-century India. Cara is further reduced to the status of pariah among the dregs of society when an accident obliterates his face, but Gopal's skill results in his being raised to the position of head sculptor of royal courts and sacred temples. Cara is hurled down among the jagged rocks of a slippery, seaside cliff; Gopal is elevated to the sides of an ascending mountain of a temple. Cara must reconstruct his own face with no help other than self-injected novocaine and a manual of plastic surgery pilfered from a library. Gopal has the task of reconstructing the story of Buddha, literally the face of the holy one, on the friezes of a foreign temple, with the help of a manual of sacred stories and the assistance of a slave. In the end, both experience a type of reversal of their situation; ironically, Cara, the pariah, returns to the city and renews his former life of work, and Gopal, the privileged artist, retreats further into the social periphery as a blinded artisan capable of executing only the simplest of carvings.

In both novels, Pineda's deep structure is essentially that of the ascetic journey of self-discovery through suffering, degradation, renunciation, and disciplined work. Both men learn to see and accept themselves better during the experience. Through the act of recall forced on each of the protagonists by their experience, they and the readers discover a forgotten incident from early life that can be interpreted as the true origin of their fate. In both cases, it was probably not understood by the individuals while in the process of living the event itself or in mature life that followed. At this level of signification, Pineda's is an ancient message meant for our time; the true meaning of life is found only through sacrifice, self-encounter, and rebirth. In *Face*, she directs it to all those who search for significance through money, sex, pleasure, and social position; in *Frieze*, she aims at those who allow their skills to be utilized by power brokers in exchange for the relative privilege of position and the promise of riches in the future. In both, the vanity of social prestige and economic rewards is denounced, and the goal of spiritual and existential satisfaction is offered as an alternative.

The fact that both novels hinge on creative acts allows them to be read as metatexts. Further support for this comes from Pineda's indirect commentary on the connection between the object of Cara's sculpting and the narrative act in the epigraph of *Face:* "Like a novel, the face is a web of living meanings, an inter-human event, in which the thing and its expression are inextricably joined."[6] Whether the author seriously pursues the ascetic life, as her novels seem to recommend, is not the point I have in mind; rather, I would draw attention to the correlation between her implied belief in asceticism and the way she constructs the novel and manipulates strategies to make it function according to that spiritual message on several levels of interpretation.

In both novels, after the prologue or preface, readers are thrust into an ambiguous setting, one that seems to float in time because memory itself is unable to fix either the specific images of the past or the exact location in which those images should appear. Elements drift in and out of vision, their significance undetermined, like loose fragments. In this sense, Pineda deprives her readers, first in the prologue and then in the narrative, of the modern role of active participants in the narrative process. She then takes away, if not sensations, at least equivalents of sensible material: a double deprivation analogous to that experienced by the protagonists in the opening pages of each novel. Both have been excluded from their professional duties and thus relegated to relative inactivity; both have been stripped of sensation and their ability to order the world accordingly. Slowly, the narrative takes shape and direction, with the recuperation of images by the protagonist coinciding with the accumulation of information by readers. Only after the journey through the text will those initial fragments form the basis for a version of the experience, one that readers must reconstruct just as the protagonists have constructed their project with the aid of a text.

Because what we are given is partial, the image can never be complete, the meaning never entirely reducible. Yet the project is vital, for what we construct in the reading is ourselves, our identity (a metaphorical face or façade) as readers, just as the characters construct themselves as artisans. What the novelist really creates, finally, is herself as novelist. The traditional message of the story as a completed sign to be transmitted to the passive reader is subsumed by inscribing/reading itself as the signifying act. If we are willing, initially and temporarily, to lose face—accept deprivation and the loss of control—and apply our skills, with no real guarantee of reward, then we can emerge transformed and able, perhaps, to survive in a world that will probably continue to deprive us of meaningful sensations and treat us as backwater curiosities who are worthy of, at best, a quick glance. The freedom realized through, and within, the ascetic life is not for everyone, just as accepting the authoritative prologuing of these texts is not to every reader's tastes, but the profound experience is there only for those who undergo the initial defacement or temporary blindness.

If we terminate our analysis at this level we are in danger of leaving Pineda in a school of traditional thought: give up your will, obey, and all will be resolved by your omniscient guide. In literary terms, this would once again associate her with the traditional, monological novelist, one who accepts the power and authority of the centralized narrative voice. In ideological terms, this would mean that she respects, maintains, and therefore posits as a model the text of traditional social dominance, that is, the patriarchal text. It is no coincidence that the plastic surgeon who speaks the prologue in *Face* is named Teofilho Godoy, an interlingual play through which God is doubly named and adored. And we recall that the author herself, like a convinced patriarch, directs our reading in *Frieze*. However, on closer inspection these inscriptions of would-be monological voices mask another strategy, that of inscribing the traditional order so as to make possible the revolt against it that the text will realize. Pineda begins with the possibility of a traditional reading, then proceeds to deconstruct it.[7]

Pineda's use of the traditional structure of the prologued, authoritative text, subsequently deconstructed and transcended through the dialogical forces within the narrative, parallels the action of the characters—the transcendence of their situation of mortification, renunciation, relegation to the hinterland, and eventual self-realization—and, as we have seen, that of the readers. In *Face*, the protagonist Cara replaces the plastic surgeon as the reconstructor of the face, proving Godoy to be not primordial, as his prologue would lead us to believe, but substitutable, replaceable, and thus far from truly omniscient. In *Frieze*, the deconstruction begins in the preface itself when the author admits that the novel she has produced is not the one she intended to write because the material forced a change in the plan, one that the author understood only *a posteriori*. This apparent cliché—the novelist must adjust to the demands of the text—proves, however, to be an allusion to the novel's unspoken, allegorical subplot: the continual rebellion of apparently submissive matter against agents of repression—slaves vs. masters, nature vs. human edifices, the sculptor or artist vs. the dictator and the sacred text. As a result of all of these rebellions, in the end Buddha is absent from the central stupa of the glorious temple, having been displaced by vandals to a peripheral position outside the outer walls, and a chief priest is killed and buried in the vacated stupa. The temple to eternal life reveals itself as a tomb of mortal men. Thus, in both novels the prime representative of a hieratic order is displaced from the center and substituted, making Pineda's novels antimonological, with all the subversive connotations that carries.

Equally, the prologues suffer the same degradation as that experienced by the characters and readers, yet in different terms. As texts, they lose their primordial function—to speak clearly the terms of engagement with the text and the goal of interpretation—and become signifiers of a suppressed signified (the alluded-to absence of one total meaning) that would be equivalent to the supreme ideal of perfect signification: God. Lest we then attempt to read the novels as manuals of divine reorientation, we must immediately affirm that Pineda is not a mystic but just the opposite. Her asceticism teaches survival on the strictly human plane, in a world from which the Word/God/logos has withdrawn, leaving behind only worldly claimants to the privilege of spokesperson, like prologist, physicians, state bureaucrats, or high priests, who too often go as far as to usurp the divine prerogatives. In both novels, the divine logos is, as Derrida would state, the always already absent in her texts. This is represented by the primal loss of the motivating ideal in each novel; both novels begin the narration from the perspective of the degraded protagonist, defaced or blinded, who recalls a fading past, and a woman, who remains only in traces of sensations. This does not mean, however, that the spiritual or ideal has no role in human life. Both protagonists are driven by the memory of their ideals to recapture their lives, but ultimately the particular woman whose image incarnates the ideal is supplanted or accepted as a permanent absence, present only as a memory whose reality depends on the power of the narrator to recall her. And the power of the protagonists to recreate is far from divinely perfect. Although they achieve admirable feats of creative sculpture, in the end they must settle for the apparently much lesser status of producer of the ordinary. In *Face*, Cara's new face is "unremarkable," while in *Frieze*, Gopal ends up carving simple grave markers. Like the monological text, the old-fashioned artist/hero is obsolete.

Pineda's foregrounding of the sculpting act must not be overlooked in our discussion of the deconstruction of the traditional logocentric and thus dominant/patriarchal novel. In that tradition, it is assumed the author possesses the word that is held to be the ultimate source of meaning for the graphic representation in the form of the authoritative text. Both of Pineda's novels, however, are graphocentric in that they displace the word as privileged expression, or even as the goal of the artistic endeavor, substituting the sculpted object of either the face or the frieze. Both protagonists take possession of authoritative texts, not to enter into the realm of authority as a participant in the inner circle but rather to revolutionize its distribution outside the circle. And neither claims the privileges of that possession after finishing the immediate task; each creates the sculpted object as image, and it then becomes the source of meaning for any word (the novel itself) that might attempt to represent it. The novels thus attack logo and phonocentrism—both closely linked to phallocentrism—representing the functionality of the word as signifier of meaning and as conveyor of a message known to, and contained in, the speaker as origin, that is, the speaker as prologist.

Face and *Frieze* do not intend to communicate the prologued message, as we have seen, but rather are to be an experience relived in an alternative fashion, through the images recalled by a different speaker or actor. In this way, the prologue, which can also mean "synthesis of the discourse to follow" (a true philosophical first principle) is denounced as repressive and inadequate. It is not a divine but rather an all-too-human, and thus limited, usurpation of what only a true God could claim: a total vision and comprehension that would be impossible to communicate logically. Despite all claims, in particular that of the monological prologist, no human reduction can adequately convey, much less take the place of, the discourse in its multifaceted reality or even the multiple discourses that intersect the text in its phenomenological field of full intertextuality. At the same time, since that polivalent discourse is unable to have itself experienced in its entire being by readers of humanly limited capacities, its totality is fated to be a continually differed difference, always eminent, but only known as a possibility suggested, glimpsed, or perhaps recalled like the fragmentary traces of a lost lover, impalpable but real enough to excite and motivate. This ultimate meaning, impossible to capture but alluded to as an as-and-in image, is generated by the narrative but simultaneously lies beyond its purview. Its realm is that of the continuous Other, so desired by discontinuous humankind, where meaning is undebatable because all would be one and the same. Pineda imbues her novels with the tension of the possible impossibilities even as she consciously relativizes and deconstructs the ideal from the human perspective.

Cecile Pineda's fiction is a recent addition to the growing body of Latina writing in the United States, but already, with only two novels published, she has proved herself one of its most skilled and interesting practitioners. More significantly, she exemplifies a trend toward a less regional and ethnically specific, more international and universal approach. This, however, does not in the least lessen her impact on the more parochial literature. Obviously, when read past the distancing surface, Pineda's novels are allegories for our time and place, as well as being subversive texts of social renewal (see note 7).

NOTES

1   Publicity for Cecile Pineda makes no indication of her ethnicity, so, as is my custom, I corresponded with her to inquire about it. She responded: "I am the product of a union between a Mexican father who fled the 1910 revolution, and came by rail to Brownsville under an assumed name. . . . My mother was of French-Swiss origin, from the suburb of Neuchatel known as Marin. By temperament and culture I identify most emphatically with my Hispanic origins" (letter, Dec. 20, 1985).

2   Cecile Pineda, *Face* (New York: Viking-Penguin, 1985), 4. Page numbers will be cited in the text in parentheses when the reference to this text is clear.

3   Pineda, *Frieze* (New York: Viking-Penguin, 1986), 207. Page numbers will be cited in the text in parentheses when the reference to this text is clear.

4   Asceticism: a disciplinary course of conduct in which certain actions, usually of a renunciatory or penitential nature, are performed for their intellectual, moral, or religious effect; the doctrine that through the renunciation of the desires of the flesh and of pleasure in worldly things and through self-mortification or self-denial one can subdue her or his appetites and discipline oneself so as to reach a high spiritual or intellectual state. It differs from mysticism in that the latter's purpose is to achieve actual union with the divine in this life, beyond the mere state of enlightenment. Asceticism is often the preparatory stage for the mystic experience.

5   The experience of forced travel to a hinterland, to a foreignlike zone where the character is far from the security he has grown accustomed to, is similar to that of the exile or immigrant. The exploration of just such a reading of the texts is the subject of a separate paper, to be presented at the MLA conference in 1987. Suffice it to say here that this may well be a connection with Pineda's personal history, and with her father's experience as an immigrant and refugee who came to the United States from a Mexico disrupted by revolution. However, we should not lose sight of the profound links between the exile and/or immigrant experience and that of females in a patriarchal society in which they often exist as foreigners or disenfranchised residents.

6   M. Merleau-Ponty states as well that "the body is to be compared, not to a physical object, but rather to a work of art" (*Phénomènologie de la Perception* [London: Routledge and Kegan Paul, 1974], 150).

7   The construction of the dominant/patriarchal stand, and then the allowance for its deconstruction by the alternative voice, places Pineda's strategy within what Julia Kristeva calls feminist practice. "A feminist practice can only be. . . . at odds with what already exists so that we may say 'that's not it' and 'that's still not it.'" She also states that women's role "is only in assuming a *negative* function: reject everything finite, definite, structured, loaded with meaning in the existing state of society. Such an attitude places women on the side of the explosion of social codes: with revolutionary movements." "Oscillation du 'pouvoir' au 'refus,'" interview by Xavière Gauthier in *Tel Quel*, no. 58 (Summer 1974), translated in *New French Feminisms: An Anthology*, ed. Elaine Marks and Isabelle de Courtivron (Amherst: University of Massachusetts Press, 1980), 166–67.

The Ties that Bind: Women and Community in Evangelina Vigil's Thirty an' Seen a Lot

MARY JANE TREACY

Over a decade after the birth of the Chicano movement, San Antonio writer Evangelina Vigil published her first book of poetry, *Thirty an' Seen a Lot*,[1] a volume that charts the development of a poetic persona—a young Mexican-American woman not unlike, one supposes, Vigil herself—from isolated individual to committed Chicana.[2] From the beginning, it is clear that this persona suffers primarily from her "hyphenated state" as a Mexican-American, seemingly caught between a Mexican past she does not share and an Anglo world that is unmitigatedly exploitative. The poetic "I" here is engulfed by the "psychological violence" that Anglos use to keep her and all other Mexican-Americans as emotionally and economically impoverished as possible in order to create a dependent underclass of docile workers: ". . . Mexicans / do all the dirty work in this city, si / te fijas. . . ."[3] When expressing herself in the Anglo language, the persona complains of being empty, in a "hollow space,"[4] and likens herself to an actress who is exhausted from fulfilling alien roles for a public that doesn't care:

> like a good actress on a stage
> but with no props
> no supporting actors
> no friends in the audience
> and no heart for it all
> anyways[5]

82

The persona, then, is faced with the task of creating her self anew in a world characterized by "human ugliness and basic human depravity shrouded often by / greed and racism."[6] She does this through a process Julián Olivares has called "seeing and becoming,"[7] achieving a spiritual regeneration from her reevaluation of the Mexican-American community: "seeing" while accepting the political ideals of the Chicano movement and "becoming," that is, "becoming" Chicana. The poems in *Thirty an' Seen a Lot* chart the story of a persona who, ignoring her Mexican heritage, comes to make a commitment to what she calls a cultural defense. In so doing, she is able to renew herself as well as to set out a schema for the social redemption of her people.

She discovers that she is not alone in her quest for an authentic self; she has some guides, all of which lead to her own past or to a simpler time, when one's self and ethnic self were identical. She has the memories of her childhood in the overwhelmingly Mexican San Juan projects[8] while, in the present, she finds that her elders, most particularly her grandmother, still embody what hitherto she has hidden from view: the Mexican, the mestiza, the Spanish-speaking part of her being. She soon recognizes that the old people have given her a culture that forms the core of her being:

> así vivieron ellos
> una vida eterna
> de conversación
> desarrollando el pensamiento
> y la filosofía íntima
> de mi barrio y de mi ser[9]

Because elders form the link between a proud Mexican heritage and the present, it is not surprising that it is an old man who first jolts her into an awareness of her marginal position as a Mexican-American. As she is sitting alone in an expensive Anglo bar, she sees the old man go by, "los pies indios clad in dusty shoes,"[10] pushing a cart, and listening to traditional Mexican tunes from a small transistor radio. What she sees is a simple man who will not permit the dominant society to ignore his presence or to define him as picturesque. On the contrary, the persona determines that the old man blares his polka defiantly as an affirmation of his Mexican background and, inspired by him, she makes her first public commitment to cultural resistance. This entails rejection of the Anglo world in all its facets: economic domination, greed, and racism, all of which marginalize and exploit her people, as well as the English language, the code that transmits the dominant ideology to all who speak it.[11]

The persona turns to the Mexican-American community. However, the Anglo world's sprawling business interests and alien capitalist values have already encroached upon the old neighborhoods, changing the cityscape and inevitably disturbing the psychic landscape of those who live there:

> el mercado queda
> por la calle Produce Row
> y la plaza queda
> en el corazón del centro
> por la calle de Comercio
> de Comercio y Soledad[12]

Like the persona who returns to the street where she lived as a child (only to discover that it has disappeared from the city's geography as well as from the memories of its current inhabitants),[13] all Mexican-Americans appear to be in danger of losing their precarious place in the world, just as they have lost or are about to lose ties to their individual and collective pasts. As a result, the community becomes fragmented, and the once-comfortably familiar streets seem to fill with the casualties of "Americanization": elders who retreat into silence, the weak who become drunks, addicts, hobos, and madwomen, and even the young, who seem to face an inevitable assimilation into an inhospitable, even hostile, dominant society.[14]

The persona can no longer hope to find a Mexican-American haven in a specific geographical place; rather, she has to begin to develop a new sense of community based upon the strong personal relationships that unite individuals and can transform individuals into a people. To do this, she envisions a Mexican-American culture that fosters spiritual connections through the customs and traditions of ordinary daily life. Consequently, many of the poems in *Thirty an' Seen a Lot* celebrate activities so common as to pass unnoticed—women primping at the bus stop, mothers dressing their little girls in soft pastels, and people flirting at the local bar[15]—but actually reveal a pattern of social practices that promotes bonding among all members of the group. Vigil gives special attention to the sounds that emanate from her community, particularly the music that seems to pour out from homes, cars, even human hands. Everywhere one hears traditional tunes that convey the Mexican heritage, create emotional ties to the Hispanic part of the self, and, because they are played so loud, spill out into the street, becoming the invisible, acoustic boundaries of the community itself. But Vigil does not include music solely because it gives people "alma, ritmo y tradición";[16] she also hopes to demonstrate the ways in which Mexican-American culture is inclusive and nurturing. Its music is for all, played over the radio in order to communicate and maintain connections among members of the community; indeed, sometimes the tunes themselves seem far less important than the accompanying dedications that spread waves of affection throughout an entire listening audience:

> se les va
> en puro leer
> dedicaciones
> usualmente
> "bonitas melodías"
> dedicación tras dedicación
> felicidades del corazón
> a los novios
> a las quinceañeras
> a los que cumplen años
> a los que celebran aniversarios
> con mucho cariño
> de parte de sus esposos
> esposas
> madrecitas
> padres
> hermanitos
> queridos
> queridas
> amistades[17]

Having constructed a highly idealized Mexican-American community, Vigil's persona can divide the world into the "capitalists" and the "us," seeing "unmistakable confrontation" and "times of war"[18] while envisaging "modern chicano/guerrilla campsites"[19] that will carry out the resistance. However, she does not argue for armed struggle to establish a Chicano homeland or, surprisingly, even for radical socioeconomic change within the United States. Rather, her campsites are ones that eschew revolutionary violence in favor of love, equality, and respect:

> Veo modern chicano/guerrilla campsites
> en tiempos de guerra
> humeando amor
> filosofía
> estrategia
> y táctica

all of
contemporary relevance:
breeding unity
(como siempre)
para al fin
algún día en aquel futuro
que pacientemente esperamos/
anciosamente anticipamos
acabar
con el desmadre:
recrear balance
igualdad
respeto[20]

Even though Vigil enumerates the evils of the United States as a capitalist nation, she primarily attacks the Anglo world for the dehumanizing values that support its economic system. Vigil seeks a revolution, but not one that takes place in the public sphere of political action. Rather, she seeks a spiritual awakening within the inner quest for the Mexican/Chicano self. Her ideas for the salvation of the *raza* (articulated only at the end of *Thirty an' Seen a Lot* in a poem dedicated to Arturo Valdez, "el 'Paul Revere' / de la Revolución Tejana")[21] are centered on the transformation of love of one's "Mexicanness" into unity and solidarity with others of similar Hispanic descent. Vigil suggests that this love is the creative force that will save the Mexican-American community from disintegration or assimilation, just as it is also the creative force that permits the persona in the last poem to transcend national borders and join with Nicaraguans and the Salvadoran left to see a victorious future.[22] Now that Valdez, the symbol of a social movement based on love, is dead, Vigil urges the living to continue his commitment to the *raza* in whatever land:

Y el ritual indio
tiene que seguir humeando
entre conversaciones importantes
sobre ideas recién nacidas
flor de ternura y amor
que crece entre nuestra gente
"¡el carnalismo, carnal!"[23]

In spite of her rhetoric of social protest, Vigil is not content with a poetics of denunciation; rather, she urges her readers to transcend politics and develop from the rebellious resistance that characterizes a first level of

Chicano consciousness to the more spiritual center of that consciousness, called *carnalismo*. According to Chicano philosopher Elihu Carranza, *carnalismo* is "a term denoting a bond between persons, a relation of flesh and bone, of moral obligation, of moral rectitude, and of moral and spiritual significance. . . ."[24] Vigil seeks, then, a Chicano consciousness brought to its fullest and developed into a ethical stance in the world or, as Carranza states, "man as he is to coincide with man as he ought to be."[25]

Vigil writes Chicano cultural nationalist poetry to protest that "it / is damn hard making it as a Chicana in the U.S.A."[26] and to present her vision of an ideal community. What sets Vigil apart from other poets in the cultural nationalist tradition is her woman's perspective. Her poetic "I" is clearly female, a gendered voice whose experiences are as determined by sex as by ethnicity; this persona wore silk dresses and patent leather shoes as a girl, learned about life at a grandmother's knee, fell in love, and now treats a niece and nephew with maternal care.[27] Due to these experiences, she can guide the reader not only through the public sphere, where Mexican-American men and women struggle against Anglo domination, but also through the intimate spaces where women bring up and nurture the young.

The private sphere is centered in the home, usually the kitchen, where women share their feelings and care for one another. Here the grandmother taught the young girl that love and compassion toward others are of primary importance, values that later would become the core of the adult persona's Chicana consciousness and the fundamental principle of her revolution.[28] Here, too, the persona as a girl learned Spanish and, in her ordinary activities, reenacted daily those traditions that would come to form the core of her Mexican identity. As Olivares points out,[29] even the grandmother's *café con leche* teaches pride in the Mexican-American's mixed race and, therefore, is a celebration of the persona's ethnic self:

> I love to spill a splash
> of thick white cream
> into a delicious steaming cup
> of grandma's strong strong black coffee
> swirl some sweet
> then anticipatingly
> hot kiss
> the spinning wheel of brown fortune
> to a soothing, tasty
> stop[30]

It is in the home, too, that the persona's mother imparted the lessons of a feminine identity (pastel dresses, jewelry) and in doing so, created an intimate mother-daughter bond: "and I think to myself / why is it that mothers always know / what kinds of things their daughters like."[31] The daughter has happy memories of her girlhood and relates the charm of her role models: hardworking women who are both strong and even aggressively feminine as they impose their world of flowered dresses, perfume and makeup on an essentially male-dominated public sphere.[32] Nevertheless, Vigil also suggests that there is a double message for the Mexican-American girl. As she recalls her happy girlhood in the projects, she recounts the ways in which she learned of love: pop music from the radio and graffiti on the building walls: " 'Lupe loves Tony' / 'always and forever.'"[33] Yet, for every sign of affection on the buildings, there were also disturbing signs that displayed female bodies in an attempt to punish or control women's sexuality, lessons that she remembers but disregards as "innocent desmadres de la juventud":[34]

> no sooner than had the building wall/canvasses been painted clean
> did barrio kids take to carving new inspirations
> and chuco hieroglyphics
> and new figure drawings of naked women
> and their parts
> and messages for all
> "la Diana es puta"
> "el Lalo es joto"
> y que "la Chelo se deja"[35]

Although unable to analyze her childhood experiences, she does observe how sexism, both inside and outside of the community, now harms Mexican-American women. First, she sees how racism, combined with contempt for women, leads men from outside the community to objectify and to use Mexican-American women, prizing "a good piece of brown ass."[36] Then, economic exploitation and sexism foster prostitution for the "Iranians and / other foreign-exchange dudes and military types"[37] who take advantage of poverty. More problematic is the discovery of sexual harassment and threats of physical violence within her community, where the Chicano joins Anglo and foreign men to objectify and bully the Chicana.[38]

As a writer of cultural nationalist views, Vigil has to value the unity of men and women in a common battle for Chicano survival. Therefore, even though she raises questions of gender difference and men's domination of women, she is reluctant to attack men as a group. Instead, she suggests that there exists a men's sphere, pertaining to men of all ethnic and national origins, which fosters aggression, sexual swaggering, and estrangement from the world of women. Since Vigil presents the Mexican-American women's private sphere as the source of the loving relationships and nurturing behaviors that the ideal Chicano revolutionary movement will bring into the public sphere, the Chicano who is "bien perdido / en el mundo de nalgas y calzones"[39] and the "tipo / de motherfucker / bien chingón"[40] are doubly dangerous for the community, for as they engage in sexist behaviors, they also betray the hope of revolutionary change.

Although Vigil bitterly criticizes "asqueroso sexismo"[41] through the persona, she does not understand sexism to be the systematic and institutionalized domination of all women by all men but rather an individual behavioral problem, a "complejo"[42] of a recalcitrant few who still cling to outmoded or incorrect values. Therefore, she is able to divide men into two categories: all "los que piensan con la verga" and "those who do not,"[43] attacking the former while apologizing to the latter for any possible association with men with sexist behaviors. Nothing could be further from Vigil's position than a feminist analysis of men as oppressors of women, for she wants to affirm that all Mexican-Americans share a culture that is essentially loving and nurturing. Therefore, she can easily distinguish the "bad" men from the "good" and lament the condition of those good men who, due to life-long experiences in the male world, have been left unable to express their affections openly. Such is the case of two old men who encounter fear and estrangement[44] when trying to approach their small grandchildren. Although they are not able to span both the public and private spheres, they long for intimacy with the children, the first speaking in "baby-talk" to communicate with his grandson, the other trying to draw out a frightened little girl who, only many years later, senses that he was "full of so much love."[45] The poignancy of their failure condemns a disfiguring male culture rather than the individuals who partake of it.

Vigil writes women's cultural nationalist poetry using a clearly gendered female persona and presenting "Mexicanness" as essentially "feminine"; that is, it is the manifestation of a nurturing, people-oriented tradition whose source is the Mexican family, the home, and the lore passed on from grandmother to grandchild. In this way, she privileges Mexican-American women's experiences, placing them at the core of any society that would save Mexican-Americans from oppression and/or assimilation. Therefore, when she demands a "defensa cultural"[46] and an individual spiritual awakening to the importance of *raza*. Vigil is insisting that every Mexican-American develop his or her "feminine" qualities, those qualities of intimacy and caring for others that are necessary for the greater communal awakening that is *carnalismo*.

Yet if Evangelina Vigil values "women's" traditions sufficiently to make them the guidelines for public life, she also dismisses common female experiences that threaten to expose differences among Mexican-Americans within her Chicano community. Thus, she brings up, but does not probe, the oppression of women. Perhaps Vigil's revolution of love is too precarious to allow for any internal critique that could disrupt a tenuous unity among men and women. Or perhaps Vigil necessarily undermines her own spiritual and political messages when she envisions a utopian community, free of dissension, but also free of the debate that fosters personal and social change. Vigil is a poet who wants to celebrate the Mexican-American tradition and who hopes to urge her readers to transform personal awareness of the Chicano self into a social movement that can unify all Mexican-Americans, and even all Hispanics. Yet her vision seems based on a community so idealized that it cannot easily tolerate the idea of injustice or flaw embedded within the culture. So even as Vigil's persona brings to light the bonds that unite Mexican-Americans, she is also bound to silence those insights that might lead to a critique of women's position in the community.

NOTES

1   Evangelina Vigil, *Thirty an' Seen a Lot* (Houston: Arte Público Press, 1982).

2   In this paper, I differentiate between those residents of the United States who are of Mexican descent, the Mexican-Americans, and those Mexican-Americans who have consciously adopted the political stance and cultural identity forged by the Chicano Movement—the Chicanos.

3   Vigil, "evening news," 38.

4   Vigil, "spinning on solid ground," 4.

5   Vigil, "sin ganas en el primer lugar," 1.

6   Vigil, "evening news," 37.

7   Julián Olivares, "Seeing and Becoming: Evangelina Vigil, *Thirty an' Seen a Lot*," in *The Chicano Struggle: Analyses of Past and Present Efforts* (Binghamton, N.Y.: Bilingual Press/Editorial Bilingüe, 1984), 152.

8   Vigil, "was fun running 'round descalza," 62–63.

9   Vigil, "mi abuelita y su hermano," 52:

> so they lived
> a lifetime
> of conversation
> developing the thought
> and the intimate philosophy
> of my neighborhood and of my being

10   Vigil, "with a polka in his hand / a *Don Américo Paredes*," 25: "Indian feet clad in dusty shoes."

11 The persona does not abandon English altogether after this point, but she does shift to Spanish and bilingual poems.

12 Vigil, "el mercado en San Antonio / where the tourists trot," 22:

> the market is over there
> on Produce Row
> and the plaza remains
> in the heart of town
> on Commercial Street
> Commercial and Solitude

13 Vigil, "el viejito: tiempo perdido," 16.

14 Vigil, "la vida es el recuerdo," 61; "spinning on solid ground," 4; "la loca," 49.

15 Vigil, "¡es todo!" 51; "iniciación," 17; "por la calle Zarzamora," 19–20.

16 Vigil, "los radios retumbando," p. 27: "soul, rhythm, and tradition."

17 Vigil, "la gente de Hondo," 29:

> time goes by
> just reading
> dedications
> usually
> pretty tunes
> dedication after dedication
> heartfelt congratulations
> to the newly weds
> to the debutantes
> to those having birthdays
> to those celebrating anniversaries
> with much love
> from their husbands
> wives
> mothers
> fathers
> brothers and sisters
> loved ones
> friends

18 Vigil, "evening news," 37.

19 Vigil, "Para El Machete, Arturo Valdez / que en paz descance [sic]," 56.

20 Ibid., 60:

> I see modern chicano/guerrilla campsites
> in times of war
> smoking with love
> philosophy
> strategy

and tactics
all of
contemporary relevance:
breeding unity
(as always)
so in the end
some day in that future
that we patiently await
that we anxiously advance
to stop
the excesses
to recreate balance
equality
respect

21 Ibid., 56: "the Paul Revere / of the Texan Revolution."
22 Vigil, "el pésame," 67–72.
23 Vigil, "Para El Machete, Arturo Valdez," 59:

And the Indian ritual
has to keep smoking
among important conversations
over ideas newly born
a flower of tenderness and love
that grows up among our people
that's *carnalismo, carnal*

24 Elihu Carranza, *Chicanismo: Philosophical Fragments* (Dubuque, Iowa: Kendall/Hunt Publishing Co., 1978), 19.
25 Ibid., 20.
26 Vigil, "evening news," 38.
27 Vigil, "iniciación," 17; "only one," 30; "lujo," 31; "ritual en un instante," 34; "¡qué esperanzas!" 66.
28 Vigil, "kitchen talk," 41; "Si vieras que nunca me he sentido completamente feliz," 65.
29 Olivares, "Seeing and Becoming," 153.
30 Vigil, "remolino en mi taza," 4.
31 Vigil, "ser conforme," 40.
32 Vigil, "por la calle Zarzamora," 19; "¡es todo!" 51.
33 Vigil, "was fun running 'round descalza," 62–63.
34 Ibid., 63: "innocent excesses of youth."
35 Ibid., 62:

no sooner than had the building wall/canvasses been painted clean
did neighborhood kids take to carving new inspirations
and gang hieroglyphics
and new figure drawings of naked women

and their parts
and messages for all
"Diana's a whore"
"Lalo's queer"
and "Chelo is loose"

36 Vigil, "evening news," 39.

37 Ibid.

38 Vigil, "tavern taboo," 64; "me caes sura, ese, descuéntate," 46; "para los que piensan con la verga (*with due apologies to those who do not*)," 47.

39 Vigil, "para los que piensan con la verga," 47: "lost / in a world of buttocks and panties."

40 Vigil, "me caes sura, ese, descuéntate," 46: "the kind of motherfucker / a real bastard."

41 Vigil, "para los que piensan con la verga . . . ," 47.

42 Vigil, "me caes sura, ese, descuéntate," 46.

43 This is a reference to Vigil, "para los que piensan con la verga (*with due apologies to those who do not*)," 47.

44 Vigil, "momma's bosom," 15; "mente joven: nothin' like a pensive child," 36.

45 Vigil, "mente joven: nothin' like a pensive child," 36.

46 Vigil, "with a polka in his hand / *a Don Américo Paredes*," 26.

The Sardonic Powers of the Erotic in the Work of Ana Castillo

NORMA ALARCÓN

Ana Castillo, a native of Chicago, first made an impact on the Chicano writers' community with the publication of her chapbook, *Otro Canto* (1977). Written mostly in English (as is almost all of Castillo's work), it ensured her reputation as a "social protest" poet at a time when it was difficult to be anything else. As a result, some of the ironic tones already present in the early work have been easily over-looked in favor of the protest message, which in fact is re-doubled by irony. It can be argued that irony is one of Castillo's trademarks. Irony often appears when experience is viewed after-the-fact or in opposition to another's subjectivity. In this essay, I would like to explore the ironically erotic dance that Castillo's speaking subjects often take up with men. Thus, my exploration will follow the trajectory of the traditional heterosexual, female speaking subjects in Castillo's published works: *Otro Canto*, *The Invitation* (1979), *Women Are Not Roses* (1984), and *The Mixquiahuala Letters* (1986).[1]

Otro Canto portrayed the burdens of the urban poor through the voice of a young woman who had learned the bitter lessons of disillusionment early in life. Thus, in the poem "1975," we hear a sigh of relief when all those "proletarian talks"—the nemesis of many a left-wing activist—are finally translated into action. The speaker underscores the repetitiveness of mere talk by starting off every stanza with the line, "talking proletarian talks," which subsequently opens the way for details that give rise to such talk. We are not relieved from this tactical monotony "until one long / awaited day— / we are tired / of talking" (pp. 49–51). Though in "1975" the speaker is not gender-marked but is revealed as being in a "we-us" speaking position within a Marxist revolutionary stance, that speaker is trans-

formed into a "we-us" who makes "A Counter-Revolutionary Proposition." In this poem we are called upon to make love and "forget / that
Everything matters" (*Women Are Not Roses*, p. 63). Given the litany of the
things that matter in the stanza preceding the call, however, the poem
urges me to ask if the speaker is wryly alluding to the well-known Anglo
counterculture slogan of the sixties: "Make Love, Not War." As the poem
notes, what matters to the proletarian (i.e., Marxist) revolutionary speaker
is the struggle to overcome class oppression, a struggle that is spoken
through a supposedly non-gendered we. However, juxtaposing the
poem's title, "A Counter-Revolutionary Proposition," with the implicit
allusion to the slogan "Make Love, Not War," may help us to unravel a
story with a difference for the underclass female speaker who addresses
her partner, "Let's forget . . ." (p. 63).

Notwithstanding the recent involvement of women in revolutionary
struggles (i.e., Cuba and Nicaragua), it is still the case that in opposition to
the erotic, a revolution or a war is especially marked with a traditional
male subjectivity that awaits analysis. In order for a female speaker to
recover the full meaningful impact of herself, she still must address how
that self figures in the "heterosexual erotic contract," revolutions not
excepted. Within this contract, the female body continues to be the site of
both reproduction and the erotic; despite class position, a speaker and her
gendered social experience are imbricated in that age-old contract. Thus,
"A Counter-Revolutionary Proposition" may now be understood as a call
to explore the politics of the erotic. Let us actively explore the neo-revolu-
tionary implications of erotic relations that have been constantly displaced, undervalued, and even erased by masculine-marked militancy, or
at best rendered passively by the male poet, with the woman as the muse,
the wife, the mother.

From this point of view, the poem's title acquires a polyvalence that
goes beyond the private, where the erotic has often been held "hostage,"
and is placed in the political arena. In a sense, then, "Let's 'make love'" is
taken from the lips of an Anglo, male, left-wing activist by the most
unexpected of speakers—Ana Castillo's poetic persona. In retrospect,
Castillo's early work stands out as one of her first attempts to appropriate
the erotic and its significances for the female speaker, with ironic repercus-
sions. Given the assumed class position of the speaker herself, affirming
the erotic, as she takes pause from the class struggle, is tantamount to
speaking against herself, or so her "brother/lover" may attest. The implicit
suggestion that the erotic and the class struggle may be incompatible in a
patriarchal world, when both are made public, places the underclass
female in a double bind, since she may be forced to choose between areas

of life that, for her, are intertwined or indivisible. In my view, the speakers in Castillo's work refuse to make such choices. Choosing one or the other splits the subject into the domains that heretofore have been symbolically marked feminine or masculine.

In the seventies, Chicanas and other women of color had a difficult time within their fraternal group when they insisted that feminist politics, with its commitment to the exploration of women's sexuality and gendered identities, also applied to them. The supposed contradictory position of women of color, one that was between a male-identified class liberation struggle and a middle- or upper-class, white, female-identified sexual liberation struggle, forced women of color to walk a tightrope in their quest for an exploration of gender.[2] Thus, a poem such as "A Counter-Revolutionary Proposition" was politically risky, as the speaker addresses another, ostensibly male, and asks that he forget that "Everything matters." Yet, it is only within this apparent self-contradictory situation that such a speaker may be able to claim sexuality for herself and explore the significance of the female body that is always, and already, sexually marked. Such a "proposition" simultaneously opens up a gap between the fact of economic oppression and the desire for erotic pleasure and significance that faces us when we perceive the separation between the first and the second stanzas in the poem.

In *The Invitation* (1979), a chapbook-length collection of erotic poems and vignettes, Castillo's speaker no longer requests that her interlocutor forget that "everything matters" but pursues, instead, a sustained exploration of her erotic, at times bisexual, desires. The appropriation of the erotic for the female speaker is again a motivating force. The emphasis, however, is not so much on the speaker's uneasy conjunction with "proletarian politics" as it is with "textual politics." That is, the appropriative process resonates respectively against, and with, two important books of our time: Octavio Paz's *The Labyrinth of Solitude* (1950), and Maria Teresa Horta, Maria Isabel Barreno, and Maria Velho da Costa's *The Three Marias: New Portuguese Letters* (1975).[3] Consider, for example, that in the second chapter of his book, Paz affirms women's dormant and submissive sexuality that awaits discovery through male efforts, while "The Three Marias" reject this view throughout their book and protest women's political bondage that, at the core, is based on their sexuality. Notwithstanding the different approaches that each of "The Three Marias" would take to liberate women, there is very little doubt that they agree that male perception of women's sexuality pervades all levels of women's existence.

The erotic thematics of *The Invitation* openly declare the influence of those two books (pp. iii, 9). Castillo's text, when viewed in their light, becomes a purposefully glossed negation of Paz's view and an extension of the authors' own erotic vision. It is as if the relative absence of any sociopolitical debate of the Chicana/Mexicana's sexuality had made it imperative that Castillo explore instead her speaker's desire in the light of a textual milieu. Moreover, reading Castillo's work in this fashion enables us to clarify her struggle to place her erotic thematics and voices in the interstice of both her sociopolitical and textual experiences. In other words, if, due to her social position, the underclass female is called upon to address her class oppression with a ready-made, class struggle rhetoric, attempting to address her sexual/erotic oppression forces her to see it in relation to texts. Her own response to those texts enables her to give voice to her experience and make it public. If she does not make an effort to bring out that voice herself, it will remain muted, as she is forced to align herself with the heretofore masculine-marked class voice. Thus, she is reconfirming, from another angle, Gilbert and Gubar's call in *The Madwoman in the Attic* for our critical need to explore "the metaphor of experience" (in "1975" and "A Counter-Revolutionary Proposition") and "the experience of metaphor" (in *The Invitation*).[4] The speaker/writer and the critic must discern, insofar as it is possible, between the metaphors female speakers create to represent our sociopolitical and erotic experience and the metaphors these speakers inherit and that *a priori* inscribe our potential experience. Thus, a writer/speaker can unwittingly live out the experiences that the metaphors call upon her to duplicate (i.e., Paz's description of female sexuality) or she can struggle to lay them bare and thus reinscribe her evolving position (i.e., "The Three Marias" struggle to reinscribe women's sexuality).

Paz's work, as well as "The Three Marias" and *The Invitation* itself, are, in a sense, all glossed over in Castillo's epistolary narrative, *The Mixquiahuala Letters* (1986), which more closely approximates the sociopolitical images of *Otro Canto*. In a sense, *Letters* is more aggressive in its conjugation of "the experience of metaphor" and "the metaphor of experience" as it pertains to the erotic, for it is yet another link in Castillo's exploration of sexuality and its significance for women. If in *Letters*, however, the negation of Paz's view of women's sexuality is continued, even as it is ironically reconfirmed by some of the males represented in the text, the work of "The Three Marias" is honored by adapting its epistolary form. However, the letters of "The Three Marias" are also supplemented by Castillo's Anglo-American political and sexual angle of vision. Castillo's sole speaking protagonist—Teresa ("Tere")—takes up the position, initially, of a free agent, while the narrative web of "The Three Marias" starts out by recognizing that women are not free agents in any sense whatsoever. Moreover, as Darlene Sadlier's essay makes clear, "The Three Marias" did not have the political freedom to explore women's sexual oppression or question its nature even textually, let alone in practice.[5] As a result, they were placed on trial for publishing their book. Ironically, the trial itself corroborated their point; women have not been free to express an uncensored subjectivity. Ana Castillo's *Letters* supplements "The Three Marias" insofar as her protagonist projects a subjectivity, free to express and practice her sexuality, but still imprisoned by an intangible heterosexist ideology, a heterosexist ideology for which we may posit Paz's view as the model. Thus, in *Letters* we have a protagonist who, by virtue of North American political practices and feminist influence, had "forgotten" what it is like to live in the world of "The Three Marias" or even in Paz's world. As a result, Tere, the main speaker in *Letters*, undergoes a trial by fire when Mexico's cultural configuration is put into play. She is forced to recall that she is not as free as she thought. Since Teresa is a woman of Mexican descent (a Chicana), she should not have forgotten but, insofar as she wants to be a freer agent, she would want to forget. The complexities of her diverse levels of consciousness may be located in the push and pull of divergent political countries, i.e., the United States and Mexico. As Gloria Anzaldúa states in "La Conciencia de la Mestiza: Towards a New Consciousness":

> Within us and within *la cultura chicana*, commonly held beliefs of the white culture attack commonly held beliefs of the Mexican culture, and both attack commonly held beliefs of the indigenous culture. . . . In a constant state of mental nepantilism, an Aztec word meaning torn between ways, *la mestiza* is a product of the transfer of the cultural and spiritual values of one group to another . . . and in a state of perpetual transition, the *mestiza* faces the dilemma of the mixed breed: which collectivity does the daughter of a darkskinned mother listen to?[6]

Indeed, this may explain the rationale behind addressing the letters to Alicia, who was Tere's traveling companion and ought to have known what they experienced. Nevertheless, the technique enables Tere to bring out, through Alicia, the Anglo-American cultural influence that, in any case, does not save either of them in the face of the erotic, as we shall see.

Before further consideration of *The Mixquiahuala Letters*, however, other important points must be brought up that will clarify its social and literary importance as well as my necessarily complex critical approaches. The critical conjugation of "the metaphor of experience" and "the experience of metaphor" is as complex as its literary elaboration.

Selections from both chapbooks, *Otro Canto* and *The Invitation*, as well as sixteen new poems, have been made available to a wider audience in Castillo's book, *Women Are Not Roses*. As happens in "selections" books, the evolution of a writer's work is often cut short in favor of the "best" that a writer has produced, a factor that is the prerogative of editors. As a result, *Women Are Not Roses* does not provide the reader with many clues to the intertextual observations made above. Theorists of the text, of course, have taught us that one does not need to have recourse to direct intertextual sources for the pursuit of such considerations. However, it is also the case that writers do respond consciously to their textual milieus and effect a revisionary dialogue. As such, it is of paramount political importance to identify the textual milieu of culturally marginalized writers such as Chicanas, as well as to clarify the appropriative strategies at work in the struggle to construct and reconstruct an identity despite its instability, lest a writer appear to speak in a vacuum. Moreover, writers and critics often rely on a textual milieu and an actual experience, insofar as that milieu assists with the verbal translation of our cultural experience. In this fashion, a variety of discourses can be negated, supplemented, modified, and repeated, though it may not always be possible, or even necessary, to make clear-cut source identifications.[7]

Women Are Not Roses does not provide any clues to Castillo's appropriative strategies and experimentations, though the word "roses" in the title points to, and plays upon, the masculine textual production in which women are represented as flowers/nature. In this book, however, there are at least two poems that resonate intertextually and intratextually, and their examination may also help us in the reading of *The Mixquiahuala Letters*.

Both "An Idyll" (pp. 8–10) and "The Antihero" (p. 24) warrant a closer look because they not only evoke the Western romantic tradition that has underpinned women's erotic image within patriarchy but also, in this instance, further the female speaker's appropriation of that tradition to explore her sexuality and revise the image. Moreover, since Tere, the letter-writing protagonist of *Letters*, does not explicitly speak of her erotic illusions and ideals but instead reconstructs, from a ten-year distance, a period of her life that she calls a "cesspool" (Letter #2), a consideration of these two poems may help us come to terms with the nature of her failed erotic quest. Though *Letters* represents sexual encounters with men, Tere often assumes a sarcastic, pragmatic, and even distant tone that contrasts sharply with whatever illusions and ideals may have led her (Letter #1) and her friend Alicia to actively explore their sexuality. This is an exploration that falls short of erotic bliss, to say the least: hence, the label "cesspool." In a sense, the expectations of heterosexual erotic bliss constitute the partially repressed aspects of *Letters,* which on occasion contains such startling confessions as "i was docile" (p. 113) or "i believed i would be placed in the little house and be cared for . . ." (p. 118).[8] These occasional confessions are barely audible. They tend to get lost in Tere's latter-day, after-the-fact sardonic anger. As we shall see, she has been framed *a priori* by certain "semantic charters,"[9] and Castillo mocks her further by framing her with the "reading charts" offered to the reader.

"An Idyll" and "The Antihero" reinscribe two aspects of the erotic/ romantic hero—the god-like and the demonic—from the point of view of a female speaker. Their representation, however, is complicated by the different spatio-temporal positions that the speaker takes, consequently putting into question how one translates and interprets (writes/reads) the experience. Since "The Antihero" is a significant inversion of the hero in "An Idyll," the speaker's relational position to each becomes very important, adding another dimension to their inscription. A speaker's position in relation to such monumental and heroic figures cannot be all that simple. The speaker is probing not only a relationship to the symbolic, that is, how the romantic hero has figures in textual tradition, but her social experience as well, that is, how she has lived her sexuality in, and through, such figurations.

In these two poems, the speaker filters her position through an intricate use of the first- ("An Idyll") and third- ("The Antihero") person pronouns in combination with temporal distance and proximity, respectively. These spatiotemporal, positional techniques are employed in *Letters* as well; though most of the letters are first-person accounts, Letters #21 and #32 are examples of speaker shifts. "An Idyll" is a first-person narration of past experience, punctuated by contemporaneous evaluations of that experience that is represented in fantastic terms, a virtual parody of male literary figurations:

                    now
    i   can   tell
    of being swept b
    y a god a michael
    angelo's david a
    man of such phys
    ical   perfection,
    one could not be
    lieve him human.   (P. 8)

In this poem, the very columnar shape points to a phallic symmetry that distorts the potential plasticity of language for its own sake. It takes a very well-programmed machine to reproduce that form. It is akin to a divine hierarchical account that only "now," by stepping outside of it, can be apprehended. The narrator, who only "now" can represent her enthrall-ment with the beautiful stony hero, assesses that erotic dance as "truer" because it was satisfying, in some measure. Enthrallment itself may have its own temporary erotic rewards. The romantic interlude—an idyll—as a symbolic fantasy may be spellbinding, but the effort to transform it into a social reality literally enslaves her:

> i ate
> with it slept wi
> th it made its b
> ed in the mornin
> g when it disapp
> eared . . . i waited
> for its return—
> each night.   (P. 9)

Indeed, like language, she is immobilized and transfixed by "it," a god-like man. "It" has turned her into a robot. The murder of this fantastic being is due to her almost sudden awareness that her union with him, despite its insane and masochistic pleasures, is tantamount to her own self-destructive collusion. In the poem, his murder is anonymous, per-haps collective. As a crowd gathers to demand his expulsion, one of them shoots him when he refuses to leave:

> until one of us c
> ould not stand it
> any longer and
> shot him.   (P. 10)

Now that the fantasy, with its perverse truth, is over, the first-person speaker is free to recall her delusion. Indeed, it is the newer, after-the-fact consciousness that makes it possible to see the enthrallment as a delusion. The one who narrates, however, is distanced from the one who lives the fantasy, that distance itself muting the emotional charge of the actual experience that was once lived as true and is now viewed through the lens of fabulous fiction. It is as if there was something inherently ironic in an experience recollected from the now-distant point of a changed conscious-ness. This is precisely the ironic tone effected in many of the letters (see, for example, Letter #16 where Tere's attraction to Alvaro is later viewed as a weakness). Tere mocks her initial enthrallment. She "Believed that beneath his rebellion was a sensitive human being with an insight that was unique and profound" (p. 48). Years later, however, either Tere's narrative hindsight or that of an unidentified narrator reports, "This is a woman conditioned to accept a man about whom she has serious doubts . . ." (p. 48).

The ironies of "An Idyll" take a more cruel turn in "The Antihero," who exhibits a reckless disregard for his partner's erotic desires: "the antihero / always gets the woman / not in the end / an anticlimax instead" (p. 24). If the heterosexual dance in "An Idyll" is paradoxically viewed as a true fiction by the first-person narrator, the lyrical speaker of "The Antihero" views him as purposely playing his partner false. He obfuscates erotic desire by rendering sexual experience anticlimactic, as against pleasure and dénouement. He manipulates her desire so as "to leave her yearning lest / she discover that is all" (p. 24). She is double-crossed by the anticlimactic ruse into continuing to conflate desire with him. It is clear, as Luce Irigaray comments in another context, that "man's desire and woman's are strangers to each other."[10] If she discovered the infinite power of her own desire, then certainly the cruel dance would undergo a transformation or come to a stop. The poem presents the anticlimactic sexual event in the present-tense lyrical mode, through the lens of the third person. The couple is objectified in the present tense to suggest an ongoing, unsatisfactory scenario of desire that brings them together, yet keeps them apart. Thus, contrary to the dictates of the lyric, which calls for a personal account of sensual experience, the poem switches the speaker's position to suggest a model of contemporaneous behavior that distorts erotic desire. For Castillo, then, angles of perception, which may be both spatial and/or temporal, are sites for discrete eruptions of meaning that may be subsequently juxtaposed, thus effecting additional meanings. In a sense, the significance of any one thing is highly unstable and much depends on the angle of vision.

Conventionally, the letter form has shared at least two important features with the lyric, notwithstanding the fact that the first is prose and the second is poetry.[11] Both reveal the intimate events in the life of the speaker, *combined* with the speaker's emotional response to them, thus exploring the personal states of mind at the moment of the event or with respect to it. It should be noted, in passing, that *Letters* is a mixture of poetic and prosaic forms, but the speaker, who may not always be identified with Tere, does not feel bound by conventions. This disruption of conventions signals, in my view, a pursuit of narrative approaches that may be beyond Tere's simple "i." In a sense, she is undergoing an inquisition that makes her both the subject of her narrative and the object of someone else's.

Consider how, in recalling events shared with Alicia, her sole inter-locutor, Tere almost consistently shifts to a third-person, present narration to explore emotional responses to an event. Letter #21 is an example of such an instance, an account telling of Tere's breakdown as a result of her misalliance with Alexis:

> After a while, she adapts to neglecting herself more than he can. Her nails are bitten to the quick. She forgets to eat or eats when she's not hungry. Her inability to sleep makes her face droop like the jowls of an old hound dog. She is twenty-six years old. With nervous gestures, she tears an invisible thread from the edge of her slip. If she doesn't watch out, she will quietly go mad and no one will have noticed. (P. 112)

As in "An Idyll," enthrallment again leads to a slavish madness, but it cannot be stated in the first person. Who narrates? An older Tere, who fears to re-enter that period of insanity with a personal "i"? Also, as in "The Antihero," the speaker shifts to the third-person account, thus creat-ing distance with regard to speaking positions, but not to time. As a narrator of her own letters, Tere reveals that she occasionally shifts per-sonae to "create distance with the use of a personal 'i' " (p. 64). As such, it would appear to be an admission that, emotionally, events have a dan-gerous, contemporaneous power that must be objectified, displaced to a "she/her." Often, Tere can only *re*-present what has lost the power to hurt her. Romantic love, however, cannot be spoken of, intimately or directly. As she—or is it she?—coldly says; "Love? In the classic sense, it describes in one syllable all the humiliation that one is born to and pressed upon to surrender to a man" (p. 111). In our time, "the classic sense" of love is the erotically romantic one that has been popularized *ad nauseam* through romance novels or, in the case of Mexico and Latin America, *fotonovelas*—as Tere knows (p. 50). It is a genre that cuts across classes and makes many women, regardless of their economic status, sisters under the skin, daughters of patriarchy. In fact, it is the erotic quest that holds Tere and Alicia's friendship together. The true closeness of the friendship is placed in question when we read Letter #13, in which Tere emphasizes her occasional loathing of Alicia. The wedge between them is Alicia's priv-ilege, color, and worldly wise airs. Clearly, Tere and Alicia's relationship requires further scrutiny. However, what keeps them together is their shared relationship to the romantic. Letter #40 serves to additionally reiterate the erotic common ground.

In Letter #33, to further explore her relations with Alexis, Tere again shifts speaking positions. On this occasion, she switches to her fantasy of his voice. When Tere encounters Alexis five years after the breakup, she imagines what he should be thinking upon seeing her. This is the end to the affair that pleases her (p. 114). The poem, entitled "Epilogue" and attributed to Alexis, is a tribute to Tere's unequaled charms, a testimonial to his lingering affection for Tere, despite the passage of time and his subsequent involvements with other women: "It was *her. / . . . She /* was there, in the same room . . ." (p. 115). Tere is effectively converted into his Muse, the one still capable of stirring him into poetic reverie. Indeed, she reveals that being the object of his desire is something in which she is well trained, so well in fact, that she can even write poems about that object, *herself,* and assume his voice. Even as this version of the end pleases her more than the actual reported sordid end of their affair, Tere's self-con-scious posing parodies the experience of the romantic metaphor: *She,* the muse, the love object that truly moves him; *He,* the desiring lover/poet. In Tere's relationship with Alexis, the gap between the metaphor of experi-ence, insanity and abandonment, and the experience of metaphor, the enchanting muse, provides us with a variation of the chords struck in "The Antihero" and "An Idyll" (see Letter #28 for Tere's initial response to Alexis). As Janice A. Radway has told us in *Reading The Romance,*[12] roman-tic/erotic bliss is the salient promise that Western patriarchy holds out to women, a bliss that constantly eludes our hapless heroines. Why? I can only conjecture that, while both Tere and Alicia are quite adept at posing as the object of desire, they find it impossible to carry through the subse-quent social actualization of that objectification, primarily because it is not an option at all. It spells the death of their subjectivity. Ironically, that is their near-unconscious discovery. The patriarchal promise of romantic/ erotic bliss, *re-*presented in all manner of popular literature, is an ideologi-cal maneuver to kill their subjectivity and any further exploration of their own desire.

The understated, failed quest for romantic/erotic bliss effects a blis-teringly sardonic tone in the *Letters,* which are an exercise in hindsight. If, in fact, *Letters* represents the struggle to move beyond the quest, the irony is Tere's inability to succeed. In part, this is due to the fact that both the women and their string of men are still operating under a romantic/erotic heterosexist ideology that is hard to shake, notwithstanding Tere's latter-day awareness that this is so. Consider what she says ten years after the quest for "womanhood": "Destiny is not a metaphysical confrontation with one's self, rather, society has knit its pattern so tight that a confronta-tion with it is inevitable" (p. 59). The quest for "womanhood" is still socially defined in sexual terms under the popular emblem of the roman-tic/erotic. Both Tere and Alicia are pressed to fulfill the pattern. In a sense, *Letters* offers us a different version of the so-called "star-crossed" lovers.

Destiny, as such, is a socially enforced misrecognition under the guise of love that places Tere in a double bind: on the one hand, a desire for her own sexual definition, and on the other, an overly determined script in which she takes part. Tere, in short, is bitter over her unwitting, yet unavoidable, folly. The appropriation of the erotic, as enjoyed and desired in the more symbolic book, *The Invitation*, is betrayed in *Letters*. *Letters* makes evident the possibility that an appropriation of the erotic in a heterosexist society may only end up being revealed as a misappropriation.

Castillo's experimentations with shifting pronouns and appropriative techniques for the purpose of exploring the romantic/erotic does not stop with Tere's letters, however. If we return to the "real beginning" of *Letters*, we must note that the first letter is to the reader, penned by Castillo. We are directed to undertake a variety of unconventional readings—"The Conformist," "The Cynic," and "The Quixotic"—each tailored to our reading needs. We are also given the option to read each of the forty letters separately, as if they were short fiction. We are alerted that we are in for a variety of ironic and parodic plays but we are ignorant of what they might be. In short, the book brings into question our own reading practices, for the apparently unconventional suggested readings actually lead to resolutions that are more conventional than the handful of letters attributed to Tere. Insofar as each suggested reading by Castillo presents us with a resolution, we are handed an ideological nexus (i.e., The Conformist-idyllic conjugal life) that forces us to reconstruct the meaning of Tere's letters as always and already leading in that direction.[13] Was that Tere's desired end, or is it The Quixotic, or The Cynic's? If, as readers, we play along with the suggested charts, we are forced to come to terms with the notion that Tere is very much trapped by a variety of ideological nexus that she, and we, need to question and disrupt.

But it is not only our reading and interpretive practices that are in question; Tere's are, too. She constantly shifts voices in an effort to "read" and interpret her own experiences. Which one of the various selves that she explores is she? Is she the vampish one, the docile one, the clever one, the fearful one, the liberated one, or the oppressed one? Insofar as each is connected with her sexuality, she is all of them, and more. Above all, I think she is betrayed by a cultural fabric that presses its images of her upon her, and her response (as well as Castillo's) is to give them all back to us, albeit sardonically. Tere is no longer a sitting duck, as Paz or even "The Three Marias" would have it, but she still inhabits a shooting gallery in which she must wear many a mask to survive and to understand where she has been.

NOTES

1   Ana Castillo, *Otro Canto* (Chicago: n.p., 1977); *The Invitation* (Chicago: n.p., 1979; 2d. ed. n.p., 1986) (may be obtained by writing: P.O. Box 163, 3309 Mission St., San Francisco, Calif. 94110); *Women Are Not Roses* (Houston: Arte Público Press, 1984); *The Mixquiahuala Letters* (Binghamton, N.Y.: Bilingual Review Press, 1986). All cited pages are from *Women Are Not Roses* and *The Mixquiahuala Letters* and shall be indicated in body of text.

2   For testimonials regarding this predicament, one of the most accessible books is *This Bridge Called My Back: Writings by Radical Women of Color*, 2d. ed., ed. Cherríe Moraga and Gloria Anzaldúa (New York: Kitchen Table Press, 1983). Leftist feminists in Latin America encounter similar predicaments when working in a framework of "grassroots" feminism. See Magaly Pineda, "Feminism and Popular Education: A Critical but Necessary Relationship," *Isis International*, no. 6 (1986): 111–13.

3   For the purposes of this essay I have used *The Labyrinth of Solitude*, trans. Lysander Kemp (New York: Grove Press, 1961); and *The Three Marias: New Portuguese Letters*, trans. Helen R. Lane (New York: Doubleday, 1975).

4   Sandra M. Gilbert and Susan Gubar, *The Madwoman in the Attic: The Woman Writer and the Nineteenth-Century Literary Imagination* (New Haven: Yale University Press, 1979), xiii. Sigrid Weigel makes a similar suggestion in her essay "Double Focus: On the History of Women's Writing," in *Feminist Aesthetics*, ed. Gisela Ecker, trans. Harriet Anderson (Boston: Beacon Press, 1986), 59–80.

5   For an excellent discussion of both the political problems and the narrative modes of this book, see Darlene Sadlier, "Form in Novas Cartas Portuguesas," *Novel* 19:3 (Spring 1986): 246–63.

6   Gloria Anzaldúa, "La Conciencia de la Mestiza: Towards a New Consciousness," in *Borderlands: La Frontera, The New Mestiza* (San Francisco: Spinster/Aunt Lute, 1987), 77–91.

7   I am specifically referring to the work of Julia Kristeva, *Revolution in Poetic Language*, trans. Margaret Waller, intro. Leon S. Roudiez (New York: Columbia University Press, 1984), 59–60; and *Desire in Language*, ed. Leon S. Roudiez, trans. Thomas Gora, Alice Jardine, and Leon S. Roudiez (New York: Columbia University Press, 1980), 15; as well as the work of M. M. Bakhtin, *The Dialogic Imagination*, ed. Michael Holquist, trans. Caryl Emerson and Michael Holquist (Austin: University of Texas Press, 1981), 259–422.

8   The use of the small "i" pronoun throughout *Letters* is disturbing but something other than an affectation. Weigel suggests that to use the "I" in public, women will have to learn to speak "without having first to acknowledge the male definition of their gender role" (see note 4).

9   Pierre Maranda suggests that "Semantic charters condition our thoughts and emotions. They are culture specific networks that we internalize as we undergo the process of socialization." Moreover, these charters or signifying systems "have an inertia and a momentum of their own. There are semantic domains whose inertia is high: kinship terminologies, the dogmas of authoritarian churches, the conception of sex roles" (184–85). See his essay "The Dialectic of Metaphor: An

Anthropological Essay on Hermeneutics," in *The Reader in the Text: Essays on Audience and Interpretation*, ed. Susan R. Suleiman and Inge Corsman (Princeton: Princeton University Press, 1980), 183–204.

10   Luce Irigaray, *This Sex Which Is Not One*, trans. Catherine Porter with Carolyn Burke (Ithaca, N.Y.: Cornell University Press, 1985), 27.

11   Ruth Perry discusses at length the enactment of "a self-conscious and self-perpetuating process of emotional self-examination," as well as the history of the epistolary genre, in her book, *Women, Letters, and the Novel* (New York: AMS Press, 1980), 117.

12   Janice A. Radway, *Reading the Romance: Women, Patriarchy, and Popular Literature* (Chapel Hill: University of North Carolina Press, 1984).

13   Fredric Jameson's commentary on "the kind of reading which attaches itself to finding out how everything turns out in the end" provides a helpful perspective for understanding Castillo's parodic plots. See "The Ideology of the Text," *Salmagundi* 31–32 (Fall 1975/Winter 1976): 225.

Part II. Puertorriqueñas

Puerto Rican Writers in the U.S., Puerto Rican Writers in Puerto Rico: A Separation beyond Language

(Testimonio)

NICHOLASA MOHR

As a writer of Puerto Rican parentage who was born, raised, educated, and is presently living in New York City, I often get asked, "Why don't you write in Spanish?" And this question is asked not only by those persons of non-Hispanic background but also by the Puerto Ricans residing on the Island of Puerto Rico.

In the fall of 1986, I was invited to be on a panel titled "Puerto Rican Women Fiction Writers," at Columbia University. As I began to work on my presentation, I realized that I was the only Puerto Rican on the panel who writes in English. I decided to examine the differences, which include and go beyond language, that exist between myself and those other Puerto Rican writers, writing in Spanish, who live in Puerto Rico or in other Spanish-speaking environments.

My birth makes me a native New Yorker. I write here in the United States about my personal experiences and those of a particular group of migrants that number in the millions. Yet, all of these actualities seem to have little or no bearing on those who insist on seeing me as an "intruder," or "outsider" who has taken on a foreign language: perhaps even taken it

Grateful acknowledgment is made to *The Américas Review* and Arte Público Press (University of Houston, Houston, Texas 77004) for permission to reprint this article which first appeared in *The Américas Review* 15, no. 2 (1987).

on much too forcefully, using it to document and validate our existence and survival inside the very nation that chose to colonize us.

Puerto Rico continues to use Spanish as its official language in spite of its status as a commonwealth of the U.S. Puerto Ricans born in Puerto Rico, unlike other immigrant or migrant groups, hold the unique position of being United States citizens while still remaining part of the greater Latin American family. And even though their position in the hierarchy of Latin America is often assessed as one of low status because of their connected dependence to the United States (a sort of stepchild or impoverished relation of the Yankees) resulting in their government's dubious allegiance to Latin America, Puerto Rico is nonetheless considered a member of the Spanish-speaking world.

Thus, this status is singular in its kind, creating a dichotomous existence further exacerbated by the proximity of the Island and permitting Puerto Ricans as United States citizens to travel frequently and cheaply from the Island of Puerto Rico to and from the mainland United States. Contact between the Islanders and the Puerto Ricans here is a common occurrence. It follows that Spanish continues to be spoken in areas of the U.S. that are heavily populated by Puerto Ricans and today by the new political refugees from Central and South America. One of the cities with the oldest Puerto Rican population that is today inhabited by the third and fourth generations of these early migrants, as well as other recently arrived Hispanic immigrants, is New York City.

Consequently, New York is fast becoming a bilingual city. Public service messages and advertisements are now written in Spanish and English. Hispanic food is available in luncheonettes as well as in fine restaurants. Many merchants speak Spanish or have bilingual employees to meet the needs of their customers.

In the U.S. and New York in particular, there are many other immigrants and political refugees and their children who are not Hispanic. However, it is unlikely that Greek-Americans, Irish-Americans, or Asian-Americans, for example, could conceivably have monthly or even weekend visits overseas with their relatives. This frequent traveling is not unusual within the Puerto Rican stateside and Island communities. Nor is it expected that these other ethnic Americans speak and write in the native language of their countries of origin. No matter how foreign these other groups may appear, their writers, when documenting injustices or illuminating accomplishments, all do so by writing in English. Some examples are Joseph Conrad, Vladimir Nabokov, and Jerzy Kozinski. Others born or raised here are Maxine Hong Kingston, Philip Roth, and Mario Puzo.

These writers are not chastised or rejected because they use English. Nor are they expected to use another language of expression. Indeed, they are applauded for the way in which they master the English language. Because I am a daughter of the Puerto Rican Diaspora, English is the language that gives life to my work, the characters I create, and that stimulates me as a writer. It has also been a vital component in the struggle for my very survival. However, it is much more than language that separates the Puerto Rican writers born and/or raised here from the writers in Puerto Rico. And I will endeavor, from my perspective, to describe what I perceive as some of the major reasons for this separation.

In the books I've published to date, I have dealt with a period in time that covers more than forty-five years of Puerto Rican history here in New York. When I started to write in 1972 I realized that, except for a book or two that concentrated on the Puerto Rican male's problems and misfortunes, there were no books in United States literature that dealt with our existence, our contributions, or what we Puerto Rican migrants were about. I, as a Puerto Rican child, never existed in North American letters. Our struggles as displaced migrants, working-class descendants of the *tabaqueros* (tobacco workers) who began coming here in 1916, were invisible in North American literature. As I proceeded to record who we were, I addressed myself both to adults and to children—and, of course, to women.

In my first book, a novel entitled *Nilda,* I wrote about Puerto Ricans in New York City during the years of the second World War. Through the various adolescent stages of the youngest child, a girl, I trace one family's position as they deal with their alienation as despised migrants, as well as their psychological, emotional, and physical attempts to sustain the family in a traditional Puerto Rican manner. We also see the beginning of the assimilation of Puerto Ricans in the U.S.

The works that followed included books recounting the problems, failures, and successes of the greatest influx of Puerto Rican migrants that arrived on the shores of the mainland immediately after the second World War. My work continued to trace the postwar migrants, many of whom arrived as small children or were born here. As the process of assimilation began, they inevitably began to understand that there was no going back; "home" was here, where they were working to materialize their own domain alongside their peers and immediate families. The Puerto Rico that we were taught to believe in was largely based on the reminiscences of our parents and grandparents, many of whom had come from small towns and rural villages. They had nostalgically presented to their displaced offspring a "paradise" where sunshine, flowers, and ownership of one's business or plot of land brought everyone abundant food and eternal happiness. This mythical Island also boasted a population that knew no prejudice and within which neither the dark color of one's skin or one's humble birth were ever seen as a cause for rejection. All of this mythology had little or nothing to do with Puerto Rico, its inhabitants, and the reality of that culture.

Later, when some of us returned to the Island, it was clear to see that according to the position one's family held, and the color of one's skin, one could hold a better job and have a higher place in society. It was also evident that those children of the poor and dark migrants who had been forced out more than two generations before, and who returned either with intentions to relocate or merely to visit, were not always welcomed. They were quickly labeled and categorized as outsiders, as "gringos" and "Nuyoricans." Indeed, proof of the false legacy that so many of us had inherited from our elders was painfully clear.

The heart of my work has always dealt with my culture. Consequently, the players in my books have been the Puerto Ricans in this city, my people and my beloved Nueva York. Their failures and their triumphs are the core of what and who we are today.

In my work, I continue examining the values I have inherited, always aware of the fact that I have come from an Island people who have been colonized from the very onset of their being and who, to this day, continue their dependency. As a Puerto Rican woman, I must also reckon with the history of my patriarchal antecedents and work to heal the scars of machismo that have been etched into our fiber for centuries.

Within this framework, my obsession with people's ability to succeed and fail, to despise and cherish, to compromise and not yield, as well as all the other contradictions and incongruities inherent in the human species, fires me on to write. I often think I write very much as an investigative reporter, to find out in the end what happened, to get at an answer that might give me a hint of the "truth." Yet I persist in using fiction as my medium. Fiction, as it is defined in the dictionary is: "That which is feigned or imagined. As assumption of a possible thing as a fact irrespective of the question of its truth."

I am not an avid reader of the literature of Puerto Rico. However, throughout the years I have become mildly familiar with some of the work of these writers. Most of the time, I have found their work to be too obsessed with class and race, thus narrowing their subject matter into regional and provincial material. Their commonly-used baroque style of writing in Spanish seems to act as filler rather than substance. Recently, I read a story that attempted to deal with a working-class Puerto Rican woman from New York who goes to San Juan for a holiday. The use of what the author considered to be a cross between Spanish and English, which is referred to as Spanglish, was incorrect and ludicrous. No one here speaks that way. The storyline was quite silly and the story rather farfetched and stupid, much like a cartoon. This writer had very little knowledge of who we are here and, I suspect, holds quite a bit of disdain and contempt for our community. This author is not the only one with this attitude. Unfortunately, it is quite common among the Island's intellectuals.

Yet I have also recently read the work of Magali García Ramis—*Felices Días, Tío Sergio* (Editorial Antillana)—whose language is very Puerto Rican and disarmingly complex, despite her simple and unpretentious prose. Her subject matter deals with her privileged, middle-class background, containing a depth that reveals much of the sickness that is prevalent in that class system. It is a system that continues to stifle attempts to eliminate the Spanish/European-style legacy of race and class that was deposited on that Island centuries ago. I also admire the work of Manuel Ramos Otero who, without apology, self-consciousness, or inhibition writes candidly and with compassion about his homosexual community. In his last book of poems, *El libro de la muerte* (Waterfront Press), he uses symbols and metaphors to bring the reader into the labyrinthine depths of his private world. I still treasure my copies of the earlier works of fiction by José Luis González, including *En Nueva York y otras desgracias* and *Cinco cuentos de sangre*, and the matchless poetry of Julia de Burgos.

There are few writers from Puerto Rico with whom I feel I can share a sense of camaraderie. Most of what I read lacks the universality that bonds the common human family, regardless of language, class, or geography.

Here in the U.S., I find writers who continue to produce work that, although very specific, is also enlightening and inspiring. Their works introduce us to Americans who ultimately share similar goals. Let me cite a few examples. Alice Walker, in *The Color Purple*, speaks to the reader in an exquisite black English about the power of female survival against the harsh domination of black machismo. In his short stories, Raymond Carver, with his minimal but powerful prose, shares with his readers a wide spectrum of the lives of working-class white Americans. Tillie Olsen's books recount the personal struggles of European immigrants and their children, as well as the psychological and social obstacles women must overcome. Ishmael Reed's works explode with the rich vernacular of black English, creating a personal mythology that reflects the reality of the black male's struggles against emasculation in a white-dominated power structure. Finally, Denise Chávez, in *The Last of the Menu Girls* (Arte Público

Press), opens the world of the Chicana from the 1950s to the present, incorporating the richness of Chicano Spanish and thereby further enhancing our literature with the language of the peoples of the U.S.

These are but a few examples of the writers (and there are many others I could include) who are not necessarily in the mainstream of the Anglo-American writers' empire but who, nonetheless, publish and speak about the realities and complexities of the varied ethnic groups who share our nation. All of these authors write in an American English that comes straight from their people. Their language represents and validates their experiences and those of the people who inhabit their books. None of them writes English like a "British subject," nor are they in any way trying to emulate the culture or values of England.

The rhythms of our American language are ever-changing, representing the many cultures that exist in the nation. Those whose works speak to and about the peoples of color, and the other marginal communities that continue to struggle for equality in the U.S., are the writers I identify with.

Except for the attempts of a few writers, I do not see any significant literary movement on the Island of Puerto Rico that speaks for the common folk: the working-class population of the Island. I wonder if the obsession with race, class, Spain, and the use of baroque Spanish might not be a way for some intellectuals to attempt to safeguard their privilege and power against the strong North American influence that presently permeates Puerto Rico. If this should be the case, then it follows that in safeguarding such a status, a majority who are less fortunate must ultimately be excluded.

As I have stated, the separation between myself and the majority of Puerto Rican writers in Puerto Rico goes far beyond a question of language. The jet age and the accessibility of Puerto Rico brought an end to a time of innocence for the children of former migrants. There is no pretense that going back will solve problems or bring equality and happiness. This is home. This is where we were born, raised, and where most of us will stay. Notwithstanding is my affection and concern for the people and the land of my parents and grandparents that is my right and my legacy.

Who we are, and how our culture will continue to blossom and develop, is being recorded right here by our writers, painters, and composers and where our voices respond and resound, loud and clear.

Open Letter to Eliana

(Testimonio)

SANDRA MARÍA ESTEVES

July 28, 1987

Dear Eliana,

I arrived into the world half blue and feet first, through the butcher shop environment otherwise known to the world as Lincoln Hospital, in the Bronx, on May 10th, 1948, sometime before or after Mothers' Day, probably symbolic, being the mother of four extremely beautiful and intelligent daughters and five adopted and equally handsome sons. In fact, the experience of motherhood, the entire process of creativity and nurturing, is absolutely without question the primary transformative influence on my personal poetics, at least as regards its philosophical applications.

My own mother, Cristina Huyghue, es una Dominicana who arrived in New York City at the tender (but sturdy) age of sixteen, speaking only high school English, determined to be a successful immigrant, teaching herself to speak the language from the local *Daily News*, securing her survival by taking on a job "only men do" at the quilt factory. For forty-three years she stood on her feet, eight hours a day, five days a week, in perfect health, never taking a day off to do something different, always on time, took only half-hour lunches, and was a genius with a sewing machine. She was an essential part of the factory. When it was sold, she went with the equipment. When it moved, she relocated across the street. Cristina Huyghue was so important to the well-being of her wealthy bosses that when she retired, the factory eventually retired, too.

So what does all of this have to do with poetry, you ask? Plenty. The hard work, the discipline of perseverance, the conscientious dedication to service, the commitment to development, the sheer will to survive, watching my mother sweat beyond her limitations, going hungry together when the cupboard was periodically bare, waiting for my father, Charlie Esteves ("that . . ."), to make good on his daughter, were all very likely the elements that seeded the beginnings of a rebellious mind and a tempered tongue.

My personal life and my poetry have evolved simultaneously and interactively. My poems are an essential catharsis to my creative self; not only have they guided others, but me even more, providing a clearer picture into the internal dynamic of self, which is often the most difficult vision of all to perceive.

I did not plan to be a poet, or to write. It was a divine gift. Ever since I could remember, or even speak my own name, I knew that I wanted to paint, to create beauty within the confines of a painful childhood trapped in the meditative, institutional environment of a convent for Catholic grammar school girls. I wanted to create visual medicine that could turn grey walls into tropical gardens, the way God had created a universe from the darkness in seven days.

Somewhere along the way I made the transition from colors to words, from shapes to sounds, and from lines to stories. But always creating as a painter, exploring style and vision, mood and environment, intention and direction.

There were a number of catalysts that contributed to this significant change in form.

The first was when I received, as a gift, an IBM Selectric typewriter, which opened up the vast possibility of productive work.

The second was a Japanese sculptor teacher at Pratt Institute who taught us how to create visual art that could only exist in the mind of the individual reading a description off the worded page. As if someone opened a door to visual conception, I realized that words came with numerous associations, textures, colors, sounds, smells, feelings, and qualities, any combination of which could produce a graphic, moving rapidly, changing focus and direction with imagery. A visual poem became a live process of storytelling with a series of simple images leading to a focused statement.

The third was a community poetry reading at the National Black Theater in Harlem, where young and old rose to the podium to recite their creations, poems that were close to their lives and mine. I was moved this first time that I heard nontraditional, nonclassical, free-form poetry that addressed itself to the immediate issues of our collective existence. Later that night, my first eight poems were born, and I embarked on a new journey in my creativity.

My approach is as a painter approaching the void. At times, my renderings are precise, chiseled descriptions; at other times, they become boundless in the infinite. There is no one consistent form or style but rather a number of sketches rendered by using varieties of techniques.

My influences were numerous contemporaries, starting with Jesus Papoleto Melendez, a modern-day Shakespeare and man of conscience, who believed in my work enough to bring me into the circle of the poetic literati. We mingled and read poems to each other, in our houses, on university tours, at the Nuyorican Poets Cafe and the New Rican Village, at a political rally in Chicago, in the Central Park Delacourt Theater, at the gates of the White House, in schools, community centers, and other multi-purpose locations, indoors, outdoors, on buses and trains; the point is that we read to each other constantly, developing critical ears and sensitive minds to the tone, quality, and evolution of each other's poetry. Eventually we realized that there is a process of change that envelops all of us, and that one of the physical laws of evolution insists that if we keep working at something, anything, it has to get better with time. We were always in constant dialogue with other poets such as Jose Angel Figueroa, Pedro Pietri, Americo Casiano, Miguel Algarín, Miguel Piñero, Bimbo Rivas, Noel Rico, Luz Marina Rodriguez, Miguel Loperena, Lucky Cienfuegos, Tato Laviera, Zoe Angelsey, Bill Canon, Tom Mitchelson, Brenda Cannor Bey, Rich Bartee, Ntozake Shange, Tulani Davis, Jessica Hagadorn, Mbembe Milton Smith, Michael Harper, Phil George, Leslie Silko, Joseph Bruchac, Ricardo Sanchez, Amiri and Amena Baraka, Sekou Sundiata, and at least a few thousand more, each one leaving a mark, an impression, a new seed for learning, sharing an insight from their unique perspectives, communicating messages. How I write today is as much influenced by their lives and their words as my own. I cannot take credit for what they have given me by way of skill and technique but only for my own thoughts and feelings that come from that part of self that no one else can see or hear but that we all know in much the same way.

In particular, there are a number of poets I must single out as primary mentors. Louis Reyes Rivera, Julia de Burgos, Ernesto Cardenal, Nicolás Guillén, Pablo Neruda, and all the masters who emerge from Latin America, whose works are a leading source of education for guiding one through the darkness where the documents of our voices are absolutely vacant and who have remained, up even into these days of interplanetary communication, relatively unknown in the international community.

There are many whose names go unmentioned, equally important, poets who have been writing all their lives and hide their work in secret drawers, exceptional presentations by poets whose names were never remembered, spontaneous poets (à la Walt Whitman) likely to be wandering around anywhere through the streets of New York City creating spiritual encounters at any given moment, conga-playing musician poets who create verse on the spot relevant to the immediate environment, God-Poets who come down and speak directly to us and through us, or else may visit our dreams.

The source of an inspiration can come from anywhere, about any thing or person or moment in time when the mind realizes an important truth to a crucial issue, perhaps a secret about life, the kind of information generally not taught at the university, only experienced if one is willing to be receptive, interacting with the great mystery called Time. But one thing I have learned is that you cannot force a poem. It creates and calls itself into being from the deepest parts of the soul and the collective unconscious in tense dialogue with the mind. There are no rules of grammar or any such thing as poetic etiquette. A poem is a simple truth that blows up like a bomb in your head, a different type of psychoanalysis, where you confront yourself like a sleepwalker waking up in unknown territory. A poem forces you to see the past but always from a new perspective. Causes you to reevaluate that which was once so important, to be replaced by better awareness. It opens you up to accept the truth of the world, and of yourself, then sensitizes you to understand it. A poem is a different kind of visualizer, medicine with definite mental side effects that causes one to become wiser and clearer, and hopefully greater at becoming and being human beings.

Sista Eliana, and other creative peers, thank you for your continued interest in my work and for asking me to contribute to this important anthology. For those who are aware, it's not necessary to explain why we have to consistently support each other in our creative evolution, or what's more, why this is an important time for the voice of "woman," our voices, to be heard throughout the planet. Not that it was never important, we were just never listened to. Now, in the light of modern-day tragedies that destroy the quality of life for all people, it becomes critical for us to understand that the symbol of woman implies the nurturing, productive work of nature, and perhaps positive change towards environmental sanity.

If each one person assumed the responsibility for just one, then the possibilities of living could be infinitely more interesting, but since life is never ideal, more like a half-surreal imitation, that means that some of us must carry around a slightly larger load of laundry to wash at the river.

With these concepts in mind, among many others, I attempt to infuse into my creative work some of that fire that animates the mind into more positive thought, in recent years taking the form of reproducing six seasons of theater as Executive Director for the African Caribbean Poetry Theater, a nonprofit, Bronx-based arts organization, committed to the evolution of the literary, graphic, and performing arts, in particular, those created by us. But before I get carried away elaborating on the dynamics of group creativity, I must acknowledge that it is through the recognition and integration of the personal "I" with the fire and source of creativity, that the group "I" can focus itself effectively.

I hope these few insightful thoughts about my poetic approach have answered some of your questions. It is now time to attend to the children, a few other things, and get back to minding the store at the African Caribbean Poetry Theater.

I thank you again for this opportunity to share some of my perspectives with some of our future thinkers and motivators toward a more powerful interaction and consciousness.

Sincerely,

Sandra María Esteves

Poetic Discourse of the Puerto Rican Woman in the U.S.: New Voices of Anacaonian Liberation

ELIANA ORTEGA

(To my students in La Unidad at Mount Holyoke College)

INTRODUCTION

"Anacaona, india de raza cautiva, de la región primitiva . . ."; so begins Tite Curet Alonso's song, made popular during the seventies by Cheo Feliciano and exported from San Juan to New York and to the rest of Latin America.

Because "Anacaona" is an integral element of a popular song, it is also a manifestation of Latin American daily life and historic experience. Once more, a voice is given to a Latin American historical figure who had heretofore been silenced by the official discourse of the dominant culture. The popularization ("cultura popular" vs. mass culture of the consumer society) of this historic event/subject functions as a collective model and representation, reconnecting the people to their cultural baggage in the re-actualization of an *areyto*:[1] "Anacaona, india de raza cautiva, de la región primitiva . . . Anacaona, areyto de Anacaona." The Indian woman, a mother figure, initiates a collective and rebellious voice in a liberation dance for her enslaved, captive peoples.

The present reading of the poetic discourse of Puerto Rican women in the U.S., that is, what I call new voices of Anacaonian liberation, goes hand in hand with the song's recovery of the historical figure of Anacaona, the Indian woman poet. My purpose is to concentrate on her as a matriarchal model in order to define a subversive poetic discourse written by women since the seventies. In my reading, the figure of Anacaona takes these poets back to a pre-Hispanic origin, a mother origin, an Afro-

Antillean origin: that is to say, to "Borinquen," the indigenous name for Puerto Rico. This is not simply a historical consciousness of an Antillian past, but also a direct confrontation with an oral tradition that keeps the history of a people alive and palpable. This orality demonstrates the importance of popular culture in the construction of an identity as a people, the formulation of a collective subject, and the representation of its artistic expression. In this way, oral discourse is superimposed over the exclusively literary one that belongs to the intellectual elite.

The return to original sources based on orality is central in establishing a definition and interpretation of female literary discourse. It is well known that the dominant ideology prevents a woman from establishing connections with her own traditions or else prevents her access to them. The editors of the anthology *Cuentos: Stories by Latinas*, one of the few published anthologies, refer to this problem in their introduction:

> . . . we are heirs of a culture of silence. Even so, women have managed to write—from Sor Juana Inés de la Cruz in the seventeenth century on through to Rosario Castellanos, Clarice Lispector, María Luisa Bombal, and Julia de Burgos in the twentieth century. These writers, however, are virtually unknown in the United States. "El" so-called "Boom" del escritor latinoamericano has only meant that norteamericanos have discovered that Latin American *men* can write. Because of this, the Latina in the U.S. not educated in Spanish, is deprived of any knowledge of her own female literary legacy.
>
> The question remains, however, to what extent can most Latin American women writers be considered our literary legacy when so many, like their male counterparts, are at least functionally middle-class, ostensibly white, and write from a male-identified perspective.[2]

What this passage illustrates is the exclusion of the U.S. Latina from the writing of Latin American women who belong to an intellectual literary elite. That is to say, if women are inheritors of a culture of silence and if those who have dared to break the silence in Latin America belong to the *ciudad letrada*[3] (literary citadel), it is obvious that such a discourse is a distortion mirror that fails to interpret the historical reality of the non-bourgeois Latina within the United States. For these women in the U.S., it is the oral, matriarchal tradition that gestates their discourse a priori.

It is useful, therefore, to define the socio-historical context in which this discourse is produced. It is one that stems from the concrete experience of second-generation Puerto Rican women, daughters of working-class immigrants, or else belongs to those who do not necessarily come from the working class but who do identify with it. They are women who also choose to name themselves within the social and racial context of the U.S. as "women of color." This identification is not simply an anti-bourgeois position but rather stems from factors of racial and economic oppression in the U.S. Moreover, the definition of this group is further complicated when we consider that the members of this second generation of Puerto Ricans enter literary circles, crossing the barrier from the oral to the written, from the ghetto to the campus, from one social class to another. With such socioeconomic, political, ideological, and cultural complexities and divergences, how can these women establish their own discourse? How can literary criticism articulate an explanation and interpretation of their work in Latin American terms at the same time? We must take into account that the official Latin American canon doubly marginalizes and silences them: first, for being that of a woman and second, for the colonial and linguistic conditions of the Puerto Rican people. How, then, will this woman-subject be represented both symbolically and discursively? There is no doubt that the intellectual citizens of *la ciudad letrada* have excluded her from their midst. Therefore, before undertaking a study of these women, we must first stop in this *ciudad letrada*, even at risk of getting lost in it. Likewise, we must remember that this citadel is labyrinthine and solitary, with women not allowed to go "walking around" in it alone.[4]

Let us have a look at the hegemonic and phallogocentric discourse in the symbolic patriarchal gallery of this city. Let us consider, for example, the figures that have interpreted and represented Latin Americans, thereby establishing a literary tradition. If the symbol for 1900 was Ariel, projected for various decades as a symbol of Latin America's positivist liberalism, and if it appeared previously in 1894 in Zeno Gandía's *La charca*[5] (to situate ourselves in a Puerto Rican context), that symbol was still only a partial definition of Latin Americanness. Thus, *Ariel*[6] represents the perspective of a dominant class who defines Latin American culture from a racial, determinist ideology in which women simply do not appear; or if they do, as in *La Charca*, they are reduced to simple objects of sexual pleasure.

In the same way, *Ariel*'s counterpart, the contemporary *Calibán*,[7] is also a partial representation that excludes Latin American women. It is true that Calibán represents a symbol of recognition of the colonial and neo-colonial condition of Latin America. If it is also true that Calibán is acknowledged as a rebel slave, we must be aware that he only half interprets us. Calibán is still the voice of one side of "Nuestra América," the voice of the Latin American man, and he still is a symbol that is dependent on European literary conventions. He is a sign that is named by Europe. However, what is so attractive about Calibán (both for Latin American women and men) is precisely his potential for rebellion from slavery. For this very reason, even Latin American women have felt interpreted by this European sign, from which many have made a Latin American symbol. At the moment that we detect the lack of voice from Calibán's mother in *The Tempest*, we perceive how she, Sycorax, is silenced in the text. The only view of her we get is through Próspero and Ariel, his echo. For them, Sycorax was an evil witch, born in Algeria, sovereign of an island before Próspero's arrival. It is Calibán who remembers this fact: "This island's mine, by Sycorax, my mother,"[8] thereby acknowledging his matrilineal heritage. But she does not appear as a character; rather, she dis-appears, deformed and monstrous. The text of the civilizer, Próspero, has silenced her, establishing her as non-text, yet still threatening because of her autochthonous knowledge that could destroy the civilized world and, with it, Próspero's white magic. Although Roberto Fernández Retamar's "apuntes sobre la cultura de Nuestra América" in *Calibán* consolidates a necessary Latin American liberation, Calibán is still a questionable symbol of Latin America for two principal reasons. Initially, Calibán's mother is never mentioned, thereby silencing women. And then, toward the end of the essay, Fernández Retamar suggests that the Latin American intellectual has two masculine options (both European): "serve Próspero, like Ariel" (who would be the intellectuals of an "anti-America," as he calls them), or "unite with Calibán in his struggle for a true freedom."[9]

For the Latin American woman intellectual, uniting with Calibán signifies only a half liberation, because as long as the mother figure remains forgotten, as long as women continue to be silenced, there can be no liberation for an entire people. However, to incorporate Sycorax would imply, for Latin American women, that they continue to be associated with the imposed dominant discourse. It would be a continuation of her definition within the mythological, colonizing codes imposed by Europe that convert woman into witch/goddess, Eve/Ave, exploited/adored by men. Therefore, the most viable alternative for Latin American women and men is the recovery of the rebel autochthonous mother, Anacaona, original owner of the land, invoker of the *areyto*, the original collective voice: as the song says: "Anacaona, india de raza cautiva . . . oí tu voz cómo lloró . . . tu libertad nunca llegó." She is the mother of a colonized people who lost their mother tongue and their land, stripped from them by the most insidious expressions of patriarchy, conquest and colonialism.

Although popular song and oral tradition obviously assist collective memory in returning to its origin, they are not sufficient in reconstructing the image of the indigenous mother and her land. For that, we must also turn to the *crónicas*, the only official manuscripts in which historical protagonists, made captive in America, appear. The *Crónica* of Fernández de Oviedo, in the books referring to Puerto Rico, "captures" the *persona* of Anacaona:

> En el tiempo que el comendador mayor D. Frey Nicolás de Ovando gobernó esta isla, hizo un areyto ante él Anacaona, mujer que fue del cacique o rey Coanabo (la qual era gran Señora): y andaban en la danza más de trescientas doncellas, todas criadas suyas, mujeres por casar; porque no quiso que hombre ni mujer casada (o que oviese conocido varón) entrassen en la danza o "areyto."[10]

In this first depiction of Anacaona, we perceive an essentially female character, the centrality of the female voice, and the collective nature of her *areyto*. This collectivity coincides with the popular tradition in Puerto Rican and Caribbean cultures that recognizes the matriarch as a central figure, carrier, and continuer of the race as well as its culture. Additionally, Anacaona is a woman in full possession not only of her land, her voice, and the destiny of her people but also of her body and her own discourse. Oviedo, astounded, describes her:

> . . . y assi era esta Anacaona en vida de su marido y hermano; pero después de los días dellos fue, como tengo dicho, absoluta señora y muy acatada de los indios; pero muy deshonesta en el acto venéreo con los cristianos, y por ser esta y otras cosas semejantes quedó reputada y tenida por la más desoluta muger que de su manera ni otra ova en esta Isla. Con todo esto era de gran ingenio, y sabía ser servida y acatada y tenida de sus gentes y vasallos, y aún de sus vecinos.[11]

It is clear from the above description that we may begin to perceive Anacaona as a sovereign of "great ingenuity," a sovereign of her land and people, her own mistress in body and soul, respected by all in spite of the misogynist criticism implicit in the European writer's account of her sexual liberation. There is no doubt that the negative frame in which the chronicle writer places her is one more patriarchal strategy whose purpose is to de-authorize her power and control by devaluing her in terms of sexual dishonesty.

But this strategy falls flat when interpreted from a socio-cultural feminist reading. Instead, Anacaona imposes herself by usurping the power of European heroines and, above all, displacing Ariel and Calibán.

Thus, Anacaona becomes the symbol of a feminine voice, a collective and rebellious voice that includes the entirety of a people, both in their histor-ical and contemporary contexts. If Anacaona authorizes a collective origin of liberation recovered by the popular song, Anacaona's rebellion is a paradigm in this article for the new voices of Anacaonian liberation:

> And I am a woman, not a mistress or a whore
> or some anonymous cunt whose initials barely left an impression
> on the foreskin of your nationhood.[12]

In Sandra María Esteves' poem, it is the speaker who defines herself as whole (woman) in counterpoint to how the dominant culture perceives her. She is a woman whose matrix force enables her to transform society's negativity into vital strength and love. That same creative force is evident in a poem by Luz María Rodríguez that appears in the anthology, *Nuyori-can Poetry*. The figure of the mother/grandmother is so important in this discourse of female self-affirmation, self-definition, and self-perception that the poem is preceded by the following introduction reinforcing the centrality and positive value of the mother as a transforming power:

> Luz once told Vilma Linares, an actress in the Nuyorican
> Theatre Festival that whenever her father showed no love she
> had to be patient and show him love. That's how Luz taught
> her to absorb aggression and transform it into strength.[13]

The following poem synthesizes and illustrates the strength of character of the Puerto Rican woman within a United States space, a woman who, in turn, projects outward from herself and toward a community that values the feminine:

> I feel the we
> of my body
> flowing through
> the cycle of woman.
> blood rush down
> cleanse my womb.
> My hair at motion,
> limbs in stimulation,
> effecting sensation
> submerging in love.[14]

From the example above, we can see how this poetic discourse embarks upon a persistent questioning of western culture and the concept of bourgeois motherhood that defines the mother both in and by her domestic role: passive, submissive, servile, and silent in front of men. In such a definition, the mother is seen as an intermediary for men but never as an active agent of her own life or that of her descendants. The Puerto Rican women's poetic discourse renders a creative and subversive response to the bourgeois concept of motherhood. In Sandra María Esteves's well-known and much-debated poem, "A la mujer borrinqueña," the speaker destroys the image of the passive mother/grandmother, converting her into an agent of collective change:

> . . . I do not complain about nursing my children
> because I determine the direction of their values
> I am the mother of a new age of warriors . . . (P. 63)

Motherhood, then, takes place and is lived in terms applicable to a community of indigenous struggle, going beyond the western concept of motherhood embedded both in and by the construction of the nuclear family. It follows that the Anacaonian mother, then, is in direct contact with her people and her motherland, expressing herself in a communal and by no means solitary voice. The lyric "I" in Salima Rivera's poem, "Ode to an Island," is actually a "we" that identifies with its indigenous origin, the *borinqueña* woman:

> Preciosa, We sing in profound adoration,
> A nymph in green velvet
> enshrined by the sea.
> Borinken, mi madre,
> Like a child who worships
> the goddess who bore her,
> My words are jewelled offerings
> I lay at your feet.[15]

As we can certainly appreciate from this poem, poetic discourse emerges from an identification with the indigenous mother, Preciosa (whose precursor, in fact, was Anacaona), transcending the purely domestic sphere and projecting herself into a historical-political-national one that she traces to her origins. These mother-speakers are neither silent martyrs or tearful *lloronas*[16] but rather rebels with a very specific cause: liberation, not simply individual liberation, but also liberation of their motherland:

> Y si la patria es una Mujer
> then I am also a rebel and a lover of free people
> and will continue looking for friction in empty spaces
> which is the only music I know how to play.[17]

In this manner, Puerto Rican women poets in the U.S. continue the Anacaonian tradition of song as a rebellious voice and act of liberation. It is a discourse that is otherwise an integral part of the continuum established by Luz María Umpierre when she notes the existence "of a correlation between the idea of freedom for women in anti-domestic terms, and the idea of social revolution."[18]

At the same time that these poets demythify the patriarchal discourse of dominant culture, they also produce a dynamic poetic discourse in a dialectic process, creating new myths that are, in turn, a product of the circumstances of a very specific everyday life as Latina women residing in the U.S. For these poets, writing itself is a double process; they deconstruct the deforming myths imposed on them by the dominant culture while at the same time creating a new, energetic, vital, mythic world that is autochthonous. In this process, the unity of woman with Nature is paramount and the presence of Borinquen is a constant theme. Yet the motherland is not a nostalgic invocation of Paradise Lost but rather the recognition of the close relationship of woman and Nature and the importance of such a relationship since both are a source of life. This is the reason why even in a barren land—the urban space made of concrete in the immense mercantile cities of the U.S.—the images of fertility abound in these poems. "Mambo Love Poem," by Sandra María Esteves, begins:

> Carlos and Rebecca move
> and the room fills with blazes of red flaming
> pianos breezing spicy tunes as coconuts fall
> from palm trees ancient to those children
> as coconuts fall from imaginary palm trees
> ancient to Boricua souls. (P. 31)

Not only is the "imaginary" tropical landscape represented, but even snow and wind, mythical ideologemes that suggest negativity and Anglo-Saxon coldness, acquire a function of positive and creative beauty in this discourse:

> Who is he
> who would call the snow ugly?
> Who is she
> who would reject the breathing wind
> carrying the spirit of life
> perhaps the soul of her next mother. (P. 69)

Additionally, the images of fertility not only refer to woman's reproductive

fecundity but also to her creative power. In her poem dedicated to Ntozake Shangé, Esteves combines the double power of woman as both
procreator and creator of a poetic discourse:

> Fertile woman is fire and thunder
> The voice of justice bringing the people up
> The new day
> A new way to live
> Breathing hope into our children's souls
> Green
> Green
> Fertile woman is green
> Sea of fertility
> Creator of destiny
> Fertile woman rise
> Reaching to the sky that fills us with being
> Fertile woman rise and harvest the earth
> With natural creativity
> Motion of majesty. (P. 69)

It is necessary to emphasize once again that the voices of Anacaonian
liberation refuse to succumb when faced with the risks and challenges
presented to them by the power structures of the dominant culture. In this
struggle, and especially when referring to the oppression and exploitation
inflicted upon the Puerto Rican people in the U.S., the speakers of the
poems once again break with yet another myth imposed on the Puerto
Rican woman. They are not submissive, they are not docile, nor do they
use the "ploy of the weak"[19] to enunciate their discourse. In other words,
they no longer perceive themselves as powerless. Therefore, their word is
direct, aggressive and, above all, ironic. Their criticism of a dehumanizing
and technological consumer society is categorical and without hesitation,
as is established in Amina Muñoz's poem, "welcome to san juan, oldest
city in the U.S.":

> . . . on T.V. the politician smiles
> an ultrabrite smile, saying
> you've come a long way baby—
> unemployment has risen from 15% to 25%
> three families
> that live in the same house
> watch him, amazed.
> T.V. has become very popular here.
> The beach has a sign—

KEEP OFF—
U.S. PROPERTY it says
meanwhile a young student
at rio piedras lies on her concrete grave.
the national guard decided
she got in the way
of the 51st star of the yanqui flag.[20]

Resorting to irony is a defense mechanism against a culture perceived by the writers not only as anti-vital but also as destructive to their people. Their anger is manifested against the situation of violence and destruction that characterizes the life of Puerto Ricans under U.S. colonialism. The speaker of Salima Rivera's "Fruits of War" could not be more explicit:

A poisonous bile of hatred
fills my veins as I see you sprawled
bleeding into the scorched foreign soil
giving sustenance to the thirsty earth—
                              Murdered!
for an undefinable cause
                    dying
                    a lonely
                    ignoble death.[21]

Hélène Cixous has already pointed out that a feminine text cannot be anything but subversive. But the subversion that emerges from the texts by Anacaonian poets is not an isolated revolt. Rather, it is rebellious voices that form an essential part of a total poetic discourse, consisting of hope and rooted in the collective struggle of the Puerto Rican people. In this respect, this discourse is an integral part of one denominated "dusmic poetry," in which woman is acknowledged as a vital component:

A dusmic poem fortifies and centralizes the reader. It gives hope without deceptive illusions. . . . She [Sandra María Esteves] makes the "i" the center stone, the grinding stone. She is the place from where all definitions of self in time and place evolve . . .[22]

It is clear, then, that the woman/poet is central in this discourse, as well as in the collective struggle against the imperial power that is the direct cause of the "ghettos" in the U.S. When confronting power, the speakers of the poems join men in order to create a space of beauty, in contrast to the surrounding world that oppresses them both; love and beauty is what the couple reaps in Esteves' poem, "for tito":

together
we reap the mystical sugarcane in the ghetto
where all the palm trees grow ripe
and rich with coconut milk.[23]

But in female/male relationships, not everything can be, or is, viewed through rose-colored glasses. Just as the woman confronts the man in a sexist society, once again the Anacaonian poets refuse to remain silent. "Irate and rebellious, anti-Virginian,"[24] is the speaker of the poem entitled "False Idols" by Salima Rivera:

> I can't dig you
> when you say
> "It's a man's destiny to rule."
> That would make me
>   a subject
>   an object
> and the Lord knows
> I don't believe in weak deities.[25]

Reading these poems requires us to confront an anti-bourgeois world vision in dramatic opposition to the decadence of the dominant authoritarian and traditional bourgeoisie that promotes a static condition, bringing with it only inertia and death. In contrast, these poets propose a world in motion, a process, a dialectic, a vital discourse in which one can find hope for a better life. The poetry these women forge is then a non-essentializing practice, an optimism rooted in collective struggle and forged in creativity. In this way, their world is also part of that Anacaonian struggle because these poets consider themselves to contain the life force.

The song that prompted our encounter with Puerto Rican women's voices reminds us that Anacaona, too, was a vital force in her original *areyto*. With the simultaneously historical and popular figure of Anacaona, we are now able to stroll through the streets of the Barrio, accompanied by a female chorus that is obviously situated at the margin that is very different from the one belonging to the woman writer of the elite. The problem of the latter is that these canonized writers are on a dead-end street because they continue to be situated, if not within the center, then definitely in the suburbs of the *ciudad letrada*. The Anacaonian voices (Puerto Rican women poets in the U.S.) have been systematically placed outside that citadel and that is why their discourse has not been listened to and read but rather silenced. Yet these voices are not silent; theirs is, indeed, a rebellious shout of liberation. These are voices that shout and weep, sing and dance, and rejoice in their liberation. And their dance is not some nineteenth-century aristocratic "danza"; it is bomba, it is plena, it is salsa, it is rumba, it is mambo. It is "A Chant":

> it's on the roof
> 100 proof
> plátanos
> bacalao
> and a million african gods
> bump their way up madison ave.
> to 116 st.
> cause
> it's in my sneaker
> a bag of reefer and
> willie colon knows
> the dominoes
> on the table
> merengue to
> ave maría and la plena
> and when they party
> they drink bacardi—
> cause puerto ricans are bad
> uh-huh
> puerto-ricans are bad
> uh-huh.[26]

Their canto/dance is a ritual that re-enacts the original dance: the Caribbean *areyto*. As in the beginning, the new voices of Anacaonian liberation carry with them the true word that is united to the motherland and rooted in the concrete reality of the Puerto Rican woman "born in el Barrio."[27] This word sets in motion the total liberation not only of the woman but also of the Puerto Rican community in the U.S. "Anacaona, oí tu voz," says the song, and the new Anacaonian voices from the Barrios of the U.S. make themselves heard in the historical Latin American present.

Translated by the author and Nancy Saporta Sternbach

NOTES

1   A meeting with religious, educational, and political goals, accompanied by dance and song/poetry in order to tell and re-tell history.

2   "Introduction," *Cuentos: Stories by Latinas*, ed. Alma Gómez, Cherríe Moraga, and Mariana Romo-Carmona (New York: Kitchen Table, Women of Color Press, 1983), viii.

3   I am referring to Angel Rama's *La ciudad letrada* (Hanover, N.H.: Ediciones del Norte, 1984).

4   Pablo Neruda, "Walking Around," *Residencia en la tierra* (Santiago: Ediciones Ercilla, 1939).

5   Manuel Zeno Gandía, *La charca* (San Juan, P.R.: Instituto de Cultura Puertorriqueña, 1970).

6   José Enrique Rodó, *Ariel* (Madrid: Biblioteca Anaya, 1971).

7   Roberto Fernández Retamar, *Calibán: Apuntes sobre la cultura de nuestra América* (Buenos Aires: Editorial La Pleyade, 1973).

8   William Shakespeare, *The Tempest* (London: Cornmarket Press, 1970), 20.

9   Fernández Retamar, *Calibán*, 82.

10   "In the time that Commander Fray Nicolás de Obando governed this island, Anacaona did an *areyto* in front of him. She was the wife of the tribal leader or the king Coanabo, and a great Lady. More than three hundred young women accompanied her, all maids of marrying age because she didn't want any man or married woman (or one who had been with men) to enter the dance or *areyto* with her," Eugenio Fernández Méndez, *Crónicas de Puerto Rico: Desde la conquista hasta nuestros días (1493–1955)* (San Juan: Editorial Universidad de Puerto Rico, 1976). I have also consulted with *Tesoro de la lengua castellana o española* (Madrid: Ediciones Turner, 1984), 696, for verification of old Spanish.

11   "And Anacaona was like this with her husband and brother; but after that, she was the absolute mistress and obeyed by the Indians. But she was also sexually dishonest with the Christians, and for these and other similar reasons she was repudiated as the most dissolute woman on this Island. With all of this, she showed great ingenuity, knowing how to be served and respected by her people, her servants and her neighbors." Gonzalo Fernández de Oviedo, "Fragmentos" de *La historia general y natural de las Indias, 1535,* Libro XVI, in Fernández Méndez, *Cronicas de Puerto Rico*, 76.

12   Sandra María Esteves, *Yerba Buena* (Greenfield Center, N.Y.: Greenfield Press, 1980), 49. All subsequent references to this volume shall be contained within parentheses directly after the quoted passage with the corresponding page number.

13   Miguel Algarín and Miguel Piñero, *Nuyorican Poetry: An Anthology of Puerto Rican Words and Feelings* (New York: William Morrow, Inc., 1975).

14   Ibid., 129.

15   Salima Rivera, "Ode to an Island," in *Nosotros, Revista Chicano-Riqueña* 5, no. 1 (1977). "Preciosa" must be read as a representation of Puerto Rico as it appears in the original traditional song.

16   Mythical crying mother figure.

17   Sandra María Esteves, "From the Commonwealth," cited in Margarite Fernández-Olmos, "From the Metropolis: Puerto Rican Women Poets and the Immigration Experience," *Third Woman* 1, no. 2 (1982): 47.

18   Luz María Umpierre, "De la Protesta a la Creación—Una Nueva Visión de la Mujer Puertorriqueña en la Poesía," *Imagine: International Chicano Poetry Journal* 2, no. 1 (Summer 1985): 134–42 (my translation).

19   Josefina Ludmer, "La tretas del débil," in *Lar sartén por el mango,* ed. Patricia González and Eliana Ortega (Río Piedras, P.R.: Huracán, 1984), 47–54.
20   Algarín and Piñero, *Nuyorican Poetry,* 109–10.
21   Salima Rivera, "Fruits of War," *Revista Chicano-Riqueña, Nosotros* 5, no. 1 (1977).
22   Algarín and Piñero, *Nuyorican Poetry,* 129.
23   Ibid., 133.
24   Rosario Ferré, "La cocina de la escritura," González and Ortega, *La sartén,* 137.
25   Salima Rivera, "False Idols," *Revista Chicano-Riqueña, Nosotros* 5, no. 1 (1977).
26   Amina Muñoz, "A Chant," in Algarín and Piñero, *Nuyorican Poetry,* 111.
27   Esteves, *Yerba Buena,* 63.

"Señores, don't leibol mi, please!!: ya soy Luz María Umpierre"

ASUNCIÓN HORNO-DELGADO

Translated by Janet N. Gold

The Puerto Rican writer Luz María Umpierre–Herrera has been living in the United States for several years, working as a professor of Hispanic Literature at Rutgers University in New Jersey. She has published three books of poetry: *Una puertorriqueña en Penna* (1978), *En el país de las maravillas* (1982), and *Y otras desgracias. And Other Misfortunes* (1985). Forthcoming is her collection, *The Margarita Poems*. She has also published a considerable number of essays on literary criticism. Umpierre has always considered herself a dissident from the mainstream of the so-called bourgeois society of the two cultures she shares: that of Puerto Rico, where she was born, and that of the United States, where she lives.

Throughout her creative work she is not only critical of the American system but intends to break new ground for a more pluralistic society, one that will allow the defiant woman, the lyric voice created in all her work, to speak out and set forth another way of being human in political, intellectual, and sexual arenas. The metaphor of always providing an alternative to already accepted values has pervaded her entire creative work. It is precisely this aspect that makes her an important and controversial figure. In this essay, it is my intention to concentrate on her second collection of poems, *En el país de las maravillas*.

Luz María Umpierre posits this work as a meditation on Puerto Rican marginality.[1] For this reason, she has subtitled it "kempis puertorriqueño." The concept of "kempis" has been interpreted by Eliana Rivero, in the prologue of this volume, as "manual de vida de una creyente iconoclasta" (guidebook to life of an iconoclastic believer).[2] The idea of a break with the establishment and the severance experienced by the lyric voice, as well as a yearning for freedom, preside over the entire book. The concept of bilingualism is achieved not only through the medium of language (she employs English, Spanish, and "Spanglish," as well as a transcription of the Puerto Rican vernacular) but also through the transgressive elaboration of the concept of ritual in the sense that, on a rhetorical level, she takes familiar rituals and gives them a specific significance in accordance with the idea she is expressing. I refer, in particular, to poems such as "Pase de lista" and "Jaculatoria in Nomine Domine," among others. The lyric voice appears with a combative tone, governed by bitter humor and irony. These are the only weapons she carries in her battle with the establishment—the American way of life that threatens to encase her and thus reduce her to a coherence within a norm.

It is important to keep in mind that Luz María, besides being a poet and a literary critic, is a professor of Spanish at a U.S. university, and so the panorama of her discourse is elaborated within this environment. She takes us by the hand from the first poem, "La receta," to discover her firm opposition to labels, helping us see our habitual activities in the academic environment with a different eye. We read her and position ourselves in relation to her implicit vision of a transformed Academy. *En el país de las maravillas* is a collection of poems that testifies to the painful experience of not adapting to a society that, as Rivero has defined, is "de gente amaestrada que impone reglas de conducta a la efervescencia latina" (made up of tamed people who impose rules of conduct on Latin effervescence).[3] Nevertheless, the poet claims her space from which to proclaim her own voice after having read (experienced) all the various discourses that amaze and anger her. It is true the reader is faced with poems full of rage and sarcasm, belligerent poems. While we may close the book and leave it to stew in its own juices, choosing to read it will mean we want to appreciate its worth and determine what Luz María is trying to say to us, even while she is letting us have it.

Beyond the level of anti-Americanism and nonadaptation, we find the defense of one's own identity, the evocation of the discourse of history, and the fully conscious acceptance of marginality as one's own space to be understood as the area of expressing, reaffirming, and dignifying that which "Gringolandia" has considered exotic. Umpierre's poetic bifurcates between the discourse of power and marginality and, precisely by means of the rhetorical use of irony, she discredits the canonical to make way for a creative laconism that flowers with dignity and seriousness. This laconism (a combination of dryness and brevity) is jarring for having arisen from the apparent apposition of trite situations and languages with euphemisms, voices of protest that are raised to create something other than a "masquerade" of life, as in the following:

Mascarada la vida . . .
Como cuando tienes que callar y reír, tragar y reír, llorar
adentro y lanzar una carcajada externa para sentirte afin con un
mundo al que poco le importas.
Mascarada la vida . . .
Como cuando quieres gritar pero te callas, quieres callar
pero discurres para seguir con el mundo y que éste siga contigo
Mascarada la vida . . .
Cuando te dicen que no puedes sentir lo que sientes, que
debes callar lo que opinas, que no debes pensar lo que piensas . . .
Mascarada interminable. (P. 32)[4]

Structurally, this collection of poems projects three levels of referentiality: 1) the allusion to situations that call forth the Puerto Rican experience in the United States; 2) reclaiming the Island through memory and by juxtaposing that memory with her present situation; and finally, 3) those poems that consciously reconstruct the tension between the two worlds and concretize a solution. A clear example of the first level of referentiality is the poem, "La receta":

Moody, Puerto Rican
Spic, Hot Tempered,
Difficult, Unconformist,
Perfunctory and Sketchy,
Rebellious and Violent,
    Regionalist

Prepararon su receta las Betty Crocker gringas
y decidieron cocerme a fuego bajo y a lumbre lenta.
Había que cocinarme y amoldarme,
envasarme al vacío con benzoato y BTZ
y mantenerme enlatada para que no me saliera.

Y fue cuando prepararon aquel label,
una maldita etiqueta con el símbolo de Goya
con sus cuatro enormes letras.

Quisieron meterme en la caja bring maltita,
bien marcada y atadita con sus signs en rojas letras:

EXPLOSIVE

HANDLE WITH CARE

Quisieron etiquetarme, las Julia Child cocineras,
para luego señalarme en supermarkets y tiendas
como aquel producto raro que vino de lejanas tierras.

Pero yo no quise amoldarme, ni conformarme a su esquema,
y yo misma me forjé una bonita bandera
que leía una palabra, seis letras:

HUMANA[5]

This poem leads us to the recent tradition in women's writing of using the metaphor of the kitchen and its confines as a feminine space that is transgressed in postmodern discourse in order to fashion a free woman.[6] This particular poem creates a woman, adapted to an Anglo society she refers to as "gringo," who still retains the leftovers of Hispanic marginality. The ingredients are adjectives that the Anglo-Saxon society has relegated to the woman in question. From the start, this rhetoric proclaims the establishment's will to undermine the subjectivity of the being to whom it refers in an impersonal and degrading way. The woman actively present in the poem is the perfect housewife and wonderful cook, as befits women who value their place in the system: the Betty Crockers, the Julia Childs. With their technique and assimilation to the established order, they destroy the identity of "unrefined" humanity, of those who would be different and thus be who they truly are. Of note in the rhetorical construction is the process of intensification, extended to achieve an exotic product, and use of the poetic voice as raw material. We witness the mechanization of the packaging process. To emphasize the obsession with identifying, the poet repeats synonyms in English, as well as in Spanish: "label—maldita etiqueta—signs." The style alludes to a demeaning of the Puerto Rican context in the U.S., where, in the uniform world of the supermarket, Puerto Rican means "Goya"; in the United States Goya refers not to the art world but rather to "ethnic food," specifically to Puerto Rican food. The poem parodies the anxiety to categorize from which American society suffers, one that pursues hygiene (asepsia) and standardization. The parody includes the "esquema" (schema) to which the poetic voice alludes in its rebellion, thus meshing its semantic field with the "receta" (recipe) of the title. There is a binary tension within the poem in terms of this configuration; the poetic voice, as one of the ingredients, is described as "sketchy." Nevertheless, this same system accuses her attempts to convert her into "conserva adaptada" (assimilated preserves), another type of schema. In her response, the lyric voice proposes just the opposite. She says: "yo misma me forjé" (I forged myself), which conveys an experience of independent construction of the self, a maturity incompatible with schemas of any kind.

Within the second group (poems that recall the Island of Puerto Rico), we can include her calligrams: "Writer's Block," "Sol Boricua," and "Título sobreentendido." In the first, "Writer's Block," we find a reclaiming of history on her own terms. The poem is dedicated to Pedro Juan Soto. Stylistically succint (Padre. Hijo. Asesinos—Father. Son. Murderers), the context of the poem is the Puerto Rican independence movement. The son of the novelist Pedro Juan Soto was shot to death by the police on Maravillas Hill in 1978. Through this poem of homage, the lyric voice unites with the defenders of liberty. Within her calligrammatic or concrete

Writer's Block

A Pedro Juan Soto

PADRE   PADRE

HIJO   HIJO

HIJO   HIJO

HIJO   ASESINOS   HIJO

HIJO   HIJO

HIJO   HIJO

PADRE   PADRE

poems, her disagreement with the political situation is expressed by means of a cutting succinctness. Her spatial configuration, as well as her title, recall a page from a writer's notebook: the writer's mission must be the defense of freedom, the unveiling of injustice. It can also be read as a gravestone whose only possible epitaph is the single word, "asesinos" (murderers). The poem's visual effect is one of solemnity and respect; it honors the voice not only of the disappeared son but also of the father, stunned in the face of the circumstantial reality of death. The voice comes forth from the most profound depths of those who have been silenced and is elevated with anger and dignity by the written "asesinos."

In "Sol Boricua," the uniqueness of Puerto Rican and Borinquen people is made up of the vital energy that music and sun produce on the Island. There is in this depiction an attempt to return to aboriginal connotations:

SOL BORICUA

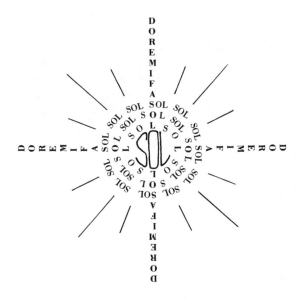

The indigenous element is elaborated by the superimposition of the elements of primitivism (rhythm, the eternal sun) and the reduction of the poetic concept to a graphic design, thereby recovering an ingenousness lost in the menacing metropoli.[7] By remembering these absent elements, Luz María establishes a process of emotional nourishment.

Because of its graphic configuration, "Título sobreentendido" takes us directly to the Island of Manhattan, homeland of Puerto Rican immigration. The idea of the "ghetto" unfolds like a rhythm, like "happiness" that engulfs those who surround themselves with "salsa." A concept as historically negative as "ghetto" becomes positive and is assimilated by the lyric voice as a weapon of strength. If traditionally this word carries with it the

TITULO SOBREENTENDIDO

```
      C L A                                   ONE TWO THREE    BONGO  BONGO   CONGA CONGA    S  A  L  S  A
   L A       V E                            
  L              E    E              E     E                                                                  
                      R                                                                          
                      H    ONE TWO   H    H  ONE TWO                                
        LA            T              T    T                         BONGO           CONGA       HAPPINESS      HAPPINESS
 N               C    O              O    O  ONE TWO               BONGO           CONGA                      
  v           v  L    W              W    W                                                                  
    w  a  v  e   A    T              T    T  ONE TWO THREE          BONGO           CONGA        S  A  L  S  A
                 V    E              E    E                                                                  
                 E    N              N    N                                                                  
                      O              O    O                                                                  
```

idea of something segregated, with Luz María it extends itself throughout and beyond Manhattan, reaching utopian levels and becoming a dream for which to fight. She extends "Puerto Ricanness" to different environments and social spheres. There is a longing to reside in undemarcated space, being whatever one may be, giving the best of oneself. The tension between the Puerto Rican context and that of the colonizer, frequently represented in Luz María's poetry in the world of academe, can be seen clearly in "Pointing Marginals":

ANGLICISMO

COCHE NOT CARRO

PUERTORRIQUEÑISMO

CENA NOT COMIDA

REGIONALISMO

MISCONCEPTION

LOOK THIS UP IN A DICTIONARY!

MISPELLED

WRONG

YOU OBVIOUSLY DON'T UNDERSTAND THE CONCEPT

X

IGNORANCE OF TERMINOLOGY

ARCHAISM!!
FAMILIARIZE YOURSELF WITH THE CASTILIAN WORD!
I DON'T UNDERSTAND WHAT YOU ARE TRYING TO SAY!
UF!

(¡mierda!)
(bullshit!)

If we contextualize this poem, we find comments made by a Hispanist with Peninsular inclinations, written in the margin of a paper whose author is Puerto Rican. The discourse of authority is emphasized in several ways: the use of capital letters and the curtness present in every line, coupled with a marked absence of humor or congeniality. This confers on the academic voice a serious, biting, and one-dimensional tone in its representation of the discourse of power. The exclamations raise the voice level, the attendant wrath, even the annoyance, and the snorted "UF!" enhances that vocal anger even more. In response, the lyric voice marginalizes herself, puts herself in parentheses. But her interior voice gathers force to emit a fierce rejection: only direct obscenities are possible in the face of academic intransigence. The use of lowercase letters indicates a change of voice, irritated in tone, yet one whose will it is to isolate herself from the pompous tone that identifies A C A D E M I A. The English language represents this institution and is used in an attempt to have the receptor assimilate the authoritarian discourse of Castilian or standard Spanish as the only acceptable norm. In the metropoli, it is only possible to pronounce a Spanish that is allied to power. It is a way of once again taking on the discourse of the Conquest. Nevertheless, in her brief response the lyric voice construes an anti-establishment discourse that is laconically bilingual: "mierda, bullshit." Through its use of the metaphor, "comments in the margin," the poem insists on Puerto Rican space as a discourse voluntarily marginalized but from the *base*—the place of the lyric voice's parentheses. Inflexibility prevents the discourse of power from a reading that does not apply its arbitrary rules a priori. As far as the establishment is concerned, if those marginalized have anything to say, it should be prepackaged, as in "La receta," but maintained within the rhetoric and voice of the colonizer.

To end my discussion of these groups of poems, I would like to include some pronouncements by Luz María, made in the journal *Third Woman*. Her statement deconstructs the English language to accentuate her position as critic "in the belly of the beast." Thus, she shows clearly, in repeated use of the prefix "pro-" that the Anglos will impose their own ways on any and every alternative:

The Atlantic side of this nation booms with professionalism, pro-Americanism, pro-liferating, pro-fuse, pro-phylactic, pro-miscous, pro-motion, pro-ductive. Individually and globally these words are a true definition of the East Coast and this pro-longued country. And I view my work and that of my sisters and our living there as anti-establishment, anti-climatic, anti-biosis, anti-C, anti-venin.[8]

She continues this sentiment in one of her poems:

> My name is not María Cristina.
> I speak, I think
> I express myself in any voice,
> in any tone, in any language that conveys
> my house within.
> The only way to fight oppression is through resistance:
> I do complain
> I will complain
> I do revise
> I don't conceal,
> I will reveal,
> I will revise.

Luz María, then, is an iconoclast—but one in defense of her identity and in the process of constructing a liberated space where the rest of the world is marginalized, a space that is contaminated in order to free it from limiting schemas in the healthy world of salsa for the sake of a commit-ment to difference.

NOTES

1   Luz María Umpierre, *En el país de las maravillas* (Bloomington, Ind.: Third Woman Press, 1982). All subsequent quotations from Umpierre's poetry are from this edition.

2   Umpierre, *En el país,* 2.

3   Eliana Rivero, "Notas sobre las voces femeninas en *Herejes y mitificadores: muestra de poesía puertorriqueña en Estados Unidos,*" *Third Woman* 1, no. 2 (1982): 92.

4   LIFE MASQUERADED:

> like when you have to be quiet and laugh, swallow it and laugh, cry
> on the inside and laugh on the outside to feel an affinity with
> a world to whom you hardly matter.
>   Life masqueraded . . .
> like when you want to scream but you say nothing, you want to say
> nothing

but you talk so as to be part of the world and so it will stay with you
>   Life masqueraded . . .
when they tell you you can't feel what you feel, that
you shouldn't say what you think, that you shouldn't think what
you think . . .
>   Interminable masquerade.

5

>   The recipe
>   Moody, Puerto Rican
>   Spic, Hot Tempered,
>   Difficult, Unconformist,
>   Perfunctory and Sketchy
>   Rebellious and Violent,
>   Regionalist

The gringa Betty Crockers prepared their recipe
and decided to cook me slowly over a low flame.
It was necessary to cook me and mold me,
vacuum pack me with benzoate and BTZ
and keep me in a can so I wouldn't get out.

It was when they prepared that label,
a damned sticker with the Goya symbol
with its four enormous letters.

They wanted to put me in the box bring maltita,
well marked and bound with its signs in red letters.
>   EXPLOSIVE
>   HANDLE WITH CARE
They wanted to label me, the Julia Child cooks,
in order to then show me in supermarkets and stores
like that rare product that came from distant lands.

But I didn't want to be molded, nor conform to their schema,
and I myself forged for myself a pretty flag
that read one word, six letters:
>   HUMANA

6 See, for example, the short story "Lección de cocina," by Rosario Castellanos, in *Album de Familia* (Mexico: Joaquín Mortiz, 1971); "La cocina de la
escritura," by Rosario Ferré, in *La sartén por el mango*, ed. Patricia González and
Eliana Ortega (Río Piedras: Ediciones Huracán, 1984), 133–54; and the section "Con
las manos en la masa," in *Bordando sobre la escritura y la cocina*, ed. Margo Glantz
(México: Bellas Artes, 1984).

7 When I use this term "metrópoli," I refer not to the city of New York, but to
a space full of neo-colonial implications and to its effect upon the immigrant
population.

8 Umpierre, "An Anti-Pro," *Third Woman* 1, no. 2 (1982): 5.

A Commentary on the Works of Three Puerto Rican Women Poets in New York

YAMILA AZIZE VARGAS

Translated by Sonia Crespo Vega

The purpose of this essay is to study the feminine and/or feminist perspective in various poems written by three Puerto Rican women of New York, with special attention given to the influence that the migratory experience may have had on the development of this perspective. In this way, we hope to begin also a comparative study of poetry written by Puerto Rican women in the United States and poetry written in Puerto Rico, a topic that could contribute to a better understanding of the history and contributions of the Puerto Rican community in the United States.

The personal experiences of thousands of Puerto Ricans who have emigrated to the United States throughout the twentieth century have left a mark that we have only recently begun to investigate and study. One of the fundamental and pioneering books on this topic is *Memorias de Bernardo Vega* [Memoirs of Bernardo Vega], edited by the Puerto Rican writer and journalist César Andreu Iglesias in 1975.[1] Until then, this "history of the Puerto Rican community in New York" was almost totally unknown to the great majority of Puerto Ricans. Vega, a cigarmaker (and therefore a member of the most select sector of the proletariat) emigrated from Cayey (P.R.) to the United States in 1916. Before him, other Puerto Ricans had already begun to establish the community of "forced emigrants"[2] that would continue to grow rapidly throughout the twentieth century. Eugenio María de Hostos, Ramón Emeterio Betances, and Pachín Marín (among others) produced important patriotic works from New York, together with other Antillians and Latin Americans during the nineteenth

century. But the North American invasion of Puerto Rico, as a consequence of the Spanish–North American War, produced significant
changes in the socio-political life of the country, one of which would be the
emigration of thousands of Puerto Ricans to the United States, particularly
to the east coast.

This migratory process lived by Bernardo Vega was, from its beginnings, different from that of other groups already established in the
United States; "more complex", Bernardo called it, with important and far-
reaching effects on Hispanic culture:

> When I arrived in this city in the middle of 1916, there
> was little interest in Hispanic culture. For the ordinary citizen,
> Spain was a country of bullfighters and dancers. Nobody was
> concerned about Latin América. . . .
>
> The formation of the rapidly growing Puerto Rican com-
> munity caused disturbances, scandals, controversies, hatred.
> But there is one fact that stands out: when we were merely
> half a million, our impact on the culture of the United States
> was much greater than that of the four million Mexican-Amer-
> icans.[3]

The Puerto Ricans living in the great urban centers had more possibility
for cultural exchange and diffusion. The Latin District (Barrio Latino),
recalls Bernardo, "was forming its own profile . . . a typical culture was
rising forth from the common experience of a population that was surviv-
ing in spite of the hostility of the environment. In the long run, that culture
would bear its special fruits."[4]

New York became an active center of socio-cultural exchange for the
population of Hispanic residents, and it was also for others, nonresidents
who saw in this city a fundamental space—a stage for new processes that
had particular and far-reaching effects on the Latin American, as well as
the North American, communities. If we think, for example, about Puerto
Rican women writers (which is the topic of this essay), we see that some of
them (Luisa Capetillo and Julia de Burgos, for example) visit and/or live in
New York, where their different and radical ideas find a more open and
tolerant climate. The experience of visiting or living in New York in some
way affects them, leaving a mark on their writing as well.

The life of another woman, Genara Pagán (probably less known
because she was, like Bernardo Vega, a tobacconist), clearly illustrates the
effects of the social struggles of Puerto Ricans living in the United States.[5]
Genara began to work in the tobacco industry, in a factory in San Juan
called "La Colectiva," where one of the first strikes of women tobacco

workers in Puerto Rico broke out. In these strikes, Genara stood out as a labor union leader. The death of her husband in World War I (in which it was mandatory to serve, according to the new regime) propelled her decision to go to New York in 1917 because she wanted to "advance the Puerto Rican Feminist Movement." There, Genara experienced firsthand the struggles for women's suffrage. She worked as a machine operator in a women's blouse factory where, as a result of the quality of her work and her leadership, she soon became a supervisor. As in Puerto Rico, Genara continued to serve militantly in the labor union movement, working with the tobacco unions in New York. When, in 1919, the Congress of the United States granted women the right to vote, Genara and other Puerto Rican feminists were surprised at the ignorance of those in the government concerning the applicability of that amendment to Puerto Rico. Genara Pagán proposed to clarify those doubts. She traveled to Puerto Rico at the beginning of 1920 and decided to defy the applicability of the law, registering as a voter since she was over 21 years of age and a North American citizen. Genara's action created a "state of emergency," forcing the government of Puerto Rico to consult the Bureau of Internal Affairs in Washington, who decided that the new amendment to the constitution was not valid for Puerto Rican women. Her action, probably motivated by the fiery suffragist struggles lived in New York, made evident two of the most conflictive facts that would affect feminists and Puerto Ricans during the following decades: the colonial situation of Puerto Rico and the stubborn unwillingness of the state to pass legislation in favor of women. Genara, taking advantage of her experiences in New York, upset the traditional order and advanced the cause of Puerto Rican feminism.

As Bernardo Vega prophetically states, the presence and participation of Puerto Ricans in the United States evolved to such an extent that it began to bear its own cultural fruits. At this point there are many Puerto Ricans who distinguish themselves in artistic and literary creation. The growing number of newspapers, magazines, and books since the beginning of the century are testimony to this, constituting overwhelming evidence of Latin American cultural affirmation.

At present, this literary work is one of their richest cultural contributions. In spite of the fact that this work is not easily accessible in Puerto Rico, a small number of testimonies are offered in magazines and literary periodicals. However, through this example we are able to acknowledge that, more than cultural affirmation, this migratory experience of almost a century can continue to contribute (as in the case of Genara Pagán) visions and ideas to social struggles that, like feminism, make up a contemporary international issue.

PUERTO RICAN WOMEN POETS IN NEW YORK

Carmen Valle was born in Camuy, Puerto Rico, and went to New York in the seventies. Like many others, she did not think she would stay so long. Her commitment to poetry took place while still in Puerto Rico, where she was co-editor of the literary review, *Ventana*. Arriving in New York, she continued her cultural work as a writer and as editor of the *Bulletin of the Association of Latin American Writers*. A large portion of her published work has been written in New York. The three books of poetry to be considered in this essay,[6] *Un poco de lo no dicho* (1980), *Glenn Miller y varias vidas después* (1983), and *De todo lo que da la noche al que la tienta* (1985), all bear a particular feminine and feminist perspective also present in other works by Hispanic women and emigrants that have been studied recently. On one hand, it is critical poetry that attempts "to destroy myths and construct new realities," and on the other, it is literature that tells "a truth charged with emotion" and that should be "read and analyzed as a different literary text."[7]

In her poetry, Carmen attacks authority and the dominant culture. In her first book, *Un poco de lo no dicho*, we see forbidden judgments and verdicts that she rebels against and also condemns humble submission in the presence of tradition and custom:

Cuando vivimos de rodillas ante
   el poder
todas las agujas del reloj
apuntan a un solo lugar;
nos metemos un buho en los ojos
y se nos abre
la más grande vidriera
en el corazón.
Nos hacemos turistas de la vida
y terminamos pagando
el pasaje
a plazos mensuales
por toda la eternidad.

When we live on our knees in the
   presence of authority
all the hands of the clock
point in only one direction;
we stick an owl in our eyes
and the largest showcase
opens up
in our heart.
We become tourists of life
and end up paying
the trip
on monthly payments
for all eternity.[8]

We also find evidence of protest and rupture with the established norms in the language of her poems, a language that breaks away from those formal and rigid poetic forms that inhibit and prevent her from stating her vital truth:

... Sin ninguna vergüenza lo digo
ya estoy enferma
harta
de no poder decir
lo que dicho
se convierte
en un poco de lo no dicho.

Without any embarrassment I
    say
that I am sick of
fed up with
not being able to say
what, when said, becomes
a little of what has not been
    said.[9]

In two other poems, Carmen explains the motivation behind her writing and her struggle to regain its reality through words:

Cómo
voy a poder escribir
si no es
de lo que a mí me sangra
hasta la última vena.
***

How
am I going to be able to write
if it isn't
about what makes me bleed
to my very last vein.
***

. . . .
Tal vez
después

. . . .
Maybe
afterwards

. . . .
Puede que con paciencia
encontremos
alguna palabra
que no nos haga mentir.

. . . .
Maybe with patience
we will find
some word
that will not make us lie.[10]

This process of "purification," which makes it possible to state her truth in authentic language, also transforms her vision of the feminine world, making her recognize the various forms of repression to which others have attempted to subject her:

Imágenes
del Catecismo,
de revista fina
para gente encantadora
o del periódico de papá
desfilan
y van llenando esa ciudad
que llevamos dentro
y se adueñan
de los ojos
y las manos

Images
of the Catechism,
of a fine magazine
for charming people
or of Dad's newspaper
parade by
and begin to fill up that city
we have inside us
and they become owners
of our eyes
and our hands

y nos obligan	and they make us
a oír sus eternos cantos	listen to their eternal songs
de alabanza propia.	of self-praise.
Amamos y deseamos con ellos.	With them, we love and wish.
Nosotros nos secamos	We dry up
nos hacemos polvo	we turn to dust
y siguen habitando	and they continue to live
hasta nuestro último	until our last
grano de tierra.	bit of earth.[11]

During "these years," concludes the last poem in the book:

". . . convertí mi ignorancia . . . aclaré varias cosas . . . que me dejaron algunas líneas en la cara pero me dieron un zafacón para los engaños."
(Translation)
"I converted my ignorance . . . I cleared up a few things . . . which
left some wrinkles on my face, but gave me a wastebasket for deceit"[12]

Carmen confesses that the process of growth was painful—away from home, alone—but she recovered through learning and the written word.

This growth and development as a woman and a Puerto Rican is again the fundamental theme of her second book, *Glenn Miller y varias vidas después*. The musical memories of Glenn Miller are the images that lead to the recalling of past experiences. They also lead to new realities that she wants to construct. That maturity, which she achieved in a place different from where she is now, gives her the vital strength to continue struggling against and defying the established order. She wants to be a "lepidop-terous" (butterfly) in order to:

. . . jugarme mis maromas;	. . . do my somersaults;
arriesgar la visión del precipicio;	risk the vision of the cliff;
dejar de escudarme en mi color;	stop hiding behind my color;
volar todo lo más arriba;	fly as high as I can;
atrever la llama.	dare the flame.[13]

What had begun as an instinctive rebellion now becomes a vital necessity: "I need to defy the few days I have left." In *Glenn Miller*, the poet proclaims, firmly and proudly, a different and atypical reality that she has been forming. Consequently, in her confession, "Con el siquiatra," she sings her original ideas joyfully:

Entre otras cosas—	Among other things—
Bebo para recordar	I drink to remember
. . . .	. . . .
Bailo bajo la lluvia	I dance in the rain
. . . .	. . . .
Prefiero un amante	I prefer a lover
a un marido	to a husband
. . . .	. . . .
Temo de las palabras	I am afraid of formulas . . .
obligadas . . .	
Estoy aquí,	I am here,
por ser persona no-grata	because I am not well-liked
y haber empezado a creer	and because I have begun to believe
que debo alterar	that I should alter
mi biografía.	my biography.[14]

Essential in that change in her biography is her rebellion against the traditional feminine role. That is why she insists on making fun of the feminine stereotypes. She ridicules the woman who has been programmed with formulas with which to be attractively appealing, who humbly submits herself to family control, who is a piece of property for a man, the "plastic" or superficial woman who is afraid of what people will say:

Untándonos perfume entre los senos	Rubbing perfume between our breasts
coqueteamos en el espejo	we flirt and mimic before the mirror
las sonrisas	the smiles
de mujer conocedora	of a knowing woman
y la vocecita incapaz	and the incapable little voice
del tú a tú.	of a social chat.
Memorizamos lo que dijo Mami	We memorize what Mommy said
y lo que agregó Tití;	and what Auntie added;
añadiéndonos el Señora de . . .	adding to our names Mrs. So-and-So
con cada—Hola, ¿qué tal?	with each—Hello, how are you?
Jugamos a que vivimos mamá y papá	We play at being Mom and Dad
y así parimos juguetes, pasando de salón en salón	and thus give birth to toys, going from room to room
en la punta de los pies	on tip-toe
mientras limpiamos	while we clean
con esmero, la pared de plexiglass	very carefully, the plexiglass wall
ante la audiencia.	in front of the audience.[15]

It is easier now to evaluate past experiences critically, such as those of the family in Puerto Rico, once a stand has been taken on the feminine question. There is no place for the romantic nostalgia of the countryside left behind. That is why, when she remembers Tía Mei (Aunt Mei), she can then tell her:

tu marido hacía planes	your husband was planning what he
con tu herencia	would do
y se emborrachaba	with your inheritance
hasta estrellarse	and he drank
. . . .	until he got stoned
tu hija reprimía	. . . .
para que los demás	your daughter held herself back
no hablaran otra vez	so that people
de la familia;	would not talk
y todos dirigían y actuaban	about the family again;
esa película, en la cual	and they all directed and acted in
te fueron llegando	that movie, in which
las arrugas,	your wrinkles started to appear,
el pelo ralo,	your hair began to thin,
y esa manera de mirar	and you got that look
que te dió el título	that gave you the title
'La pobre Melania,	'Poor Melanie,
tan buena ella.'	such a good woman.'[16]

The vision of reality achieved has widened and deepened because now, like the butterfly (the image with which the book opens), she can look at the world she lives in more freely and objectively.

Carmen continues to explore this process of breaking with established dogmas and inventing alternate worlds in the last book, *De todo lo que da la noche al que la tienta*. Although it is painful to challenge and defy traditional norms and structures, this challenge enables us to discover other realities. This discovery is possible only when we are willing to run certain risks and face the consequences of the struggle. Then one can celebrate, with loving passion and without fears, one's militancy in life:

Tengo el horizonte de mi piel.	I have the horizon of my skin.
Tengo lo que me sobrevive.	I have what is left after me.
Tengo un tiempo muy corto para tanto.	I have such a short time for so much.
Entonces, tengo los regalos de la vida.	Then, I have the gifts of life.[17]

Carmen Valle proposes an alternate feminine world, governed by challenge, struggle, and the endless search for new experiences. Disagreement, doubt, and invention grows. A poem called "Patente" says:

Muy pocas cosas sé.	Very few things do I know.
De lo que más tengo: preguntas	What I have most of: questions
y lo que a todos	and what life ends up
termina regalándonos la vida—	giving us all—a letter of marque.[18]
patente de corso.	

All of Carmen Valle's poetry is written in Spanish because she believes this is the language in which she can best create literature. Spanish is her native language, as it is also the language (first or second) of the immense Hispanic population living in the United States. Therefore, the use of Spanish has not limited the diffusion of her work, which is written, published, and circulated in the United States. The next woman poet we will be considering has written the greater part of her work in English.

Sandra María Esteves was born into an immigrant community in the South Bronx, New York, the daughter of a Dominican mother and a Puerto Rican father. Her mother tongue is English; that is why she has written more poetry in English than in Spanish. She has published two books of verses, *Yerba Buena* (1980) and *Tropical Rains: A bilingual downpour* (1984).[19] A constant theme in almost all of her work is the testimony and denunciation of prejudice against Puerto Ricans, Dominicans, and Latin Americans in general who live in the United States. Like many other Latina/o writers who live in New York, Sandra María uses literature as a tool to defend her cultural roots. "Heretics and creators of myths" are the titles Efraín Barradas[20] has given to those Puerto Ricans who, from "the other shore," contribute to the strengthening of their national identity with their literary work. The poetry of Sandra María also follows these trends, which clearly appear in various poems about feminine and feminist themes.

In a poem dedicated to Julia de Burgos, entitled "A Julia y a Mí," the author assumes a "heretical tone" when she delivers a critical tribute to one of the most respected women poets of Puerto Rico, admired by Puerto Ricans, male and female alike. Women, in particular, feel close solidarity with her sensual poetry, born of an amorous experience with a new poetic language in Puerto Rican poetry. In the United States, Julia's figure reaches even greater proportions because she was, like so many others, another Puerto Rican emigrant. As the years go by, her image has grown to the dimensions of a "woman-myth." For this reason, any rebuke or criticism of her life can constitute a heresy.

Although the poem shows admiration, influence, and identification with the life and work of Julia, it also questions and reproaches the desperation and defeatism that pervades her work, especially towards the end of her life:

Me fui a la obra y te vi Julia	I went to your work and I saw you Julia
en tus versos camine tu río	in your verses I walked along the river
ande los pisos de la tierra	with you
roja.	I walked over the red earth

The following verses, written originally in English, read:

> But why did you let the dragon slay you
> why did your visions suffocate
> in suicidal premonition you could not die
> within the flesh beat the heart
> and my child needs no image of despair
> or too much poetry of this and that
> but not enough to rise above the clouded cross.[21]

With the alternate use of Spanish and English, the poem achieves the illusion of a dialogue that switches languages, according to the tone of the conversation. Thus, for example, Spanish is used to express admiration and solidarity with Julia, but employs English when formulating questions that, as the poem progresses, turn into critical statements:

Y tú Julia?	And you, Julia?
te perdiste en palabras no	You got lost in words, not in life.
en la vida.	
you let the dragon slay you	
and let life cut your sorrow from wrinkles young	
you let the wine mellow your hatred	
dissolving the fuel that nourished your fires of wisdom[22]	

However, further on in the poem, the poet insists again on the fascination that she feels toward Julia (again in Spanish):

Miro a tu cara, tus ojos	I look at your face, your eyes
mirando el mundo	looking at the world
el mismo que miraba mi madre	the same world my mother looked
siento el ritmo de tu pecho	at I feel the rhythm in your bosom
. . . .	. . . .
oigo tus versos del universo,	I hear your verses about the
humanidad y de mujer.	universe, humanity, and
	woman.[23]

The poem then goes on to develop a "heresy" that has historical reasons. The Puerto Rican woman emigrant, forced to leave her country in search of a better economical situation, generally faces a society, such as the one in North America, which discriminates against her because she is both a woman and a Puerto Rican. The struggle for survival is definitely more difficult for women. Consequently, they will have to assume a more aggressive attitude. Julia's world, like today's world, continues to oppress women (written originally in English):

> it is the same world that has not moved
> but an inch from your suffrage
> women still tend fires that men burn
> and lovers still imprison dreams
> and truth remains cold like your bones yet bittersweet[24]

For this reason, the struggle must continue to demand more than the right to vote or protest. The struggle must continue to affirm and defend a dynamic, aggressive, and transforming vision of the feminine world. The poet proclaims her vision:

A ti Julia, ya será tarde	For you, Julia, it will be too late
pero a mí no	but not for me
Yo vivo!	I live!
y grito si me duele la vida	and I shout if life hurts me
y canto con la gente	and I sing with the people
y bailo con mis hijas	and I dance with my daughters
no soy lágrimas de ser	I am not tears of being
soy el río	I am the river
la mariposa y la culebra.	the butterfly and the snake.

The rest of the text, written originally in English, reads:

> my fist is my soul
> it cuts into the blood of dragons
> and marks time with the beat
> of an afrocuban drum.[25]

The switch from Spanish to English underscores the sources of learning behind the formation of the feminist consciousness. The images of nature and moods, so frequent in the poetry of Julia de Burgos, are presented in Spanish because they are the product of a cultural legacy in Spanish. The verses in English summarize the new experiences and resolutions that have molded the contemporary Latina woman as an immigrant in the United States.

But while this "heretical act" may well contribute to a critical reevaluation of the feminine archetypes in Puerto Rican culture, it does not free the
poetic text from mythicizing a traditional feminine behavior that is sup-
ported and strengthened in the dominant ideology. The poem, "A la mujer
borrinqueña," praises the woman who, born in "el Barrio," has been able
to endure discrimination and continue to cultivate her Caribbean cultural
identity. Women are admired because it is they who teach the men to be
strong, and also because they respect the customs and traditions of the
patriarchal tradition. This woman, named María Cristina, feels proud of
herself because (written originally in English):

> Our men . . . they call me negra because they love me
> and in turn I teach them to be strong
> I respect their ways
> inherited from our proud ancestors
>
> . . . .
> I do not complain about cooking for my family
> because abuela taught me that woman is the master of fire
>
> . . . .
> I teach my children how to respect their bodies
>
> . . . .
> I teach my children to read and develop their minds
>
> . . . .
> I teach them with discipline and love[26]

In this way, women will play a fundamental role in the struggle for
cultural and national affirmation but also continue to assume those typical
roles to which they have been subordinated in the patriarchal society: the
house, the kitchen, the education of the children. The mystique presented
in this poem contrasts with the vision in the previous poem, which insisted on women's active participation in the struggle for social change. If
the "heresy" towards the Julia-myth presents other possible options for
the Caribbean woman immigrant, the myth of Latin femininity suggests
the acceptance of those models that perpetuate women's submission.
However, the defense of Latin cultural values does not necessarily justify
those traditional models, as we shall see in the poems of our last woman
poet.

Luz María Umpierre was born in Puerto Rico, later going to the United
States to pursue graduate studies in literature. At present, she lives in the
States and works as a professor. The feminine and feminist themes appear
in her three published books: *Una puertorriqueña en Penna* (1978), *En el país*

de las maravillas (1982), and *Y otras desgracias / And Other Misfortunes* (1985). In these three books, Luz María emphasizes specifically the problems of Puerto Rican and Latina women.[27] The critical feminine perspective that she develops in various poems intends, above all, to combat prevailing stereotypes, emphasize different forms of behavior, and destroy myths that have traditionally dominated the education of Latina women. These ideas are worked very originally into a poem entitled "In Response," which was written in answer to a poem by Sandra María Esteves and mentioned earlier in this essay. Luz María's poem criticizes the model named María Cristina, presented in "A la mujer borrinqueña." Luz María defends another model (written originally in English):

> My name is not María Cristina.
> I am a Puerto Rican woman born in another barrio.
> Our men . . . they call me pushie
> for I speak without a forked tongue
> and I do fix the leaks in all faucets.
> I don't accept their ways,
> shed down from macho ancestors.[28]

Using a structure parallel to the poem by Esteves that she criticizes, this verse presents a woman that rebels against Latino patriarchal ideology. The speaker in the poem claims her right to think, to speak, and to fight (written originally in English):

> My name is not María Cristina.
> I speak, I think,
> I express myself in any voice,
> in any tone, in any language that conveys
> my house within.
> The only way to fight oppression is through resistance:
> I do complain
> I will complain.[29]

The alternative of defiance and the development of a feminist consciousness necessarily cause anguish and pain, but this is part of the complex process of conquering personal liberation (written originally in English):

> My eyes reflect myself
> The strengths that I am trying to attain,
> the passions of a woman who at 35 is 70.
> My soul reflects my past,

> my soul deflects the future.
> My name is not María Cristina.
>
> . . . .
>
> for I speak without a twisted tongue
> and I do fix all leaks in my faucets.[30]

The poem (the first in the book) strengthens the position of an anti-traditional speaker who, through many other texts (in English and in Spanish), will comment on the condition of women in our contemporary society. Through satire and irony, the author criticizes the woman-robot who is dominated by social etiquette, as in her poem, "The Astronaut" (originally written in English):

> You have seen her!
> Haunted.
> With her taut braids,
> her liturgical expression,
> trepidating in her elevated shoes,
> hermetically tightening her tights
> the fear of expression is too cumbersome.[31]

The poem progresses from "you" to "we," making the reader be a witness and accomplice to the same vision. It then energetically condemns the woman who, through her submission, betrays the well-being of her group (originally written in English):

> Yes, we have seen her!
> And her actions bequest honor,
> and she loathes the word sister
> and she is never to be seen
> in pink or lavender.
> She is a sell out,
> She is a locker,
> She is a clam,
> a woman who no longer answers to her gender,
> A patriarchal tool,
> a matriarchal break-up,
> Someone in need of transcendental etude;
> the man in the moon who is a lady.[32]

Other poems attack marriage or the couple relationship and question the roles and chores traditionally assumed by gender (originally written in English):

What if I broke in,
tore down your vaulted contract?
What if we took down turns
for nourishing the children;[33]

In the poem "Cocinando" the author mixes daily life and unexpected images to create a sense of contradiction and mockery in the reality that she criticizes:

Quiero escribirte un poema,	I want to write you a poem,
pero la cuenta del banco no me lo permite.	but my bank account won't let me,
. . . .	. . . .
Quiero dedicarte un escrito,	I want to write something for you,
pero ¿te apesta el sofrito?	but, does the seasoning stink?
. . . .	. . . .
No, no quiero embarazarte,	I don't want to embarrass you
	(make you pregnant)
Y ya estás, pues llegaste,	And you are here, you arrived,
¿cerraste con cerrojo la puerta?	Did you lock the door?[34]

The author, however, employs the elements of satire, irony, and unexpected or surprised association more forcibly in the poems, where she proposes to explode those myths spread by religion and children's tales. She constructs her criticism of the myth of original sin around an everyday conversation about a stain in a garment. While talking about the difficulty of getting the stain out, the question about the possible origin of sin is raised:

¿Dirán que fue la serpiente?	Will they say it was the serpent?
¿la manzana de la vida?	or the apple of life?
¿O la trastada de Adán	Or Adam's dirty trick
cuando se vino aquel día?	when he came that day?

The poem concludes ironically:

Cuando se trata de manchas,	When getting stains out,
si no sale con el cliner	if it doesn't come out with cleaner we
nos toca ser lavanderas hasta	wind up being laundry women
que nos llegue el día.	till our dying day.[35]

Religion is again the theme in "Sacrilegio," a sort of modern and feminist litany of irreverence to the Virgin Mary:

Virgen sin virginidad,	Virgin without virginity,
virgen gorda y flaquita,	virgin fat and skinny,

Virgen plástica, rosada,	Virgin pink and plastic,
virgen de mármol o astilla.	virgin of marble or wood.[36]

The poem suggests that the Virgin Mary does not constitute a real model for the contemporary woman. The author thus poses the validity of sacrilegious acts to criticize false religious rites in a consumerist society that has commercialized even our sexual behavior:

Deja que yo te masturbe	Allow me to masturbate
la cabeza tan bendita	your so holy head
con una ilusión que te haga	with an illusion that will make you
menos de piedra, menos niña.	less stone-like, less girl-like.
. . . .	. . . .
Necesito tu milagro,	I need a miracle of yours,
y la paga ya se explica.	and the payment is self-explanatory.
Déjame que te perturbe,	Allow me to perturb you,
mientras tu cristo dentro de mí	while your Christ inside me
grita.	screams.
Virgen de Woolworth's	Virgin from Woolworth's
virgen de Penny's	Virgin from Penney's
virgen barata,	cheap virgin,
icon que todo lo quitas.	icon that takes everything away.
. . . .	. . . .
¿Dónde dejaste tú a Eva?	Where did you leave Eve?
¿Por qué no arbitraste la porfía,	Why didn't you mediate the
entre manzana y culebra	treachery
para que yo hoy ya no exista?	between apple and serpent
	so that I would not be today?[37]

In two other poems, the author invents (as in the case of the virgin) an alternate story, based on a well-known children's tale that we have all heard in our childhood. The innovation in one of the stories is achieved through the juxtaposition of fantasy and everyday reality. The fairy tale becomes a tale without fairies and, therefore, poses the real crisis that the institution of marriage is going through presently in our society:

El matrimonio perfecto—muñeco	The perfect marriage—tin boy
y muñeca de hojalata.	doll and tin girl doll.
El entierro de lujo, pompa, vino y	The fancy, pompous funeral,
champaña.	wine and champagne.
La combinación perfecta—hijos	The perfect combination—rag
gemelos de trapo y chatarra.	and scrap-iron twin children.
. . . .	. . . .

Mesa bien puesta, sirvientes, cubiertos de plata.	Well-set table, servants, silverware.
Debut social, visitas a los psiquiatras, figuras en los periódicos,	Social debut, visits to the psychiatrists, personalities in the newspaper,
. . . .	. . . .
La muñeca se destripa; el muñeco se desbarata.	The girl doll's insides fall out, the boy doll breaks.
Los niños flotan con el viento	The children float in the wind
. . . .	. . . .
El apocalipsis de la Biblia, mucho fuego, poca agua, y el mundo se contorsiona;	The apocalypse of the Bible, lots of fire, little water, and the world writhes;
. . . .	. . . .
Y el colorín, colorado ya no sirve, ya no encanta.	And they all lived happily ever after. It's no good any more, it doesn't delight any more.[38]

In the second poem, "A Rizos de Oro" (To Goldilocks), a feminist and Latin American vision is worked around the traditional story. Here, all the characters are women; instead of the three traditional bears, we have three female Latin American bears who confront the ostentatious behavior of the Anglo-Saxon Goldilocks and defend their Latin American identity jointly:

La primera vez que te vimos venías a robarnos la sopa de la mesa;	The first time we saw you you were coming to steal the soup from our table;
. . . .	. . . .
La primera vez que te tocamos querías provocar desmayos graciosos ante tus dorados rizos para poder así ponernos al cuello la cadena y en el pie, el grillo. Nosotras, las tres ositas, la última vez que te miramos no pudimos resistir tu blanca seducción, goldeada y despertándote de nuestras camas	The first time we touched you you wanted to overwhelm us with your golden curls so you could then put the chain around our necks and the fetters on our feet. We, the three little female bears, the last time we looked at you couldn't resist your white, golden seduction and, waking you up from our beds in Bolivia, El Salvador, and Puerto Rico, sent you home

en Bolivia, el Salvador y
    Puerto Rico
te mandamos a casa
a ser nuevamente común en
    vez de mito.

so we could again be one instead of a
myth.[39]

CONCLUSION

In the poetry of the three authors studied, the theme of women manifests itself repeatedly. It appears very closely linked to the effects that the migratory experiences to the United States has had on these women. The confrontation with a society, in which racism and discrimination against Latins prevails, definitely gives rise to the defense of their cultural heritage and national identity as central themes in their poetry.

But as women, they will also suffer from the oppression generated by the patriarchal ideology that dominates innumerable aspects of daily life. The daily personal and social experiences of these women show this ideology to be archaic and ineffective, thus contributing to the development of a feminist consciousness in a place (country) that, because it is new and distant from its place of origin, will also facilitate a particular vision of the feminine problem.

The definitive rupture with the norms and dogmas imposed upon women presents itself as one of the outstanding characteristics of these poems. The irreverence toward the myths of religion and marriage upsets the traditional feminine world and, in turn, proposes another world founded on a counterculture of feminist and Latin American affirmation. The defense of nontraditional love, the certainty of the necessity of a militant struggle, the sacrilegious acts toward the religious world, and the reinvention of children's tales are some of the new elements that begin to give shape to this proposed alternate world. The radicalism and originality of these proposals suggests that the migratory experience could have served as the catalytic agent in the feminine and feminist perspective, presented in the poetry of these women. In this sense, a comparative study of the poetry written by women in Puerto Rico could shed more light on the effects of the migratory experience in the formation of that feminist consciousness.

The determination to create new worlds that we see manifested in the poetry of Carmen Valle, Sandra M. Esteves, and Luz María Umpierre evidences how the written word can contribute to invent additional tools that also form part of the struggle for more justice in the construction of human relations and societies.

NOTES

1 César Andreu, ed., *Memorias de Bernardo Vega* (Río Piedras, P.R.: Ediciones Huracán, 1977).

2 José Luis González uses this term in his Prologue to *Memorias de Bernardo Vega*, 11.

3 Ibid., 23.

4 Ibid., 24.

5 For more details about the life of Genara Pagán, see Yamila Azize, *Luchas de la mujer en Puerto Rico, 1898–1930* [Women's Struggles in Puerto Rico] (Río Piedras, P.R.: Editorial Cultural, 1985), 180–82.

6 Carmen Valle, *Un poco de lo no dicho* (New York: Editorial La Ceiba, 1980); *Glenn Miller y varias vidas después* (México: Premia Editora, 1983); *De todo lo que da la noche al que la tienta*, manuscript provided by the author, New York, 1985.

7 These concepts are developed by Eliana Ortega and Marta Traba in their essays published in the anthology *La sartén por el mango* (Río Piedras, P.R.: Editorial Huracán, 1985), a valuable volume for the critical literary study of the feminine and feminist perspective. In the essay, "Desde la entraña del monstruo: voces 'hispanas' en EE.UU.," Ortega describes this poetry as one that "attempts to destroy myths and construct new realities" (163–69), while Marta Traba, in "Hipótesis de una escritura diferente," points out that the literature written by women frequently bears witness to a truth charged with emotion that should be read and analyzed as a "different literary text" (24, 26).

8 Valle. *Un poco de lo no dicho*, 10.

9 Ibid., 1.

10 Ibid., 14–15.

11 Ibid., 19.

12 Ibid., 20.

13 Valle, *Glenn Miller y varias vidas después*, 9.

14 Ibid., 11.

15 Ibid., 17.

16 Ibid., 45.

17 Valle, *De todo lo que da la noche al que la tienta*.

18 Ibid.

19 Sandra María Esteves, *Yerba Buena* (New York: Greenfield Press, 1980); *Tropical Rains: A Bilingual Downpour* (New York: Caribbean Poetry Theater, 1984).

20 Efraín Barradas, *Herejes y mitificadores* (Río Piedras, P.R.: Editorial Huracán, 1980).

21 Esteves, *Yerba Buena*, 50.

22 Ibid.

23 Ibid., 51.

24 Ibid.

25 Ibid.

26 Ibid., 63.

27 Luz María Umpierre, *Una puertorriqueña en Penna* (San Juan: Masters, 1979). Umpierre utilizes a play on the world *Penna* in her title. It refers to Pennsylva-

nia, as well as to pain or suffering from the Spanish word *pena; En el país de las maravillas* (Bloomington, Ind.: Third Woman Press, 1982); *Y otras desgracias/And Other Misfortunes* (Bloomington, Ind.: Third Woman Press, 1985).

28 Umpierre, *Y Otras Desgracias*, 1.
29 Ibid.
30 Ibid.
31 Ibid., 5.
32 Ibid., 5.
33 Ibid., 13.
34 Ibid., 33.
35 Ibid., 35.
36 Ibid.
37 Ibid., 37.
38 Ibid., 45.
39 Ibid., 47.

Other works I have consulted for the writing of this essay are: María M. Solá, ed., *Yo misma fui mi ruta,* an anthology of poems by Julia de Burgos (Río Piedras, P.R.: Editorial Huracán, 1986); various essays by Juan Flores, "Rappin, Writin and Breakin: Black and Puerto Rican Street Culture in New York City" (CUNY, forthcoming in *Callalao,* 1986); "One assimilated Brother, Yo soy asimilao: The Structuring of Puerto Rican Identity in the U.S.," *The Journal of Ethnic Studies* (Fall 1985), 1–16; J. Flores and A. Cortés Falcón, "The Cultural Expression of Puerto Ricans in New York: A Theoretical Perspective and Critical Review," *Latin American Perspectives* 3, no. 3 (1976): 117–50; Asela Rodríguez de Laguna, ed., *Imágenes e Identidades: el puertorriqueño en la literatura* (Río Piedras, Puerto Rico: Editorial Huracán, 1985); Mario Maffi, "Loisaida, New York: Una cultura alternativa en el Lower East Side" [An alternate culture on the Lower East Side], *Revista Quimera* (Barcelona) (October 1986).

Latinas at the Crossroads: An Affirmation of Life in Rosario Morales and Aurora Levins Morales' Getting Home Alive

LOURDES ROJAS

The need for self-definition is one of the most recurrent themes in Latina writings today. Many and varied are the paths chosen by these writers in their search for identity.[1] In *Getting Home Alive,* Aurora Levins Morales and Rosario Morales, daughter and mother, respectively, embark on a multifaceted process of re-creating their own stories in an attempt to acquire a fuller sense of themselves as women, writers, and Latinas.[2]

This very recent sense of urgency to write autobiographical and/or testimonial accounts that will validate the Latina, both as subject and object of the literary creation, constitutes a departure from the Latinas' oral tradition, as well as a signal for the development of a new literary canon. The Levins-Morales book exemplifies the shift from a mainly verbal construction of Latinas' life stories to the use of the written word, both as a tool and a weapon, in the reconstruction of Latina identity in literary texts.

In the Preface to *Cuentos: Stories by Latinas,* the editors state the purpose of their publication as the need to create a body of literature that would truly express Latinas' experiences. Oral stories are no longer viable testimonies of these women's existences, for they can no longer endure to bear witness to a reality defined by the constant struggle to survive at the crossroads:

> But we can no longer afford to keep our tradition oral. . . .
> This way of life that kept our tales re-told is falling apart. . . .

> We need una literatura that testifies to our lives, provides
> acknowledgment of who we are: an exile people, a migrant
> people, mujeres en lucha. . . .[3]

In this essay, I propose a reading of the Levins-Morales text within the general framework of testimonial literature from the perspective of the Latina experience. I intend to identify what themes are more prevalent in their writings, the use of text as a political and ideological tool, and to what extent Levins Morales and Morales are proposing a redefinition of the literary canon.

In her essay, "And Even Fidel Can't Change That," Morales stresses Latinas' need to examine and redefine the mother-daughter relationship, which she considers crucial to any significant transformation of the role of women in Latina and Latin American cultures: "The relationship between mother and daughter stands at the center of what I fear most in our culture. Heal that wound and we change the world."[4]

Although Morales does not elaborate on the meaning of the relationship as a wound, the image brings to mind a poem by Rosario Castellanos, where the poetic persona (a mother), in describing the act of giving birth, uses the words "wound" and "hemorrhage" to summarize the end of the physiological process of gestation. The expulsion of the baby through the vagina carries with it the mother's loneliness as she opens up to the world through this new experience: "I remained open, manifest / to visitations, to the wind, to presence."[5] For Castellanos, the wound signifies a new possibility for communication with the child and with others; for Morales, it implies a rupture that needs to be healed. The image of a "wound" could also represent the condition of Puerto Rican immigrants who, as victims of the socio-economic and political blows inflicted upon them by the power structure in mainland U.S.A., offer a struggle of resistance from the "entrails of the monster."[6]

The gender difference accounts for the contrast in the rapport established; in the Levins-Morales narrative, the subject is a female child, trying to free herself from the violence and anger of a rupture with the mother that is determined by the hierarchical lines imposed by society. The powerlessness transmitted from mother to daughter becomes a "shared open wound" upon which a false sense of unity, rather than a bonding, develops. The daughter's task is to create new grounds for this bonding, to refuse the cultural inheritance of women's suffering as definer of the female condition, and to develop a trust among women in general and between mother and daughter in particular: "A revolution capable of healing our wounds . . . If we are the ones who need it most, then no one else can do it."[7]

Castellanos, on the other hand, writes the poem re-creating the birth of her son from the perspective of the mother. Her entire approach is more a demythicization of motherhood, portraying a realistic picture of the biological process rather than a reflection on the actual mother-son bonding. There is no sharing of a wound; neither is there a transmission of a gender-determined condition. Yet both visions of motherhood participate of the same need to reexamine and redefine women's experience as creators of life.

In her introduction to *Getting Home Alive*, Levins Morales uses the image of a telephone cord that links them across the miles as a symbol of the conversation between mother and daughter that will become the basis of the book and that replaces the umbilical cord as the image of the bonding between them. The telephone conversations are the beginnings of a process of mutual discoveries and exchanges of learnings that are at the basis of the mother-daughter's equal partnership in literary creation: "This book is the blossoming of that cross-fertilization. My mother taught me how to read. Together, we have taught ourselves to be writers."[8]

The structure of the text itself proposes a nonhierarchical relationship based on the reconstruction of mutual and individual memories, with equal degrees of intensity and creativity. Both authors interchange their biologically determined roles by becoming creators of each other's and their own stories in an ever-fluid and interchangeable experience of awareness.

In the short narrative piece entitled "Wolf," Levins Morales, using the first-person narrator, describes a dream where she greets a wolf that appears at the doorway of her clay house with the words: "This is my true self" (p. 16). The animal approaches her while it changes shape: it becomes a buffalo and an anteater, but always changes back to its true shape of wolf. The protagonist finds joy at the sight of the animal, motivated by a strong sense of identification with it. Nevertheless, she becomes painfully aware that the wolf's search for self-preservation through its changes of shape will not be effective, since the new forms it adopts are also doomed to extinction. The dream ends with the protagonist's anxiety to convey to her younger friends the importance of this revelation in order to save everyone's life: "For their survival and mine and the world's, I must make them see the wolf's nature. I must tell them this story" (p. 16).

This literary motif of constant transformation as a symbol of the protagonist's defense against total destruction, as well as the narrator's expressed need to write her story to ensure survival, are vehicles of the general processes of self-awareness and cultural identification that permeate Levins Morales's writings. Like the wolf of her dreams, the author sees the universal beauty as a synthesis for movement, change, and transformation. Also like the wolf, she values an identity whose very essence is rooted in change: "My totem is the wolf" (p. 16).

Levins Morales sees her story as an increasingly common tale for children in American society: "My children will be born in California. It's not strange any more, in this part of the world, in this time, to be born a thousand miles from the birthplace of your mother" (p. 27). Nevertheless, being born far away from one's mother's home is not equivalent to being born without a history or tradition. On the contrary, as a "child of many diasporas" born at the crossroads, Levins Morales sees her place in the world at the apex of a very rich cultural platform from which to draw strength, a wealth of cultural tradition with which she will communicate these stories to a younger generation:

> My children will hear stories about the coquis and coffee flowers, about hurricanes and roosters crowing in the night, and will dig among old photographs to understand the homesick sadness that sometimes swallows me. . . . Perhaps they will lie in bed among the sounds of the rainforest, and it will be the smell of eucalyptus that calls to them in their dreams.
> (P. 27)

Morales' writings, like her daughter's, are built upon the conceptual premise that considers diversity as a means of self-empowerment and realization. For Morales, the written word also represents a bridge from isolation into a world of women's solidarity. Her stories, both biographical and fictional, are testimonies to her struggle for survival. Furthermore, they also constitute an overture for a diversified network of women based upon trust and mutual acceptance.

In "Double Allegiance," Morales, while denouncing the hierarchy of oppression, proposes a pluralistic women's allegiance based precisely on their diversity and held together by their awareness of a shared condition of marginality as daughters and granddaughters of immigrants in American soil.

The need to affirm one's own identity and the urgency to retell one's history of oppression does not, or should not, asserts Morales, be turned into a mechanism of destruction and separation among women: "A workshop, to heal our differences, I'd thought, but the noises were war cries, were competition for the one-down spot, each trying to prove to the other how much more oppressed she was, to prove she was the *only* one oppressed" (p. 157).

Instead of "scissors" to separate and accentuate the different shapes, colors, and forms of oppression, Morales offers a unifying "thread" for women's solidarity that will bring together an awareness of each and all the different textures of the fabric of women immigrants:

> So that I had to go home to sew myself together with the thread we'd spun, my jewish girlfriends and I, made out of our games and fantasies, of tastes of each other's foods and each other's tears, of our parents' memories of cities hastily abandoned—Naranjito, Kiev, Munich—of yiddish-spanish accents in our speech, of browning photographs, of grand-parents we hardly knew, of the feel of our arms around each other. I ran small running stitches up my scalp, small chain stitches down my face, then stopped and wound what thread was left carefully onto the spool. It was about time, I thought, to give part of it away. No, all of it. I can make more. (P. 158)

Another aspect of Morales's writings that is very much a part of her story is her social awareness and political activism. She sees her socio-political commitment—part of the cultural legacy she now shares with her daughter—as a result of her solidarity with the poor: "The fighting is so people can have what I want, can count on the warmth of their room, can slip into the rhythm of their days . . . I get furious that we can't have that, that people in so many places can't have that. And sad" (p. 159).

In her piece entitled "My Revolution," Morales builds upon a theme explored by her daughter in ". . . And Even Fidel Can't Change That." Levins Morales calls for a true revolution, changing women in order to change society: a change by women and for women. Morales proposes a revolution free from stultifying dogma, one that would allow for creativity and self-expression:

> My revolution is not cut from a pattern, I designed it.
>
> It's homemade and hand-crafted
> It's got seams to let out
> and hems to let down
> tucks to take in
> darts to take out. (P. 161)

The imagery of the entire poem is derived from the act of sewing. A well-fitted dress becomes a metaphor for a fitting revolutionary process. This revolution, like the dress, allows for changes according to need. And also, like the dress, it is an article created by those who will wear it. These social changes are not designed according to foreign models, for there is no established pattern for them; the final product will depend on the need and wishes of those who develop the new socioeconomic structures.

The idea of piecing together, of sewing up, the different materials to create a united product is also present in Morales' "Double Allegiance"; in both works, it stands as a metaphor for solidarity within diversity. It is also a call for a collective women's action and for constructive tasks in a joint effort for change toward a better world. "My revolution is comfortable/ hardwearing/long-lasting/versatile . . ." (p. 161).

Examining the book as a visual object in itself, it is possible to establish a correspondence between the picture on the front cover and the main theme of the text. The design constitutes a graphic synthesis of the book's main *raison d'être:* unity within diversity among women. The picture in question depicts a quilt—that is, a cloth stitched together with pieces of different colored and textured materials. It is also interesting to point out that the verb "to knit" is "tejer" in Spanish, and is from the Latin *texere,* which has the same linguistic root as "texto," the Spanish word for text. The visual symbol refers to both: a text made up of a variety of genres, coauthored by mother and daughter who explore, in the text, the many and varied components or textures of their own histories.

Another space shared between mother and daughter is their memories of the lands of their ancestors. For both authors, the senses become a vehicle of remembering. For Morales, the smell of garlic, the sight of trees, and the sound of coquis are symbols of her adult nostalgia for the land and people of Puerto Rico, nostalgia for what she remembers of her years in Indiera, and also for what she imagined about it even before getting there:

> I grew up with nostalgia for a place I did not grow up in, nostalgia for the family I'd missed, uncles and aunts and cousins—and grandparents . . . I grew up with nostalgia for landscapes and tropical fruit, . . . For the smell of coffee roasting, the sound of cock's crowings and hens scratching behind the house. (Pp. 87–88)

Morales' cultural nostalgia is an adult invention that partakes, at times unevenly, of both her recollection of actual events of the childhood years in Puerto Rico and her imaginary creation of a life and time she, the adult writer, wished she had lived as a child. By re-creating part of her past, Morales appropriates a culturally defined and artfully created time-space unity that, like her own history, becomes a product of mixture.

Inventing a past is as important as remembering it, since Morales wants to rescue a part of her history that was denied to her. Through this mechanism of imagined memories, fed to her by her own mother's tales, the author also re-creates her parents' childhood, and through those stories she partakes at will of the experiences of children growing up in the valleys and mountains of Puerto Rico. Both time and space become a magic moment, where several generations of women enjoy a childhood together:

> I was in Naranjito, in my father's dreams, in my mother's stories, and she was young like me, skinny, barefoot, riding bareback in the special heat of the Naranjito hills . . . I will run barefoot just this once, run wild like any titere in the hills of Puerto Rico, bathe in the creek past the pasture with my mother, make mud pies with my aunts, steal tangerines with my daughter, play house with her and Tita . . . I will jump from the tall rock into the springy ferns below, jump with them all, into the green of their summers again and again. (P. 125)

Although there is a strong sense of nostalgia for an almost idyllic past, Morales is very aware of the fact that those real and invented memories address only a part of her story; they belong to a time-gone-by that fails to explain her whole reality. On a trip back to Puerto Rico, Morales realizes that although she carries her island tucked inside her, she is never totally at home there, either:

> *Home*, like Australians talking about an England they have never seen—The home country: Italy, Ireland, Poland, Puerto Rico. Photographs, someone else's memories and my vivid dreams as I grew up. Home? A place where I am never completely at home. But then where am I completely at home? . . . (P. 76)

The nature of her memories, which are a blend of reality, dreams, and desires, constitute an impediment to her sense of being totally at home in Puerto Rico. The Island she could conceive as her home does not exist outside her imagination and hence, her writings. In addition, she has spent most of her formative years in the U.S., a place she also recognizes as home. For Morales, to be totally at home means to live in the border-lands, where one never belongs totally to one place, yet where one is able to feel an integral part of many places; home is at the crossroads.[9]

The tropical vegetation is the element with which Morales closely identifies in her return to the land: "I'm more at home with the vegetation than with this city's street" (p. 76). But her distance from the land goes deeper than a lack of affinity with the streets and the relatively short time (eleven years) spent in Indiera Baja. The gap is made more evident by the women with whom she cannot identify. In trying to understand this separation, Morales acknowledges the enormous importance of her experience in mainland U.S.A. in her own formation:

. . . it has to do with the kind of woman I am. Nothing so crude as docile, catholic womanhood . . . Lots of women here are strong and independent. And yet. . . .

I don't know. Maybe it has to do with not having been a little girl in this place. I was shaped on Manhattan Island. (P. 79)

Furthermore, gender relations dramatize for Morales how her different behavior endowed her with a "non-entirely Puerto Rican' identity as a woman: "I remember in the mountains how women said 'Mi marido no me deja,' . . . It was unanswerable, everyone understood that . . ." (p. 79). The author's rejection of the patriarchal attitudes still held on the island can be summarized by the woman's defiance of her husband's authority, and by the author herself, when pointing out women's complicity in her own enslavement to the reader: "¡Pero tú lo dejas que no te deje!" (p. 79).[10]

What the author fears most, in her return to the island, are both the societal constraints imposed on her as a woman and the male code still prevalent today. The pressure to conform is very strong, the possibility of doing something different almost nonexistent for a woman: there is a price to be paid for disobedience, for "home" is ". . . full of predatory males who punish you for being female" (p. 80).

The awareness of the double standard in gender relations produces in the writer a sense of a painful distancing from the place she wanted to call her home, plus the realization that she will never totally be at home in one place: ". . . I look forward to my own life as to a rest cure. I've been anticipating the return home so mucch, and now as I pack for it, I'm sad about leaving. Ah me, no peace" (p. 82).

Levins Morales' memories and concept of "home," on the other hand, are threefold: her Puerto Rican birth and childhood (which ties her to the culture of the Island), her paternal grandmother's stories about the Old country (which establishes, for her, the connection with her Jewish background), and her mother's stories about growing up in the barrio. In a way similar to her mother, Levins Morales wants to rescue her past in an attempt to understand her identity.

The process of anagnorisis (that is, recognition, which has a strong resonance with María Luisa Bombal's protagonist in "The Tree") is triggered, in Levins Morales' text, by the author's sensorial memories. This bridge to the past serves to bring to the narrative present, images of places and situations rather than of people. While in her California kitchen, for instance, she remembers a childhood in the kitchens of Puerto Rico: "From the corner of my eye, I see the knife blade flashing, reducing mounds of onions, garlic, cilantro, and green peppers into sofrito . . ." (p. 37).

Cooking sofrito or frying plátanos becomes a magic ritual that connects her two worlds and gives her a sense of continuity and belonging: ". . . bathing in the scent of its cooking, bringing the river to flow through my own kitchen now, the river of my place on earth, the green and musty river of my grandmother . . ." (p. 39).

While Morales' nostalgia for trees represents her link to her parents' land, with Levins Morales there is a longing for streets. Her strongest memories are full of her city experiences as she seeks her connections to the past through life on the streets, both remembered and imagined:

> I am mountain-born, country-bred, homegrown jíbara child.
> But I have inherited all the cities through which my people
> passed, and their dust has sifted and settled onto the black
> soil of my heart. (P. 90)

For Levins Morales, the immigrant experience is crystallized by an imagined life on city streets (and, hence, the concomitant diversity associated with them), but for Morales, "trees" replace "city streets" as a similar symbol. Levins Morales continues:

> I didn't yearn for the cities the way my mother did for green-
> ness and quiet trees. But I dreamt of them. The markets and
> neighborhoods . . . the stories hidden in their names. . . .
> The bustling variety of life, of languages, of foods, of cus-
> toms—the meeting of so many roads. (P. 91)

Both authors also see language as a factor of cultural identification. Although, for Morales, English is the language that informs most of her writings, she feels Spanish is also very much a part of her; additionally, Yiddish words have been incorporated into her everyday vocabulary. For Levins Morales, the same holds true. The amalgam of English-Spanish, and sometimes Yiddish, is within easy reach for both authors, the linguistic mixture being a means to reaffirm their cultural pluralism:

> I am what I am, I am Boricua as Boricuas come from the isle of
> Manhattan, and I croon sentimental tangos in my sleep and
> Afro-Cuban beats in my blood . . . I mean there it was yid-
> dish and spanish and fine refined college educated english
> and irish which I mainly keep in my prayers. . . . (P. 138)

In the text, language is presented as a valuable searching tool. Through their various languages, the authors define themselves at the sociocultural and linguistic crossroads that stand for the nondefinable and irreducible essence of mixture.

By calling themselves Latinas at the crossroads, Morales and Levins Morales are proposing a culturally syncretic identity that aims at obliterating the lines of separation among all immigrants. This movable composite of realities is paralleled by the visual structure of the text that conveys a sense of both fluidity and amalgamation in the mixture of the various genres: poetry, narrative, newspaper clippings, letters, diaries, as well as photographs. Yet, this multiplicity of elements is rooted and held together by the unifying thematic thread of self-definition. By creating this multi-genre literary structure, they are inventing a text that mirrors the culturally multiple essence of their own definition as Latinas.

The best example of this multifaceted cultural definition appears in a dual poetic composition produced by both mother and daughter:

I am what I am
A child of the Americas
A light-skinned mestiza of the Caribbean
A child of many diasporas, born into this
continent at a crossroads . . .
I am an immigrant
and the daughter and granddaughter of immigrants. . . . (P. 212)

Both authors are equally proud of their historical past and cultural present. They are aware of being a product of many diasporas, drawing strength equally from all of their roots and they also are cognizant of, and committed to, their historical present. They are not Africans, although Africa contributed to their making; neither are they European, although European history explains their present as well. And neither do they, as Latinas in the U.S.A., consider themselves Tainas, although they share with them the Latin American heritage. Together, they are new entities like their texts, culturally and socially, rooted in an integrated plurality. They represent a cohesive and meaningful voice for the powerful heterogeneity of the immigrant woman:

I am a child of many mothers . . .

We are new.
They gave us life, kept us going,
brought us to where we are.
Born at a crossroads . . .
We will not eat ourselves up inside anymore.

And we are whole. (P. 213)

Whereas the concept of "mestizaje cultural" could presuppose a fragmented cultural definition, the mixture constitutes an identity in itself for

Levins-Morales. Both authors reject the attitude of cultural ambivalence and the self-denial that characterized some of their literary predecessors and/or contemporaries, as the penultimate verse of this last poem states: "We will not eat ourselves up inside anymore" (p. 213).

The poem "Not Either," by Sandra María Esteves, could serve as an example of a contrasting view of Latina identity. Like Levins–Morales' "Ending Poem," Esteves' poem evolves around a theme of self-definition. However, though Levins-Morales give the reader a defiant and positive affirmation of Latina identity ("I am what I am"), Esteves communicates a negative, or at best doubtful, tone of her cultural self image:

> Born in the Bronx, *not* really jíbara
> *Not* really hablando bien
> But yet, *not* Gringa either
> Pero *ni* portorra, pero sí portorra too
> Pero *ni* que what am I? (My emphasis)[11]

The use of the negatives *not* and *ni* carries the tenor of self-denial, of an identity that is defined in terms of what it lacks, of what it is not. The final verse is a negation, followed by a question mark, which synthesizes the poet's cultural uncertainty. In Levins-Morales' texts, the question of "What am I?" finds an answer in the joyful vindication of the "mezcla"; in so doing, the "not eithers," articulated by Esteves, now become "yes and also."

> I am Puerto Rican. I am U.S. American.
> I am New York Manhattan and the Bronx.
> A mountain-born, country-bred, homegrown jíbara child,
> up from the shtetl, a California Puerto Rican Jew. (P. 212)

In *Getting Home Alive*, Levins Morales and Morales give a positive meaning to life in the borderlands. Being a Latina means to be able to share in the richness of a culturally diverse heritage. Their home is at the crossroads, where all the points converge, and where the magic of being one and all can still take place, as they themselves affirm: "A multilingual, multireligious, many-colored and -peopled land where the orange tree blooms for all" (p. 208).

NOTES

1 In their Introduction to *Cuentos: Stories by Latinas*, Alma Gómez, Cherríe Moraga, and Mariana Romo-Carmona state the purpose of their work: "In *Cuentos* our intent is to mention the unmentionables, to capture some essential expres-

sion—without censors—that could be called 'Latina,' and 'Latina-identified'"
(New York: Kitchen Table, Women of Color Press, 1983), ix.

2   For purposes of clarification, I shall refer to Aurora Levins Morales as
Levins Morales, and to Rosario Morales as Morales. "Levins-Morales" would refer
to both, daughter and mother respectively.

3   Gómez, Moraga, and Romo-Carmona, *Cuentos,* vii.

4   Cherríe Moraga and Gloria Anzaldúa, eds., *This Bridge Called My Back* (New
York: Kitchen Table Press, 1983), 56.

5   Rosario Castellanos, "Speaking of Gabriel," in *Contemporary Women Authors
of Latin America,* eds., Doris Meyer and Margarite Fernández-Olmos (New York:
Brooklyn College Press, 1983), 21.

6   "The wound that never heals" is also the title of a poem by Sandra María
Esteves, in which the image of the wound stands for the condition of life in exile
and the endless pain of longing for the motherland, in *Tropical Rains: A Bilingual
Downpour* (New York: African Caribbean Poetry Theater, 1984), 2.

7   Meyer and Fernández-Olmos, *Contemporary Women Authors,* 56.

8   Aurora Levins Morales and Rosario Morales, *Getting Home Alive* (Ithaca,
N.Y.: Firebrand Books, 1986). All further quotations are from this edition. Page
numbers are indicated in the text.

9   The title of the book, *Getting Home Alive,* could be read as an allusion to the
authors' need to survive in a perilous world while searching for a safe place to call
home, a place that will have to be of their own creation; home is also in their
writing.

Another reading of the title suggests the car accident in which Levins Morales
almost lost her life and her subsequent struggle to regain control of all of her brain
functions.

10   But you allow him not to let you!

11   Sandra María Esteves, "Not Either," 26.

Part III. Cubanas

The Show Does Go On

(Testimonio)

DOLORES PRIDA

Over ten years ago, when my first play was produced in New York City, I dragged my whole family down to a dank basement in the Lower East Side to see it. My mother, who never really understood what I did in the theatre, said to me after the show was over: "Todo estuvo muy bonito, m'ija, pero, en todo eso que yo vi, ¿qué fue exactamente lo que tú hiciste?" I explained to her that I had written the play, that I was the *dramaturga*. She just said, "ahhh," and shook her head.[1]

I fantasized about her, next morning, telling her coworkers at that factory in Brooklyn where she used to sew sleeves onto raincoats all day long, "¿Oye, Rosalía, tú sabes que mi hija, la mayor, es dramaturga?" And Rosalía answering, "¿Dramaturga? ¡Ay pobrecita! Y eso, ¿tiene cura?"[2]

My mother passed away three years ago, and I regret I never took the time to explain to her what being a *dramaturga* meant to me, and why it can't be "cured," that once bitten by the love of the theatre, you are infected with it for the rest of your life.

Now it is too late to share with her why I put up with the long hours, the lack of money, the unheated basements: the thrill of opening night, the goose pimples when an audience laughs at the right lines, or when you can hear a pin drop at the right moment.

It is not too late to share some of it with you.

I didn't start off as a playwright. As a teenager, I wrote poems and short stories that nobody read. In fact, nobody knew I wrote them because

This article is partly based on a lecture given at Rutgers, The State University of New Jersey at Newark, February 1987.

I didn't tell anyone. Writing poetry wasn't the "in" thing among my peers. I am from a small town where there was one single bookstore and one single library, which was closed most of the time—I don't know why, maybe because it was right next door to the police station.

We had two movie houses, one that showed Mexican and Argentinian films, mostly three-hanky tearjerkers. In the other one—*el cine América*—you could watch the latest Hollywood films, with subtitles or dubbed into Spanish. I actually grew up believing that John Wayne was really from Madrid by watching movies in which he would speak perfect Castilian: "Alzad laz manoz, matonez."[3]

One thing we didn't have in Caibarién, Cuba, was a theatre. I didn't get to see a live play until I came to New York. That was in 1961. It was a musical, and I became fascinated forever with the idea of people bursting into song and dance at the least provocation.

The first play I wrote—*Beautiful Señoritas*—was a play with music. And I wrote it in English.

In 1976, I went to Caracas, Venezuela, to cover an International Theatre Festival for *Visión*, the Latin American news magazine. It was my first festival and I enjoyed every minute of it. I saw plays from over thirty different countries, many in languages I did not understand. But one peculiar thing caught my attention: not one of those plays dealt with "the women's issue." At the time, I was quite involved in the women's movement in New York and knew that *la liberación femenina* was also being hotly debated in Latin America and Europe. Yet, the stages of an international theatre festival didn't reflect it. I decided, then and there, that when I got back to New York I would write a play about women. And I did.

Beautiful Señoritas was produced by DUO Theatre in 1977. It was a modest one-act musical play that poked fun at long-standing Latin women stereotypes—from Carmen Miranda to Cuchi Cuchi Charo to suffering, black-shrouded women crying and praying over the tortillas to modern-day young Latinas trying to re-define their images. The play was extremely well received—it went on to have many productions throughout the country, including a special performance at the National Organization for Women's national convention in San Antonio, Texas, in 1980.

From then on, most of my plays have been about the experience of being a Hispanic in the United States, about people trying to reconcile two cultures and two languages and two visions of the world into a particular whole: plays that aim to be a reflection of a particular time and space, of a here and now.

Of course, not all of my plays are women-oriented or totally Hispanic. Being a woman and being a Hispanic is neither an asset nor a handicap but a fact. And, as an artist, I do not wish to be categorized just as a "Hispanic

Playwright" or a "Woman Hispanic Playwright," but rather as a person, a playwright who happens to be a woman and a Hispanic and who feels committed to writing on those subjects because they are part of the universe.

I find it particularly rewarding being able to write non-Hispanic characters, male or female, who are believable and authentic. And writing believable and authentic characters is what theatre is all about. Of course, good theatre also springs from writing about subjects and situations one knows best. And what I know best are the ups and down of being a Hispanic woman playwright living in New York City. And I am not contradicting myself.

THEATREWORKS

I consider myself a "theatre worker" rather than a "theatre literata." Theatre is not literature; theatre is to be "done," not read, seen, not imagined. Theatre is people. Theatre is team work. We need each other: playwright, director, designers, actors, choregraphers, technicians, carpenters, composers, ticket takers, audience. We don't exist without each other. And I have tremendous respect and admiration for the skills and talent of everyone involved in bringing a production to the stage. I love actors. I adore choreographers. I am awed by composers and musicians. Directors? Putting your play in the hands of a good director who has vision and understands your work—well, that's icing on the cake. Good directors, however, are few and far between.

The first thing I did at Teatro the Orilla, a collective theatre group in New York's Lower East Side, was to sweep the floor and collect tickets at the door. Then I ran the sound equipment, made lights from empty tomato juice cans and supermarket light bulbs, went shopping for costumes and props, filled out endless forms for grant money, and then, only then, I began to think I could write a play that would appeal to that particular audience: people who had never been to a theatre before.

My theatre life came into being soon after various Hispanic theatre groups began to get established, thanks to newly available public funds in the late sixties and early seventies. It was all part of a process, a side effect of the ethnic and racial reaffirmation that followed the black civil rights movement, the women's liberation movement, the anti-war demonstrations.

I did not get into the theatre for the "let's-put-on-a-show" fun of it, but because I felt I had things to say about immediate and relevant issues and I wanted to say them with comedy, with music, with songs. Live.

Besides those already mentioned, I have also written about gentrification (*Savings*), about anti-poverty agencies (*The Beggars' Soap Opera*), about Hispanic theatre itself (*La Era Latina*), about Latin soap operas and nuclear war (*Pantallas*), about cultural assimilation (*Botánica*). Waiting their turn are plays about AIDS (so many of my friends are gone) and teenage pregnancy (What happened to women's liberation? Have we failed the younger generation of women?).

Also, I've had plays canceled for the alleged "insidiousness" of my politics. "Maligned in Miami" is the Hispanic community's equivalent of "Banned in Boston."

The need to use the theatre as a medium to discuss relevant and immediate issues and experiences is not new, except in one sense; today, many Hispanic playwrights are writing about these experiences in English, whereas the earliest examples were in Spanish (of all my plays, only two, *Pantallas* and *Botánica*, are in Spanish).

There are two stories I always like to mention when speaking of the origins of Hispanic theatre in the New World. One is fact, and one is fiction.

The fictitious event I like best, because it concerns the earliest example of Hispanic American musical theatre. It comes from a passage of *El arpa y la sombra*, by the Cuban novelist Alejo Carpentier. One of the sections of the book, "La mano," is written as the travel diary of Christopher Columbus. Let me share it with you in its original splendor:

> Más adelante—fue durante mi tercer viaje—al ver que los indios de una isla se mostraban recelosos en acercarse a nosotros, improvisé un escenario en el catillo de popa, haciendo que unos españoles danzaran bulliciosamente al son de tamboril y tejoletas, para que se viese que éramos gente alegre y de un natural apacible. (Pero mal nos fue en esa ocasión, para decir la verdad, puesto que los caníbales, nada divertidos por moriscas y zapateados, nos dispararon tantas flechas como tenían en sus canoas. . . .)[4]

So here we see that one of the first, although fictional, Hispanic theatre performers in the Americas (Christopher Columbus, producer) was a musical comedy, and that it was panned by the audience.

The second—and much-quoted—story is fact, according to researchers. It documents the actual first performance of what could be called a play, in what is today U.S. territory. In 1598, a group of conquistadores, led by Juan de Oñate, crossed the Río Grande from Mexico to take formal possession of all the kingdoms and provinces of New Mexico in the name of King Philip of Spain. They struck camp on a spot near the present-day city of El Paso, Texas.

Among the group was a captain of the guard named Marcos Farfán de los Godos (how's that for a stage name!), who, besides being a soldier, dabbled in the art of "dramaturgy." That evening, he prepared *un espectáculo* to entertain his fellow conquistadores. The theme of this presentation is reported to have dealt with the question of how the church would be received in the newly "discovered" lands of New Mexico.

This presentation is considered to be the first theatrical piece ever performed in what is today the United States of America. It predates, by sixty-seven years, the first recorded English play produced in the New World. It predates, by eight years, the French masque perfomed in Acadia, Canada, in 1606.

Both these theatrical events, whether fact or fiction, also sprung from the immediate reality of those first "Hispanics," and their experiences as conquistadores in a new land. Had they not come here, they would not have written those particular plays. Therefore, they are "American" plays.

Today's Hispanic American playwrights, arriving at, or being born on, these shores more like *conquistados* than conquistadores, continue that tradition.

From a Miguel Piñero, who writes *Short Eyes* from the inside the nightmare of a prison, to Eddie Gallardo's family in the South Bronx's *Simpson Street*, to Eduardo Machado's upper-class Cuban families arriving in Miami with suitcases chock-full of jewels, to Manuel Martín's working-class Cubans celebrating Thanksgiving in Union City, to Gloria González' *Café con leche*, to my own *Coser y cantar*, which deals with how to be a bilingual, bicultural woman in Manhattan and keep your sanity, to a host of as-yet-unproduced new plays by young Hispanics developing in the wings, Hispanic American theatre is slowly becoming a hall of mirrors in which our society and ourselves are reflected, sometimes documenting the intangibles of being a minority in the United States with more subtlety and depth than many an expensive sociological research paper.

However, much of this work is unknown or ignored, both by the Hispanic and the general community. For Hispanics, going to the theatre is a tradition that generally we do not bring along from our countries of origin. There the theatre is, in most cases, for the social and intellectual elites. In coming here, we find that the arts are not necessarily considered a luxury but perceived as being somewhat irrelevant, something for which one usually does not have time.

The need for many immigrants to struggle, survive, and adapt does not allow them the luxury of attending the theatre. Going out means going dancing or to the movies—what they think is accessible and "fun." Regular escapist entertainment is found nightly in the never-ending *telenovelas* and in the weekly convulsions of Iris Chacón's hips. Only a minority within our community goes regularly to the theatre. Many of our 99-seat houses are half-empty many a night.

Although non-Hispanics come to see our plays, it is more like a novelty, or a duty—as in the case of the classics. I mean, you have to see a García Lorca or a Lope de Vega play at least once in your lifetime, and, of course, the latest effort by novelist Mario Vargas Llosa.

In the Hispanic theatre community, we are aware of the need to further develop our audiences. I believe the type of plays we are now writing, in which Hispanic American audiences can identify with the characters and situations they see on stage, is contributing to that development (in 1986, *Bodega*, Federico Fraguada's first play, broke all box office records at the 20-year-old Puerto Rican Traveling Theatre in New York City. Nearly every New York City *bodeguero* and his family went to see the play. It was presented again in the 1987 season). Musicals and comedies are attracting younger audiences who used to think that going to the theatre meant they were in for a boring evening and opted to stay home and watch music videos.

Adding to the problem of lack of visibility and audience growth, we face the sad fact that in the Hispanic community we don't have a responsible media with responsible, knowledgeable writers who can discuss art and culture intelligently. American critics are, in most instances, either patronizing or insensitive to the work produced by Hispanics, even if it is English.

THE UNIVERSITY'S UNIVERSE

I feel the academic community has a large role to play in bringing Hispanic American theatre and literature into the mainstream of this country's cultural life. Fortunately, today there are many college professors who have a deep interest in our work, are studying it, writing papers, and struggling to include it in their curricula. This is a must. Because they are not only trying to enrich the lives of their students by exposing them to the art and culture of the soon-to-be largest ethnic minority in this nation, but also building theatre audiences for the future.

Unfortunately, these few pioneers face many obstacles from within and without the walls of academia. From the outside, there is the problem of not enough published literary and theatrical works by U.S. Hispanics. From inside the walls, opposition, confusion, misunderstanding, and — why not say it?—plain, ugly racism from faculty and administrators.

Because, they ask, what is "Hispanic literature"? What is "Hispanic drama"? Is there such a thing? And if so, where is it? Where does it belong in the curriculum? They don't know, or don't want to know, what to do with the whole darned big enchilada.

This metaphorical enchilada, like the small real ones, is meant to be eaten, and enjoyed! You can't worry about heartburn a priori! I say, what's wrong with bringing U.S. Hispanic literature and drama into the American Drama Department, along with black and Asian-American works? It also belongs as an interdisciplinary subject in Latin American departments. ¿Por qué no?

My increasing theatre contacts with Latin America and Spain reveal that there is a tremendous interest in what is happening in Hispanic theatre in the United States. One of my plays, *La Era Latina,* a bilingual comedy I cowrote with Víctor Fragoso, won an award in Venezuela. Right now I am busy preparing an enormous amount of information on Hispanic theatre in the U.S. for a book on Latin American theatre, to be published next year by Spain's Ministry of Culture.

YES, BUT WHAT IS IT?

I define Hispanic American theatre, or literature, as that written by Hispanics living and working in the United States whose subject matter, whether written in Spanish or English or both, reflects their expressions in this country in the same manner that, before us, the Jews, the Irish, the Italians documented their experiences and their histories that came to be part of *the* history of this nation.

Hispanics are here for many different reasons. Many have been born here. Many were here before parts of this land came to be called the United States of America. Some came a lifetime ago. Some came yesterday. Some are arriving this very minute. Some dream of returning to where they came from. Some will. Some have made this place their home for good and are here to stay.

Millions of Americans live next door to a Rodríguez or a Fernández. They go down to the corner bodega and buy Café Bustelo and Goya Beans. They eat tacos and enchiladas (big and small) as if there were no tomorrow. They work shoulder to shoulder with millions of Hispanics at every level, every day.

However, in the schools, in the universities, these same Americans learn nothing about those strangers they ride the elevator with. They are not taught who they are, what they think, why they came here.

This is the place, and this is the time. And theatre, and painting, and dance, and poetry can help bridge that gap.

In the theatre, we have that saying—you know the one: "The show must go on." As I said before, soon Hispanics will be the largest ethnic minority in the U.S. Our presence here promises to be a long-running engagement—despite the bad reviews we get most of the time, despite the problems we may have with the lights, and the curtain and the costumes, and the enter and exit cues. Despite all that, this show will go on, and you might as well get your tickets now.

NOTES

1   That was all very nice, dear, but what exactly did you do in what I just saw? *dramaturga* = playwright.

2   "Hey, Rosalía, did you know that my oldest daughter is a dramaturga?" "Dramaturga! Poor thing! Can it be cured?"

3   Hands up, you bullies.

4   Later on—it was during my third trip—when I noticed that the Indians of a certain island were suspicious of us and reluctant to approach us, I improvised a stage on the stern of the boat, forcing some Spaniards to dance noisily to the sound of drums and castanets, so they could see that we were happy and peaceful people. (But to tell the truth, it was not a very fortunate occasion. The cannibals, unamused by all the heel-tapping and arm-waving, shot all the arrows they had in their canoes at us.)

From Immigrants to Ethnics:
Cuban Women Writers in the U.S.

ELIANA RIVERO

For those readers who are not in touch with the wide diversity of literary traditions present in American society, many of the artistic works produced in the last two decades are hidden behind mirrors. Texts that reflect the readers' own selves and ideas are very visible, but others, beyond the silvery white surfaces, simply do not exist. Minority writers are routinely ignored, even when they are published by mainstream presses. And if this happens regularly with male ethnic writers, it occurs even more often with the large numbers of female writers of varied nationalities that populate the literary landscapes of this country; women of all colors are even "more invisible" than men. The appearance of publications such as *The Third Woman: Minority Women Writers of the United States* in 1980 was a landmark, with a message that is yet to be recognized in its entirety within canonical circles.[1]

More recent books, such as the widely distributed reference compilation, *American Women Writers*,[2] the much-touted *Norton Anthology of Literature by Women: The Tradition in English*,[3] and the "comprehensive" *Stealing the Language: The Emergence of Women's Poetry in America*,[4] either totally ignore the notable contributions of U.S. Hispanic female authors who had already appeared in the *Third Woman* anthology (while at the same time recognizing the ever-growing production of African-American, Native American, and Asian American women), or severely misrepresent the numbers and importance of Hispanic women writers in our midst. Ostriker, in *Stealing the Language*, makes only a brief mention of two poems by

Cherríe Moraga.[5] And yet Ostriker's book appeared five years after the prestigious Pitt Poetry Series (University of Pittsburgh Press) had published Lorna Dee Cervantes' *Emplumada,* the first important book in English by a Chicana poet. Important fiction by Hispanic women, such as Sandra Cisneros' *The House on Mango Street* (Arte Público Press, 1983, recipient of a recent American Book Award), remains on the fringes of the canon—even the revised Anglo canon—despite the increasing attention given to it by feminist critics.

The work of Hispanic women writers in the United States has been ignored, in quite a few instances, due to an uninformed linguistic argument; the bilingualism barrier is deemed insurmountable. This, of course, does not address the prevalent absence of research about such women in departments of Spanish and Latin American studies. In many cases, the subject of U.S. Hispanic women writers is referred to its "natural habitat," i. e., women's and ethnic studies departments. But after reading works by many Hispanic female authors, especially Chicana and Puerto Rican women writing in the continental U.S., one realizes that any efforts to sustain the "linguistic handicap" criterion can only be proven ludicrous. More and more Hispanic women are writing in English, their works appearing in monolingual publications, and translations of poetry and prose are increasing by women who prefer to speak with a Spanish literary voice. Ultimately, the most powerful argument for inclusion of Hispanic minority women within the parameters of what passes for "American literature" might be the latter's characteristic pluralism. Some critics argue that since the so-called American mainstream is basically multiethnic and pluralistic, it, in fact, constitutes the "macro context" for all ethnic minority literary manifestations within the U.S. border; Jewish, Afro-American, and Chicano writings, for instance, have been called the American "counter literatures."[6] For years, this has also been the contention of MELUS (Society for the Study of Multi-Ethnic Literature in the United States). One of the underlying assumptions for this article is, then, that women writers of Hispanic ethnicity are as much an integral part of the North American literary scene as Alice Walker or Isaac Bashevis Singer.

And yet the generating conditions and surface features of literary texts produced by Hispanic women writing in the U.S. differ greatly from those that appear in the traditional mainstream publishing houses of this country. Further, particular idiosyncracies can be noted for each subgroup of Hispanic women writers: from those who write in standard Spanish and speak from an experience of immigration and middle-class origins, to those who write in standard English and speak from the conditions of a working-class background. In between, there appears a wide spectrum of bilingual and/or bicultural writers who, although with diverse origins and in very different literary modalities, seem to unfailingly address themselves to what it means to be female *and* Hispanic in this pluralistic society.

In discussing the subject of Hispanic subgroups in the United States, I make a distinction between the "native Hispanic" and "the migrated Hispanic." The first category comprises Mexican-Americans or Chicanos, as well as Puerto Ricans who live on the mainland (Neorricans); the second reflects the waves of migration that, for political or economic reasons, have deposited on these shores a vast contingent of Cubans, Central Americans, and South Americans.[7] Most writers who are in the latter category have been born (and often raised) outside the borders of the United States; however, some among them, especially younger individuals, are in the midst of effecting the transition from emigré, exile, or immigrant/refugee categories to that of ethnic minority members. In a special sense, this transition entails coming into a personal awareness of biculturalism, and takes for granted the reality of permanence in a society other than the one existing in the country of birth. For some Hispanic women writers, a link with the native country and its literature can be maintained if return to the homeland, however short or temporary, is possible: such is the case of a few Argentine, Central American and, lately, Chilean writers who reside in the United States. They, as a rule, consider themselves as Latin American "emigré" or transplanted writers and have a niche in their own national literatures, whether these are written inside or outside the homeland.[8] Among Cuban women who migrated to the U.S. after the Revolution in 1959, the only one that fits adequately in this category is a writer who has been considered a significant figure in the island's literary tradition since the fifties: the Afro–Cuban folktale researcher/writer Lydia Cabrera, best known for her celebrated work, *El monte* (1956).

Some other Cuban women who were writers before being immigrants are squarely situated in the "exile" modality; in their works, they mostly re-create inner and outer landscapes of their native land: social, political, and personal. Their work is tinged with nostalgia for the homeland, as in the case of the poet Ana Rosa Núñez, or their texts live within a space populated with the inner demons of individual and social analysis; the novelist Hilda Perera and the poet Belkis Cuza Malé are good illustrations. Other Cuban women who belong in that same generation are Rita Geada, Pura del Prado, Martha Padilla, and Amelia del Castillo; a younger group of often published poets also includes Juana Rosa Pita and Gladys Zaldívar. Yet none of these names exemplify the transition from exile to ethnic minority member. Their texts often bespeak an existential alienation that denotes an inner struggle with roles and identities; nevertheless, they "neither treat nor engage the U.S. experience."[9]

A few Cuban women writers who were born around 1940 and migrated to the United States in the late fifties or early sixties began, in the mid- and late-seventies, showing in their work a consciousness of change: this was frequently a feminist awareness that at times clashed with their middle-class values and conservative ideology. Sometimes a detail as subtle as a North American geographical name or an English song title would appear in their descriptions of daily happenings; or perhaps it was a flat statement about a house in the suburbs gladly given up to return to Cuba. These authors included the poet Maya Islas (*Sola . . . desnuda . . . sin nombre*, 1974; *Sombras papel*, 1978); the poet, novelist, and short story writer Mireya Robles (*Tiempo artesano*, 1973; *En esta aurora*, 1978; *Hagiografía de Narcisa la Bella*, 1985); and the poet and short story teller Uva Clavijo (*Versos de exilio*, 1974; *Ni verdad ni mentira y otros cuentos*, 1977). *Sombras . . .* , *En esta aurora*, *Versos de exilio*, and *Ni verdad ni mentira* are among the first works published by Cuban women in the U.S. that document American society through the authors' literary *personae*, bearing witness to the cultural impact of a very different lifestyle.[10]

It was in 1976, nevertheless, that the fully conscious recognition of a "double identity" was registered in the works of Cuban women writing in the United States. Lourdes Casal, poet, short story writer, essayist, scholar, and political activist, who died in Havana in 1981 after a prolonged illness, is exemplary in marking the transition from a consciousness of immigration to a certainty of permanent dualism, existential as well as sociocultural. After living twelve years in the United States, Casal returned to Cuba in 1973 for the first of several visits; she remained there during her last one, being hospitalized and in serious condition until her final days. Her published works are many, but most important to this study are the literary texts collected in *Los fundadores: Alfonso y otros cuentos* (1973) and in the posthumous book of poetry, *Palabras juntan revolución* (1981).

Casal's experience of living alternately in two cultures, in two radically different sociopolitical systems, profoundly affected her view of reality. Her poem, "Para Ana Veltfort" (first published in 1976), best portrays the dichotomy experienced by a Cuban outside her primary cultural milieu; her poetic *persona* functions in two different environments but fits completely in neither. The text, full of recollections and nostalgic remembrances, tells about her sense of double identity:

. . . . Nueva York es mi casa.
Soy ferozmente leal a esta adquirida patria chica.

Por Nueva York soy extranjera ya en cualquier parte
. . . .
Pero Nueva York no fue la ciudad de mi infancia,
no fue aquí que adquirí las primeras certidumbres,
no está aquí el rincón de mi primera caída
ni el silbido lacerante que marcaba las noches.
Por eso siempre permaneceré al margen,
una extraña entre estas piedras,
aun bajo el sol amable de este día de verano,
como ya para siempre permaneceré extranjera
aun cuando regrese a la ciudad de mi infancia.
Cargo esta marginalidad inmune a todos los retornos,
demasiado habanera para ser neoyorkina,
demasiado neoyorkina para ser,
-aun volver a ser-
cualquier otra cosa.[11]

Havana is the "mother city" of identity but New York—cultural megalopolis—is an experience that will forever define the writer's sense of marginality. The poet feels somehow alien, a stranger and a foreigner in either place, the native and the adopted space of life, yet both sites are familiar and very much a part of her being.

Such a marked self-awareness of "hybridism" appears explicitly in the fabric of such poetic texts as the one quoted above; but it was also beginning to be interwoven by Casal in her fiction writings as early as 1973. In "Love Story según Cyrano Prufrock," a double discourse of recreation about Havana and New York, a male narrator goes in search of love and identity, and is evidently much influenced, in his speech and perceptions, by Casal's own studies of Cabrera Infante's *Tres tristes tigres*. The reader finds allusions to a complex quilt of readings, noticing an American cultural presence in which, nevertheless, Cuban/Hispanic elements are basic to an understanding of the totality of the text:

Ay poetisa, los tigres no eran tres sino miles . . . hacíamos la revolución y el amor y todo en medio de la interminable noche habanera. . . .

Y me senté a tu lado a declamarte discursos impresionantes sobre el destino de la década, lo que se nos habían vuelto los sesenta, el sueño de la razón engendra monstruos (fíjate, piba, terminamos con Nixon de presidente), los gallardos caballeros que se fizieron (te regalé un poster de Malcolm X), la sociedad de consumo lo deglute todo (te regalé un disco

autografiado por Marcuse que se estaban liquidando en Mar-
boro), Peter Paul and Mary se separaron y los Beatles ya no
existen. . . . ("Capítulo l. Beatriz encontrada with a little help
from my friends, from Johnny Weissmuller to Jean Luc God-
ard")[12]

Allusions to French film directors, Hollywood movies, Goya's "black"
paintings, American radical leaders, New York stores, and legendary
musical figures are interspersed with memories of the native city, speech
imitations of medieval literary language, references to night life, song
lyrics popular both in the U.S. and Cuba, not to mention the not-so-subtle
intertextual signs pointing to T. S. Eliot, Edmond de Rostand, Erich Segal,
Dante (J. Alfred Prufrock, Cyrano de Bergerac, *Love Story*, Beatriz), and
Cortázar's *Rayuela* (the two-city motif, "piba"). English appears still as a
point of contact, as a reference; the second language is a cultural tool that
has not yet become part of the author's "natural" literary voices and
rhythms. Casal wrote mainly in Spanish, but her texts—whether essays,
film reviews, poems, short stories, or editorial articles—are thoroughly
permeated, during the last five years of her life, with the double vision of
biculturalism. There is a sense of irony when one reads, today, her young
words of 1957, written while still in the native country:

> Todos los pueblos de Hispanoamérica están de acuerdo en
> una actitud defensiva y hasta agresiva frente a la potencia del
> Norte; pero el influjo del triunfo aparente de *ese estilo de vida*,
> *que nos es ajeno*, ha determinado, sin embargo, la duda y *la*
> *aceptación de costumbres importadas con etiquetas de "Made in*
> *U.S.A."* que se han ido infiltrando en nuestra América. . . .[13]

Finally, that "alien lifestyle" also became her own, although her basic
Cubanness was unmarred with the acquisition of cultural dualism.

To the end of her life, Casal's painful awareness of an insurmountable dual reality—one that had to be lived out daily—was still best expressed in her reiteration of motifs belonging to Havana and New York.
Her own tale of two cities reflects her ultimate fear: the erosion of time,
that inexorable leveler that makes contours disappear under the dust, that
erases all known things:

> Que se me amarillea y se me gasta,
> perfil de mi ciudad, siempre agitándose
> en la memoria
> y sin embargo
> siempre perdiendo bordes y letreros . . .
> ("La Habana 1968," *Palabras juntan revolución*, p. 49)

The same fear of not capturing reality, of losing all memories, assaults the poet, who yearns to "name" the features of her adopted city, her second identity source:

> Recorro las calles de este New York vestido de verano,
> con sus guirnaldas de latas de cerveza
>
> . . . .
>
> obsedida por la pasión de nombrar,
> azotada por la furia de fijarlo
> y recrearlo todo en la palabra,
> esta batalla irremisiblemente perdida
> contra la caducidad de todo,
> esta batalla incesante y dolorosa
> contra la erosión,
> el tiempo,
> y el olvido,
> que lo devoran todo.
>
> ("Domingo," Palabras . . ., p. 58)

It is with Lourdes Casal that Cuban women writers in the United States can fully claim their cultural dualism as immigrants. But, more importantly, her life and works give witness to the first full-fledged step in the direction of becoming Cuban-Americans, in the best sense of that term. Ethnic name hyphenation implies a recognition of existential and sociocultural hybridism, and Cuban women in the U.S. are, at present, involved in the process of recognizing themselves as such "others," not only because of the gender imperative, but, more crucially, because of their irrevocable historical situation.

In the works of other U.S. Hispanic writers, it is usually the emergence of bilingual texts that signals, for them, an established conscientization ("self-awareness") of minority status; in other words, the political consciousness of being "dual," or "other," is clearly best expressed at the linguistic level. This phenomenon was first registered for Cuban women authors with the presentation in 1977 of the play *Beautiful Señoritas* by Dolores Prida, a writer/journalist who has distinguished herself as a playwright (*Coser y cantar*) and as a poet. She was also one of the first editorial members of the Latino publication *Nuestro,* and her work for the stage in the 1970s is pioneering among Cuban women.[14]

But the establishment of ethnic awareness/affirmation as a permanent literary presence for Cuban-American women comes in the mid-eighties with the young poet, short story writer, and playwright from Chicago, Achy Obejas. At this writing, she has not published a book yet, but her promising works have appeared in *Woman of Her Word* (1983), *Third Woman*

(1984; 1986), and *Nosotras: Latina Literature Today* (1986); a 1983 play she cowrote, "Carnicería," was highly acclaimed and is considered the most successful play in the history of Spanish-language theatre in Chicago. Her texts, whether in English, Spanish, or a language-alternation mode, are highly polished, well-crafted, and evidence the bilingual/bicultural world vision that distinguishes other well-known "native" Hispanic women poets, such as the Chicana Lorna Dee Cervantes and the Nuyorrican Sandra María Esteves. Obejas synthesizes the process of searching for roots and the consciousness of "hybridism" in texts such as "Sugarcane":

> can't cut
> cut the cane
> azuca' in chicago
>
> . . . .
>
> you can't can't cut
> cut the blood
> lines from this island
> train one by one throwing off
> the chains siguaraya
> no no
> no se pue'e cortar
> pan con ajo quisqueya
> cuba y borinquen no
> se pue'en parar[15]

In this code-switching discourse, the island motif of sugarcane, with all its implied meanings for Cuban culture, draws on an intertextual past of Afro–Caribbean poetry, on song lyrics that portray the speaker's acquaintance with popular cultural icons, and with the experience of Hispanos in the barrios of midwestern and northeastern America. The words of a fifties' Afro song by Celia Cruz—noted Cuban singer, reborn as an entertainer in the heights of *salsa* fever—constitute a takeoff point for the refrain, "no se pue'e cortar." The lyrics of the song, "Siguaraya" (tree especially revered for its magic properties in the Yoruba religious belief system), repeated the refrain: "Siguaraya, yo va tumbá, con permiso de Yemayá." Obejas changes the positive affirmation of the slave chant—"I am going to cut the tree down with permission from [the goddess] Yemayá"—into a "negatively" phrased reaffirmation of radical cultural pride ("you can't can't cut / cut the blood / lines from this island"), marked at the verse level by the imitated staccato patterns of the song. Siguaraya and sugarcane, two native, life-giving plants of the Caribbean, are intimately tied to the economic, social, and cultural life of the Great Antilles. The

three islands, recognized in the text by their Taíno names (Cuba, Borinquen, Quisqueya), are equated for what they share in the "magic," the life
rhythms, and the social awareness that the poet sees as vital to her
bicultural life in the United States.

Obejas also publishes in standard Spanish, as with her poem, "El
bote" (*Third Woman* 2, no. 1 [1984]: 33): "no nos acabamos de ir del país / tú
y yo, siempre con el mapa abierto." This composition treats, in a symbolic
manner, a recurrent motif for Cuban-American women: leaving the native
country. The same theme forms the background for "The Escape," a sober
portrayal of cultural, as well as real, death, a short story that brings into
play all the elements of the Cuban experience of political flight to, and
exile in, a foreign country. A seven-year-old girl looks around her and sees
strange, pale, lifeless North Americans with blond eyelashes that seem
"fuzzy and alien" (*Nosotras,* p. 46). She kills one of them, only to fall prey
to the ocean waves, drowning herself while rafting for pleasure, at fourteen, amid the fearful, stormy Atlantic currents off the coast of Florida.

Basic distinctions between a *Cuban* woman writer in the United States
and a Cuban-*American* woman writer are, thus, the full consciousness of
dualism, the sense of belonging to a minority, and the use of English that
appear in the works illustrated above. Cuban-born women writers in the
U.S. who belong to the older generations still identify, for the most part,
with a "writer-in-exile" definition. That situates them squarely within the
realm of a Latin American *status quo* vision, whereas minority writers in
the U.S. usually speak from an experience of marginality and discrimination due to race, class, and/or sex. More to the point, Cuban "writers in
exile"—women *and* men—tend to identify with the establishment and
reject the Third World stance of many native Hispanic writers, and thus do
not feel part of an underprivileged ethnic minority.

In general, Cuban women who were writers before they migrated
preserve the literary notions and standards they learned in their intellectual and artistic formation, often considering themselves as part of the
literature of their native country and/or of Latin America. Still, some of the
writings done by Cuban women in the United States present a modified
vision of cultural reality due to the prevalence of a feminist ideology in
their texts, and to the naked, critical portrayal of sociocultural myths, such
as the submissive, petit-bourgeois wife and her pathetic Don Juanesque
husband. An excellent illustration is *Hagiografía de Narcisa la Bella*, by
Mireya Robles (now residing in South Africa, after almost thirty years in
this country). This 1985 novel is a well-crafted, avant-garde work with
similarities to some of the best productions of Latin American prose fiction
in the last decades (Puig, Donoso, Lynch, Vargas Llosa). Its locale is a

provincial town of Cuba in the fifties, and its plot ends with the terrible ritual death of the ugly, sensitive, clairvoyant Narcisa, victimized at the hands of her family. Jean Franco has praised the novel, saying of Robles that she has:

> el don genuino de la sátira y lo cómico, algo relativamente escaso en las letras hispanoamericanas.[16]

Robles represents, in the characterization of Cuban women offered in these pages, the immigrant writer who associates her craft with Latin American or Hispanic/universal canonical forms, while Achy Obejas symbolizes the other end of the spectrum: the Cuban-American in her dually grounded vision of culture and society. To put it in general terms, the most distinguishable feature that separates older immigrant generations of Cuban women from their younger compatriots in the U.S., beyond their choice of language, is the problem of their cultural/political identity and affiliations.[17] These vital connections, with their own inner and outer selves, constitute on artistic mother lode of inquiry, rejection, and affirmation.

For Cuban-American women writers, then, the process of establishing themselves in the multicultural U.S. literary scene has just begun. They are already partakers of what Lourdes Casal defined more than a decade ago as a "marginality immune to all returns"; but the road ahead promises to give them a place behind the one-mirror surfaces of the American mainstream as well. Theirs is, nevertheless, an exciting location at the margins: on the cutting edge of Latina cultural ethnicity and gender awareness.

NOTES

1   Dexter Fisher, ed., *The Third Woman: Minority Women Writers of the United States* (Boston: Houghton Mifflin, 1980).

2   Linda Mainiero et al., eds., *American Women Writers* (New York: Frederick Ungar, 1979–82).

3   Sandra Gilbert and Susan Gubar, eds., *Norton Anthology of Literature by Women: The Tradition in English* (New York: W. W. Norton, 1985).

4   Alicia Suskin Ostriker, *Stealing the Language: The Emergence of Women's Poetry in America* (Boston: Beacon Press, 1986).

5   Notes pertaining to pages 189–90 in the Ostriker volume refer to Cherríe Moraga and Gloria Anzaldúa's *This Bridge Called My Back: Writings by Radical Women of Color* (New York: Kitchen Table, 1981). On the back cover of *Stealing the Language,*

one can read a curious comment by Catharine Stimpson (founder of *Signs*, professor of English and women's studies at Rutgers University): "[this is] the first *comprehensive* appraisal of women's poetry in America" (emphasis mine).

6 Cordelia Candelaria, *Chicano Poetry: A Critical Introduction* (Westport, Conn.: Greenwood Press, 1986), 15.

7 For a detailed discussion of these categories, see my article "Hispanic Literature in the United States: Self-Image and Conflict," in *International Studies in Honor of Tomás Rivera*, special issue of *Revista Chicano-Riqueña* 13, nos. 3–4 (Winter 1985): 173–92. I make free use here of ideas I developed for that article, as well as of concepts that I have researched for an NEH-sponsored project done in collaboration with Tey Diana Rebolledo, "Unsung Women: The Identity of Chicana Literature," forthcoming publication.

8 Names such as Luisa Valenzuela, Rima Vallbona, Mercedes Valdivieso, Marjorie Agosín, and Lucía Guerra-Cunningham come to mind; some of them are now publishing their works in translation for an English-reading public. The case of Isabel Allende—as with Valenzuela, one of the most distinguished Spanish–American women writing in the continental U.S.—is a vastly different one, since she will most likely return to Chile as soon as democracy is restored.

9 Juan Bruce-Novoa, "Hispanic Literature in the United States" (Paper presented at the Hispanic Southwest Regional Conference, "Media and the Humanities"), San Diego, Calif., December 4–7, 1980.

10 In Islas, for example, "la casa de Montclair" and "el 'threshold' de mis miedos," 40; in Robles, " 'Feelings'—/una canción escrita para el subway," 27; and in Clavijo's short story, "1342 Park Road," 125–35, and her poem, "Declaración," reproduced by Margaret Randall in *Breaking The Silences: 20th Century Poetry by Cuban Women* (Vancouver, B.C.: The Pulp Press Book Publishers, 1982), 25 (English) and 31–32 (Spanish).

11 This an important poem that appeared originally in *Areito* (New York) 3, no. 1 [Verano 1976]:52, and was later included in the posthumous volume, *Palabras juntan revolución* (La Habana: Casa de las Américas, 1981). There are a few significant changes in the latter version that appear not to have been authorized by Casal ("querida" instead of "adquirida," "las piedras" instead of "estas piedras," "newyorkina" instead of "neoyorkina"). All further references to Casal's poetic work in this article are made in relation to the Casa de las Américas edition.

12 Lourdes Casal, *Los fundadores y otros cuentos* (Miami: Ediciones Universal, 1973), 72–73.

13 Casal, "Problemas hispanoamericanos," *Insula* (La Habana), 1, no. 1 (16 diciembre 1957): 19–25, and reproduced in *Itinerario ideológico: antología de Lourdes Casal*, ed. María Cristina Herrera and Leonel de la Cuesta (Miami: Instituto de Estudios Cubanos, 1982), 13–19 (emphasis mine).

14 Other Cuban writers who have published works about the U.S. experience, originally written in English, are Raquel Puig Zaldívar's "Please, Yell 'Bingo'!" in *Nosotras: Latina Literature Today* (Binghamton, N.Y.: Bilingual Press, 1986), 31–38, and Eliana Rivero's "North from the River, South Inside," in *Canto al Pueblo* (Phoenix: Arizona Canto al Pueblo, 1980), 105–9, and "Huachuca: The

Mountain Poems" and "Going West," in *Bearing Witness/Sobreviviendo: An Anthology of Writing and Art by Native American/Latina Women*, special issue of *Calyx* (Spring 1984): 22–23.

15 "Sugarcane," *Woman of Her Word: Hispanic Women Write*, ed. Evangelina Vigil (special issue of *Revista Chicano-Riqueña* 9, nos. 3–4 [Winter 1983]): 48–49.

16 Comment on back cover of *Hagiografía* . . ., (Hanover, N.H.: Ediciones del Norte, 1985) ("a real talent for satire and comedy, something relatively scarce in Latin American letters"). A paper with the suggestive title/theme of "Gender Identity and Feminine Creativity in Mireya Robles's *Hagiografía de Narcisa la Bella*" was read by Rosemary Geisdorfer Feal at the annual NEMLA (North East Modern Language Association) conference in April 1987.

17 This is hinted at by Margaret Randall in her introductory essay to *Breaking the Silences* (see note 10, above), where she includes poems by Cuban women outside the country (Lourdes Casal, Eliana Rivero, Uva Clavijo). She characterizes the three—most especially Casal—as women for whom, in varying degrees, a "search for identity became their search for their country" (p. 23).

Dolores Prida's Coser y cantar: *Mapping the Dialectics of Ethnic Identity and Assimilation*

ALBERTO SANDOVAL

In the United States, a nation that glorifies and perpetuates itself as the land of opportunity, the dominant political discourses of power propagate the ideology of the "melting pot" in order to mythicize their concept of "freedom and justice for all." In this respect, what comes to mind are the imperial celebrations of the Statue of Liberty centennial, which blurred the lines between myth and history in a theatrical, televised, naturalization ceremony for 16,000 immigrants in five cities.[1] The so-called "aliens" became citizens by patriotically reciting the oath of allegiance to the United States in a spectacular ritual, reminiscent of the choreography and monumental Hollywood sets of the thirties, situated in what I call secular sacred spaces—that is, at the feet of two national monuments: the Statue of Liberty (the Lady) and Mount Rushmore (the "Founding Fathers").

But can an immigrant leave behind her/his cultural baggage and mother tongue so effortlessly? Is it that easy, after naturalizing, to speak, interact, and transact thoughts for a monolingual life in English? Are the ideologemes of the "All-American Boy," the "American Way of Life," and the "American Dream" of upward mobility ("Making It Big," the "Bigger the Better," the "Sky is the Limit," and "Number One") gratuitously guaranteed to all immigrants? At what point do the hegemonic, fictive discourses (television, cinema, Broadway, and advertising) stereotype the immigrants' rite of passage—arrival, culture shock, psychological adjustment, cultural adaptability, assimilation, success, and acceptance?[2] How is the proverbial happy ending in these discourses contradicted when we also take into account that the historical experience of "aliens" in the United States is determined by race, gender, and class?[3] Indeed, if assimilation in the United States ensures integration, equality, and acceptance, the ethnic culture and mother tongue of the "alien" is sacrificed, dissolved, and vanquished in the "melting pot." What happens to the immigrant who refuses to give up the native culture and mother tongue, who attempts to stay attached to the ethnic umbilical cord, and continues nurturing the cultural heritage (traditions, norms, values, attitudes, sentiments, practices) of the place of origin? What becomes of the person who wants to reconcile both cultures and their respective social constructions of reality, while at the same time not succumb to Anglo-American acculturation?

The above introduction functions as the overture to a socio-cultural reading of Dolores Prida's play *Coser y cantar*. My aim is to demonstrate how subjectivity is constructed, configured, and articulated when an individual moves dialectically between two cultures. Most of Prida's plays, as she herself states, "have been about the experience of being a Hispanic in the United States, about people trying to reconcile two cultures and two languages and two visions of the world into a particular whole." Prida specifically declares about *Coser y cantar* that: "[it] deals with how to be [a] bilingual, bicultural woman in Manhattan and keep your sanity."[4]

In *Coser y cantar*, a Latina named Ella[5] shares a New York City apartment with her Anglo inner self, "She." They are two different characters, two cultural sides of a personality: the Cuban immigrant and the assimilated Anglo-American "other." Ella speaks in Spanish, while "She"[6] says her lines in English; as a result, they both experience a crisis in communication. This crisis emerges from the affirmation of Ella's Latina/o culture and linguistic heritage, and also her ability to cope with the imposition of "She" 's Anglo-American way of life. In this dialogue, which is, in effect, a monologue, the split personality of Ella surfaces. In "Important Notes from the Author," the playwright specifically states the controversial interaction between Ella and "She":

> This piece is really one long monologue. The two women are one and are playing a verbal, emotional game of ping pong. Throughout the action, except in the final confrontation, Ella and She never look at each other, acting independently, pretending the other one does really exist. . . ."[7]

If the stage design and dramatic action of *Coser y cantar* must be visualized in terms of a ping-pong game, the two players, Ella and She, each bounce their own metaphorical ball of cultural selfhood back and forth. The spectator is forced to concentrate on following the movement of the players hitting and returning their own "cultural ball." The players, actually competitors in the land of free enterprise, are expected to challenge one another until one of them is defeated in the game and the adversary claims victory.[8] But the game becomes complicated and cannot reach its goal—total assimilation[9]—because, at the end, Ella bounces back her own ball of Latina selfhood. Thus Ella's refusal to return "She" 's ball is a conscious rejection of "She" 's imposed Anglo-Americanization. In other words, Ella dis-articulates and de-centers the horizon of expectations for the spectator, an Anglo-American who anticipates a final outcome of introjection and projection of Ella's self-identity and self-image as an assimilated Anglo-American ego. Within this paradigm of competitive performance, Ella and "She" gesticulate and articulate past and present experiences, memories and fantasies, in a verbal and nonverbal confrontation of Spanish and English.

At first glance, Ella could be immediately judged as schizophrenic, but the deep structure of the character reveals a process of an individual's double articulation of the traversing, intersecting, and defining of two cultures. In this dialogic monologue, Ella and "She" struggle with their separation, in search of the fusion of their two cultural selves. Such a search produces the construction of Ella's subjectivity as a historical process marked by doubleness, oppositions, divisions, contradictions, and differences.

As I shall examine, Prida's play is but the *re*-presentation of Latina subjectivity in process: always in movement, in flux, and oscillating in the dialectics of a bi-cultural identity in the U.S. The conflict of the *dramatis persona*, Ella, is how to synthesize both cultures, how to survive and come to terms with the dilemma of a dual selfhood that is demeaned, marginalized, and silenced by monolingual-ethnocentric-white-Anglo-American systems of power.

BICULTURAL SPACES AND PROPS

Set design, props, and dress codes constitute a unified duality in *Coser y cantar*. The stage portrays an apartment divided into two ethnic territories, one for each character. The props refer to cultural artifacts, and the costumes embody referential cultural constructs:

> Couch on stage right is Ella's. The one on the stage left is She's. Piles of books, magazines and newspapers surround She's area. A pair of ice skates and a tennis racket are visible somewhere. Her dressing table has a glass with pens and pencils and various bottles of vitamin pills. She wears jogging shorts and sneakers.

> Ella's area is a little messier. Copies of Cosmopolitan and
> Vanidades and TV Guías are seen around her bed. Her table is
> full of make up, a Virgen de la Caridad and a candle. A large
> conch and a pair of maracas are visible. Ella is dressed in a
> short red kimono. (P. i)

It is evident from this description that both characters function as ethnic
stereotypes; both the Latina and the Anglo-American woman project a
framed, static, frozen configuration of rationalization, of cultural otherness.[10] "She" is the "All-American Girl": young and healthy, body-cen-
tered, and consumer-oriented. Being a body and image worshiper, she is
ego-centric and individualistic. Even her work-out clothes infer the Protestant work ethic, mediated by the competitive spirit of sports all year
round (notice that her ice skates and tennis racket are on stage). Because of
such a competitive disposition, "She"'s character emerges as a person
who is clean, self-controlled, self-reliant, efficient, fast, aggressive, as-
sertive, industrious, dedicated, goal-oriented, motivated, status-seeking,
and social climbing.

On the other hand, Ella is a reader of popular media, a T.V. addict,
and disorganized (implying her lack of concern for the Anglo logical order
of things and her obvious disinterest in the regulation of time). Ella is
oriented toward distraction and entertainment, a proponent of "hay que
vivir el momento," neglecting the work ethic and the narcissist fetishism
of keeping the body "in shape." In counterpoint to the vitamin pills on
"She"'s table, Ella possesses ethnic artifacts: a virgin, a candle, a conch
shell, and a pair of maracas. These cultural icons, rather than being self-
referential (like those belonging to "She"), concretize a communal, socio-
centric, Afro-Caribbean, and historico-cultural past in the rituals of religion and music. If, after immigration, these cultural objects have been
dis-connected, dis-membered from the whole, dis-centered toward a margin, they still empower the Latina's self-identity, providing a sense of
belonging metonymically to the mother land from a distance. The conch,
for example, particularly links Ella to nature, to the Caribbean paradise
that contrasts with the absence of nature on "She"'s side of the room,
where pure artificiality and rehearsed spectacle hold her reality together.
As for Ella's make-up and kimono, emblems of exaggerated, stereotyped
Latina femininity, they serve as props to please the gazing eye of the male.
Ella has internalized the need to be an object of voyeurism for the male;
even the conch and the maracas evoke the visualization of the "tropical
bombshell," with a performance directed to a male spectator. On the other
hand, "She," by satisfying her ego-centrism and the physical control of
her body, thus claims her sexual liberation from the male.

Although stereotypes always affix and freeze ethnic "others" in images of prejudice and discrimination, in *Coser y cantar*, once the dynamics of cultural difference and interaction are set in motion, both stereotypes are dis-mantled and, at the same time, re-constructed. However, whenever "She" devalues, subordinates, and subjugates Ella, the reverse effect is accomplished. Ironically, "She" operates as the generator to make Ella aware of her socio-cultural, historical identity. As a result, Ella's ethnic affirmation and spatial/mental positioning rely on the presence and deconstruction of "She." Nevertheless, the communication of Ella and "She" takes place without cultural exchange or a sharing of past experiences and, for this reason, when they attempt to communicate, both re-institute cultural dichotomizations. Such is the opening scene of the play.

When the play begins, Ella is listening to Olga Guillot's song, "Qué sabes tú," singing along/performing, while "She," reading *Psychology Today,*" interrupts her impatiently, "gets up and turns off the record player, cutting of Ella's singing in mid-sentence." Immediately, "She" "begins to pick up newspapers and magazines and to stack them up neatly" (p. 1). "She" 's action is an intrusion, a super-imposition, and super-ordination to silence Ella. In response to such aggression, Ella reacts passionately:

> ELLA: *(with contained exasperation)* ¿Por qué haces eso? ¡Sabes que no me gusta que hagas eso! Detesto que me interrumpas así. ¡Yo no te interrumpo cuande tú te imaginas que eres Barbra Streisand! (P. 1)

Obviously, there is a conflictive encounter of cultural selfhoods, models, roles, attitudes, ways of seeing, and ways of doing. The characters' disagreement about their taste in music delineates a polarization between Latino and Anglo-American cultures in the U.S.:

ELLA	"SHE"
Olga Guillot	Barbra Streisand
Spanish	English
Bolero	Pop music
There and then	Here and now
Absence	Presence
Recovery & affirmation of Latino culture	Rejection & exclusion of Latino culture

Ella, the immigrant, has brought with her items of her culture that make up her survival kit in exile. The song playing evokes memories, leads to the identification with Latino cultural models, and re-vivifies the mother tongue. However, "She" insists on imposing her reality, her language, and her order of things: the "American Way." "She" is not willing to understand Ella's cultural history and absences, which are condensed in language, objects, and memories brought from her place of origin. Consequently, both cultural components of Ella's self, instead of communicating (we may infer that, for Ella, communication implies assimilation), develop modes of resistance and political struggle that fluctuate between fixation and dis-placement, centralization and marginalization, acceptance and rejection, re-appearance and dis-appearance, remoteness and contiguity, unity and disjunction, interruption and continuity. In short, Ella's dilemma is not being there and not be(long)ing here.

MAPPING THE DIALECTICS OF ETHNIC IDENTITY AND ASSIMILATION

If Ella/"She" constitutes a bilingual/bicultural reality within one self, can the construction of subjectivity be totally dichotomized in binary oppositions, as politically established by the hegemonic Anglo-American system of power? Can its rejection of bilingualism be construed as the negation of the subject-in-process who, by virtue of attempts to define its self biculturally, can constitute a potential threat? To what degree does the official U.S. system of education, which favors English as a Second Language abroad, discredit bilingualism at home, conveying it as a basic antinomy? Could such a political strategy impose and install an imperialistic enterprise that comprises the elimination of all that is different or in between boundaries (such as Chicanos and Nuyoricans)? Juan Bruce-Novoa deconstructs the ideological control and intended subjugation of binary oppositions when applied to bilingualism:

> Aunque las posturas binarias llenan las necesidades del pensamiento científico y pseudoscientífico, tienen el efecto contraproducente de caracterizar el espacio entre los dos polos opuestos como si fuera una escala de valores calibrados entre signos positivos y negativos. Como resultado, cualquier punto entre los polos recibe la dudosa precisión de ser menos que los enteros; de no ser ya una cosa, ni todavía la otra . . . el estadio intermedio no es ya, o no es todavía algo aceptado. . . . Los lenguajes quedan opuestos en pares y ser bilingüe es cambiar de los códigos de uno a los del otro, no mezclarlos ni fusionarlos. Cuando hay algo menos que un salto preciso de un polo al otro, recibe el nombre de interferencia, con la carga de negatividad que el término acarrea. El espacio entre los idiomas es la zona prohibida del "ni esto ni lo otro."[11]

In this perspective, what Prida has achieved in *Coser y cantar*, by alternating Spanish and English language and culture as two contrapuntual social constructions of a character's reality, is to re-present the conflictive, bilingual situation of a bicultural existence. Ella and "She" are juxtaposed not only linguistically, but also in their respective socio-cultural realms. For example, the linguistic antinomy is specifically grasped and staged when Ella and "She" "both stand center stage, back to back," and speak at the same time:

> SHE: A E I O U (*in English*).
> ELLA: A E I O U (*in Spanish*).
> ELLA: Pirámides.
> SHE: Pyramids.
> ELLA: Orquídeas.
> SHE: Orchids.
> ELLA: Sudor.
> SHE: Sweat.
> ELLA: Luz.
> SHE: Light.
> ELLA: Blood.
> SHE: Sangre.
> ELLA: Dolphins.
> SHE: Delfines.
> ELLA: Mountains.
> SHE: Montañas.
> ELLA: Sed.
> SHE: Thirst. (P. 10)

What starts as a simple linguistic situation of double utterances and thoughts, not an exercise in translation, terminates in a confrontation of cultural difference at the moment of action:

> ELLA: Tengo sed.
> SHE: I think I'll have a Diet Pepsi.
> ELLA: Yo me tomaría un guarapo de caña. (P. 11)

Both cultural worlds are articulated by native values and ethnic foods.[12] "She" is only concerned with her body image, while Ella wants nourishment from the nutrients of tropical fruits. However, there is a radical difference between the tenses of both utterances; "She" uses the goal-oriented future tense that affirms, in advance, the realization of desire, while Ella uses the conditional and, in so doing, institutes the impossibility, the contrary-to-fact condition, and the absence of the tropical drink. In fact, "She" gets up, goes to the kitchen, and comes back with a Diet Pepsi, but Ella, who has no access to her "guarapo," instead reactivates the cultural past by concentrating on the meaning of a song from the place of origin:

> ELLA: ¿Por qué sería que Songo le dio a Borongo? ¿Sería porque Borongo le dio a Bernabé, o porque Bernabé le pegó a Muchilanga? ¿O en realidad sería porque Muchilanga le echó burundanga? . . . ¿Y Monina? ¿Quién es Monina? . . . ¡Ay, nunca lo he entendido! . . . el gran misterio de nuestra cultura. . . . (P. 11)

Although the above tongue twister/song is hilariously questioned, what Ella is really experiencing is a recovery of her historical past, her memories, and her cultural models. She does so by examining and deconstructing cultural codes in order to reintegrate them anew in her present bi-cultural horizon of experience. This cultural examination will be judgmental and critical of both the Anglo-American culture and her own. Each side of Ella's personality criticizes, undermines, and puts down its cultural adversary, in its quest to survive, by the elimination of either Ella or "She." For example:

1) When "She," obsessed with her body, condemns Ella's eating habits ("You eat all day, then lie there like a dead octopus"), the latter responds: "Y tú me lo recuerdas todo el día, pero si no fuera por todo lo que yo como, ya tú te hubieras muerto de hambre" (p. 2).

2) When "She" uses a typical Anglo-American cliché to express the beauty of the day ("Aaah, what a beautiful day! It makes me so . . . so happy to be alive!"), Ella comments sarcastically, "No es para tanto" (p. 3).

3) When Ella remembers the sad moment of departure at the Cuban airport, "She" rejects the evocation of these memories and coldly states: "Dwelling in the past takes energies away" (p. 5).

4) Both judge and attack each other for their culturally-inscribed, emotional reactions and their conceptions of body image (i.e., natural vs. artificial):

> ELLA: Si pudiera sonreir como la Mona Lisa me tomarían por misteriosa, en vez de antipática porque no enseño los dientes . . .
>
> SHE: (from the couch, still staring) That's because your face is an open book. You wear your emotions all over, like a suntan . . . You are emotionally naive . . . or rather,

emotionally primitive . . . perhaps even emotionally
retarded. What you need is a . . . a certain emotional
sophistication . . .

ELLA: . . . sí, claro, eso . . . sofisticación emocional . . .
(*thinks about it*) . . . ¿sofisticación emocional? ¿Y qué
carajo es sofisticación emocional? (*angry*) ¿Ser como
tú? Tú, que ya ni te acuerdas como huele tu propio
sudor, que no reconoces el sonido de tu propia voz!
¡No me jodas!

SHE: See what I mean! (Pp. 7–8)

While "She" strives to be self-controlled and "emotionally sophisticated"
(as the magazines she reads have taught her), Ella is spontaneous, pas-
sionate, intemperate, and natural. Ella conceives her body to be a part of a
natural process and rejects the artificiality promoted by the advertising
industry, which seeks to make it a product of/for consumption.

Indeed, such a flux and facility for linguistic back-and-forth sliding,
with its capacity for self/other examination and judgment, concretizes a
hybrid cultural identity within Ella. What appears to be an irreconcilable
opposition in her is actually a dialectic dependency, molded and vectored
toward an ideal cultural synthesis. In this synthesis, Ella will always
rescue, re-shape, re-define, and even re-familiarize herself with her native
cultural models of/for social action. Ella's struggle to affirm and incorporate her Latina identity in the United States establishes the co-existence of
both the Latino and the Anglo cultures.

DEBUNKING MYTHS AND STEREOTYPES OF WOMEN'S SEXUALITY

Whenever any immigrant crosses the border, s/he has the potential to
become liberated from ethnic gender models, values, attitudes, and ethics. This awareness of liberation occurs especially when entering the
United States, which is known abroad for its so-called sexual liberation.
For a Latina woman, it can mean breaking away from taboos and domestic
stereotypes: virginity, passivity, motherhood, and subjugation to the
male. In *Coser y cantar*, womanhood and sexuality are significant issues
when seen through the prism of cultural difference and social construction
of sexuality. For a conservative, bourgeois audience, Ella/"She"'s sexual
openness may be distasteful and even obscene. But the truth is that this
monologue of self-exegesis and cultural examination requires a manifestation of Ella's intimacies after she enters the Anglo-American domain.

Consequently, throughout the play Ella and "She" will recount their sexual experiences and, in so doing, judge each other's concepts and attitudes toward sexuality.

"She" is the one who brings up the sexual issue: "Maybe what I need is a good fuck after all." Ella responds condemningly: "Eres una enferma" (p. 12). In these two utterances, both world views contrast, and Ella/"She" move within opposing cultural horizons of gender roles, prohibitions, possibilities, and expectations regarding women's sexual politics. Given that Ella's sexual liberation constitutes breaking away from models and stereotypes of Latina womanhood, Ella immediately philosophizes about her past Latina ways of being, seeing, and acting:

> Mi mamá me dijo una vez que la vida, sobre todo la vida de una mujer, era coser y cantar. Y yo me lo creí. Pero ahora me doy cuenta que la vida, la de todo el mundo: hombre, mujer, perro, gato, jicotea, es, en realidad, comer y cagar . . . en otras palabras, ¡la misma mierda! (P. 12)[13]

Ella juxtaposes two histories, two times, two spaces: there and then, here and now. At the same time, Ella looks at the past, deconstructing the previous way of ascribed and prescribed behavior, moral principles, and ethics. But in this process of comparing past and present, Ella looks at life cynically. In order to survive and declare her independence from the Mother (embodying Latino dogma, cultural rules, and expectations), Ella laughs at life in general, and at the Latino petit bourgeois society and its values, inscribed in her mother's advice. On the one hand, she universalizes, in "comer y cagar," the biological needs of humans and animals, and rejects imposed, politically-constructed gender roles: "coser y cantar." On the other hand, laughter functions as a psychological mediation to position herself in control after transgressing and breaking away from the Latino socio-cultural order of reality. Ella, an outsider to U.S. society, utilizes irony, sarcasm, laughter, and cynicism to cope with estrangement, alienation, loneliness, abandonment, and disengagement.

With regard to the debunking of gender roles, Ella later laughs at "She" when the latter reveals that her fantasy is to be as great a dancer as Fred Astaire and Ginger Rogers. In this fantasy of embodying both genders simultaneously, her latent bisexuality is connoted, as Ella quickly points out:

ELLA: ¿Cuál de ellos, Fred Astaire o Ginger Rogers?
SHE: Why can't I be both?
ELLA: ¿Será que eres bisexual?
SHE: No. I have looked. (P. 15)

Time after time, both characters feel free to talk about sexuality. In Ella's bicultural reality (a betwixt-and-between condition), there is indeed room for bisexuality. Without taboos or euphemisms, Ella suggests sexual alternatives to her Anglo-American, sexually pseudo-liberated inner self—"She." This sexual ambivalence is portrayed once again in a graphic phase-by-phase account of a sexual scene in crescendo. The scene opens with a memory of two bodies (male and female?) that ends in either masturbation or heterosexual intercourse, thereby implying a lesbian experience as well:

ELLA: . . . olor a jazmines, mezclado brisas de salitre. A lo lejos se escucha un bolero: (SINGS) "¿Te acuerdas de la noche de la playa? Te acuerdas que te di mi amor primero . . ."

SHE: . . . I feel the smell of two bodies together, the heat of the flesh so close to mine, the sweat and the saliva trickling down my spine . . .

Both get progressively excited

ELLA: . . . y unas manos expertas me abren la blusa, me safan el ajustador, y con mucho cuidado, como si fueran dos mangos maduros, me sacan los senos al aire . . .

SHE: . . . and ten fingernails dig into my flesh and I can hear drums beating faster and faster and faster! (P. 25)

Ella is in control of her sexuality, enjoying her own body, and transgressing taboos. As a result of the awareness of her sexual desire, Ella recognizes her ability for pleasure (jouissance). Because of this, she even feels free to challenge religious dogma, and sees her sexuality as assertiveness and self-control. In these terms, sex is a biological need, not a sin:

SHE: (*Half-laughs*) . . . I remember the first time . . .

ELLA: Ja ja . . . a mí me preguntaron si yo había tenido un orgasmo alguna vez. Yo dije que no. No porque no lo había tenido, sino porque no sabía lo que era. . . . Pensé que orgasmo era una tela.

SHE: I looked it up in the dictionary: orgasm. Read the definition, and still didn't know what it meant.

ELLA: . . . a pesar del diccionario, hasta que no tuve el primer orgasmo, en realidad no supe lo que quería decir . . .

SHE: It felt wonderful. But all the new feelings scared me . . .

ELLA: (*Kneeling on the chair*) . . . fui a la iglesia el otro día . . .
me arrodillé, me persigné, alcé los ojos al cielo—es
decir, al techo—muy devotamente, pero cuando em-
pecé a pensar la oración . . . me di cuenta de que, en
vez de pedir perdón, estaba pidiendo . . . ¡aproba-
ción! . . . ¡permiso para hacerlo otra vez!

SHE: . . . Oh God, please give me a sign! Tell me it is all
right! Send an angel, una paloma, a flash of green light
to give me the go ahead! Stamp upon me the Good
Housekeeping Seal of Approval, to let me know that
fucking is OK!

ELLA: ¡Ay, Virgen del Cobre! ¡Yo tenía un miedo que se
enterara la familia! ¡Me parecía que me lo leían en la
cara! (Pp. 26–27)

Whereas "She" invokes a only male deity ("Oh God"), Ella turns to the
Virgin, a female deity whom she trusts. Both replies to the sexual experience reveal different attitudes toward pleasure, guilt, and sin. Consequently, the Catholic devotion to the Virgin, and the dogmatic Protestant
rejection of her, constitute another antinomy in Ella/"She"'s bicultural
identity. Furthermore, while "She" is individualistic and her sexual liberation borders on promiscuity, Ella's sexuality encompasses her family's
approval and her self-respect. What constitutes sexual liberation has a
different meaning to both. Sexual relations on a regular basis do not attract
Ella:

SHE: You are too romantic, that's your problem.

ELLA: ¡Y tú eres muy promiscua! Te acuestas con demasiada
gente que ni siquiera te caen bien, que no tienen nada
que ver contigo.

SHE: (*Flexing her muscles*) It keeps me in shape. (*Bitchy*) And
besides, it isn't as corny as masturbating listening to
boleros. (P. 16)

Ella is an independent woman, in control of her sexuality, but still
attached to Latino relationships and cultural modes of behavior. However,
she is not dependent upon a male and is thus capable of breaking up with
her boyfriend in a telephone conversation almost at the end of the play:

ELLA: . . . pero, ¿quién carajo tú te crees que eres para venir
a tirarme así, como si yo fuera una chancleta vieja! . . .
¡A ver si esta putica que te has conseguido cocina tan
bien como yo! . . . (*Suddenly desperate*) Ay, ¿cómo
puedes hacerme esto a mí? A mí que te adoro ciega-

mente . . . Mi amor . . . ay, mi amor, no me dejes.
Haré lo que tu quieras. ¡Miénteme, pégame, trai-
cióname patéame, arrástrame por el fango, pero no
me dejes! (P. 28)

Ella oscillates between submission/independence and passivity/libera-
tion. She alternates insults with lyrics of boleros (which stereotype the
submissive femme fatale). Nevertheless, at the end of the conversation,
Ella sees the possibility of another sexual relationship. She actually verbalizes proudly about how good she was in bed:

De veras . . . honestamente, no te guardo rencor . . . te deseo lo mejor . . . ¿yo? . . . yo seguiré mi viaje. Seré bien re-
cibida en otros puertos! Ja, ja, ja . . . De veras, te deseo de
todo corazón que, esa tipa, por lo menos, ¡sea tan BUENA EN
LA CAMA COMO YO! (P. 29)

In these terms, Ella achieves sexual liberation because, to a certain degree,
she is able to liberate herself from the cultural models of sexual roles and
behavior.[14] Her liberation goes beyond the body, beyond the sexual terms
that "She" advocates. As a result, Ella's life-journey and undetermined
future in the United States are open to new sexual possibilities.

THE CONFRONTATIONAL DYNAMICS OF BICULTURAL
EXPERIENCE

Ella's introspective analysis concludes in a confrontation with "She," resulting from the clash between ethnicity and assimilation:[15]

ELLA: . . . Yo tengo mis recuerdos. Y mis plantas en la ventana. Yo tengo una solidez. Tengo unas raíces, algo de
qué agarrarme. Pero tú . . . ¿tú de qué te agarras?
SHE: I hold on to you. I couldn't exist without you.
ELLA: But I wonder if I need you. Me pregunto si te nece-
sito . . . robándome la mitad de mis pensamientos, de
mi tiempo, de mi sentir, de mis palabras . . . como
una sanguijuela! (Pp. 29–30)

Obviously, "She" depends on, and consumes, Ella's existence, and Ella
convincingly affirms that if she were to return to Cuba, "She" would
disappear:

ELLA: Tú no eres importante. Ni tan fuerte. Unos meses, tal
vez unos años, bajo el sol, y ¡presto! . . . desapare-

cerías. No quedaría ni rastro de tí. Yo soy la que existo.
Yo soy la que soy. Tú . . . no sé lo que eres.

SHE: But, if it weren't for me you would not be the one you
are now. No serías la que eres. I gave yourself back to
you. If I had not opened some doors and some windows for you, you would still be sitting in the dark,
with your recuerdos, the idealized beaches of your
childhood, and your rice and beans and the rest of
your goddam obsolete memories! (P. 30)

In her ethnocentric attack against Ella, "She" reminds Ella that she has
rescued her from isolation, loneliness, and reactionary nostalgia. But if
Ella were to follow "She" 's advice of forgetting the past, she would be that
much more prone to instant assimilation. Their relationship, at this point,
is a separation and division of being, a dramatic suspension, and a desire
for positionality that signs the double nature of Ella's coherent psyche.
Ella's subjectivity is divided between ego and alter ego in two cultural
symbolic orders and imaginary domains: Latino and Anglo. This duality,
multiplied to the second power, is not a search for total separation (condu-
cive to schizophrenia) but rather a search to bridge, overlap, and merge
cultural borders in order to reinstall subjectivity in at least a partial resolution of reconciliation.

If Ella's Janus-double-faced being must come to terms with its self,
intercultural understanding is the solution. However, in *Coser y cantar*, Ella
and "She" achieve only a partial bonding when, in their final confrontation, they recognize that self-destruction is not the answer. Such an awareness and alertness results from the interruption of their argument by
sirens, shots, and screams from the outside. They immediately realize that
the urban Anglo social environment is destructive, hostile, violent, and
terrifying.[16] The noises and screams of horror coming through the window are not a sign of communication, but a sign of death:

SHE: They are shooting again.
ELLA: . . . y están cortando los arboles.
SHE: . . . they are poisoning the children in the schoolyard!
ELLA: . . . ¡Y echando la basura y los muertos al río!
SHE: . . . We're next! We're next! (P. 31)

When dealing with a matter of life and death, Ella and "She" can no longer
bi-polarize each other but rather, they must re-unite. I/You/Other pronoun distinctions disappear in order to become one being who must
escape death. Once they have identified themselves as potential targets,
they must find a safe place to go:

ELLA: El mapa . . .
SHE: Where's the map? (P. 32)

The map is a metonymic symbol, specifying Ella's nomadic being since she migrated to the United States.[17] Having been uprooted, separated, decentered, and displaced once from the place of origin, she will be able to do it again and again. Although throughout the play Ella has been looking for a map to get away,[18] "She" had objected to her desire to move, to find a place somewhere else: ". . . You always want to be going somewhere, but now you are stuck here, with me, because outside is raining blood and you have been to all the places you can possibly ever go to! No, no, you have nowhere to go! Nowhere! Nowhere!" (p. 21). In the final confrontation, removal from the urban spaces configures a vision: to find a place of peace, security and happiness, where both Ella and "She" can live in the United States.

Ella's immigration embodies a nomadic journey of life, a threshold situation for coping with ethnicity and assimilation, a search for cohesiveness and a sense of be(long)ing as a bicultural "minority." This is a conscious journey that also implies walking to the edge of loneliness, isolation, and death. Indeed, immigration or exile is an awareness of death: to be aware of relatives and friends, dying in the place of origin, and realizing the impossibility of being there, to become aware of one's own death, and the choice of burial place as there or here, and even to experience a cultural death, which is assimilation.[19] In *Coser y cantar*, Ella experiences the fear of a concrete, violent death. The map at the end of the play will indicate a place to go, a place to get away from a violent death (versus a natural death, as might be expected in the place of origin). In that utopian place indicated by the map, Latino immigrants could die with dignity, rather than with the violence that characterizes so many deaths in the U.S. Nevertheless, the map will not point out a fantasy place, as portrayed in Anglo-American movies:

SHE: . . . Sometimes I wish I could do like Dorothy in "The Wizard of Oz": close my eyes, click my heels and repeat three times: "there is no place like home" . . . and, puff! be there. (P. 22)

Given that Ella is conscious of her historicity and rejects the Anglo models that promote an alienation from reality, she demystifies Hollywood's philosophy of life and nonexistent fictive home:

ELLA: El peligro de eso es que una pueda terminar en una finca en Kansas. (P. 22)

Ella has her act together, lives forward, looking back at family values and the cultural meaning of the Latino home. In so doing, Ella can affirm her Latina historical subjectivity in order to position herself between the uprooted home and the yet-to-be-found home in exile: "Da gusto llegar al lugar que se va sin perder el camino" (p. 6).

Coser y cantar is a play that elaborates the construction of a Latina subjectivity in the United States. Through Ella, the struggle of bicultural individuals is exemplified, as is evidenced in the following testimonies from other Latino writers:

> I am two parts / a person
> boricua / spic
> past and present
> alive and oppressed
> given a cultural beauty
> . . . and robbed of a cultural identity.
> —Sandra María Esteves[20]

> My family came to Miami from Habana when I was 13, that means there are at least two sides to my personality—one that is conservative and relates to traditional beliefs, another side that is rebellious and secular.—Luis Santeiro[21]

> Consider me, if you choose, a comic victim of two cultures.
> —Richard Rodriguez[22]

These three voices (a Puerto Rican, a Cuban, and a Chicano) reveal a bicultural experience, a historical reality in which the Latino moves between two cultural spaces and historicities. However, it is up to each to see oneself as a political being who can determine, define, and articulate a discourse of oppositional consciousness of resistance, or simply silence one's ethnic culture into assimilation.

In *Coser y cantar*, Ella lives and feels continually her displacement, marginality, estrangement, and sense of loss; for this reason, she attempts to articulate, restore, and redefine her ethnicity—her identity and cultural past—before further dislocations occur. The contrapuntual and overlapping situation of two cultural realities, a marked divergence within a bicultural person, produces a dramatic tension/confrontation in Ella/ "She." On the one hand, she attempts to accomodate her Latina selfhood into the Anglo environment and, on the other, to adjust the Anglo ego into her Latina cultural past. The result is a series of vicissitudes, hesitancies, anxieties, discrepancies, differences, and wishes in the construction of her bicultural subjectivity. Ella, whose future in the U.S. remains vague unless she takes the "yellow brick road" to assimilation, assures a space for herself within the mental spaces of the past; but such displacement is not a reactionary nostalgia. Rather, Ella re-places her Latina identity at the axis of her historical present in the U.S., that is, at the crossroads of cultural frontiers. At this crux, the Anglo laws of assimilation collide with her Latina cultural survival instincts of disassociation, making her aware of the possibility of a terminal loss of Latino culture, memories, and past experiences. For this reason, Ella must re-construct a new subjectivity—a bilingual/bicultural self in constant making—who refuses to be decentered, discontinuous, displaced at the margin, but that is at the same time a body of differences, inconsistencies, gaps, and antinomies in the eyes of the Anglo culture. As a result of this collision, the Latina subject is constantly aware of experiencing two socio-cultural territories and living in two linguistic horizons.

NOTES

1   *Time*, July 14, 1986, "The Lady's Party," 10.

2   The media also promotes the "American dream" of "making it," especially in the case of Asian-Americans, who are supposed to be the "model minority" in the U.S. See the cover story in *USA Today*, June 12, 1987, "USA Marvels at Minority's Winning Way," p. 1.

3   It would be interesting to compare ethnic otherness in the U.S. with sci-fi minorities that are invented for the screen—Alf, E.T., Starman, Aliens—and how they displace/mediate what is different. Indeed, minorities are increasingly being replaced by the monster figure.

4   Dolores Prida's *testimonio*, "The Show Does Go On," in this text.

5   "Ella" is not the Anglo name but rather the Spanish subject pronoun meaning "She."

6   In this paper, all references to She—the character—shall be contained within quotation marks in order to distinguish the character from the pronoun, she.

7   Dolores Prida, *Coser y cantar: A one-act bilingual fantasy for two women*, (New York: n.p., 1981), i. All further references to this text shall be contained within parentheses after the cited passage. I wish to extend my appreciation to Dolores Prida for sharing all of her manuscripts with me in the preparation of this article.

8   There is no doubt that competitiveness in the U.S. is mediated in terms of sports; therefore, sportive competition constitutes a political discourse. For example, in *Newsweek*'s coverage of "Liberty Weekend" (July 14, 1986, 30), a new American citizen, originally from Japan, rationalized his success in the U.S. in terms of sports: "You can try for anything you want to" in America. He compared it to a boxing match: "You get in the boxing ring with the gloves on and [compete]

against someone. . . . In this country when you get knocked down you can get up and try again. You are given another chance." Such a statement also functions paradigmatically with Sylvester Stallone's *Rocky* movies.

9   "Assimilation occurs when a group or an entire society gradually adopt, or are forced into adopting, the customs, beliefs, folkways and lifestyles of a more dominant culture. At the intra-societal level, after a few generations of assimilation, minority members become culturally and physically indistinguishable from the mainstream of national life. Thus a policy of assimilation results in the virtual disappearance of the minority culture. At the inter-societal level, differences between cultures become eroded, diversity in lifestyles is reduced, traditional patterns tend to disappear and there is an irreversible push towards global homogeneity in cultural manifestations. . . . Advocates of assimilation may or may not realize that the policy implies a superiority of the majority culture relative to the minority, often to the extent of denying any work in the culture being absorbed. Groups undergoing assimilation do not find the process psychologically satisfying because of connotations of inferiority, self-rejection, and in extreme instances, self-hatred." Stephen Bochner, "The social psychology of cross-cultural relations," in *Cultures in Contact*, ed. Stephen Bochner (London: Pergamon Press, 1982), 24–25.

10   "Stereotypes determine our perception and judgement of others, and those who regard the content of such stereotypes as epi-phenomena, consequences rather than causes of existing inter-group relations . . . stereotypes are indeed shaped by social, economic, political and historical antecedents, and that they are used in order to justify the subjugation, exploitation and even elimination of others. They then serve as rationalizations of the *status quo*, permitting those in a position of power to persuade themselves, as Hooton (1937) puts it, that 'the act of grabbing is somehow noble and beautiful,' and they 'can rape in righteousness and murder in magnanimity'." Otto Klineberg, "Contact between ethnic groups: a historical perspective of some aspects of theory and research," *Cultures in Contact*, 48.

11   Juan Bruce-Novoa, *Imagenes e identidades: El puertorriqueño en la literatura*, ed. Asela Rodríguez de Laguna (Río Piedras, P.R.: Huracán, 1985). "Although binary positions fulfill the needs of scientific and pseudo-scientific thought, they have the counterproductive effect of characterizing the space between the two opposite poles as though it were a scale of measured values between positive and negative signs. As a result, any point between the poles receives the dubious classification of being less that the whole, of no longer being one thing, nor yet the other. . . . The intermediate phase is still not, or no longer, acceptable. The two languages remain in a state of opposition and being bilingual requires changing the codes of one language for those of another without mixing or integrating them. When there is anything less than a precise leap from one pole to another, it is classified as interference, with the negative connotations that this term implies. The space between any two languages is that forbidden territory, designated as "neither here nor there." Bruce-Novoa further specifies the dilemma that the hegemonic system of power imposes upon immigrants in USA: "A los inmigrantes se les juzga desde extremos opuestos y se proyectan sobre ellos las exigencias de las

estructuras. Se tornan en nativos menos que auténticos de ambos lados; su mera existencia se le considera como una interferencia y como una amenaza a la identidad de cada polo. Los intentos de desarrollar ciertas costumbres o modalidad de lenguaje dentro del ámbito en que se encuentra el inmigrante y que reflejen sus vivencias materiales e ideales, son rechazados por los puristas de uno y otro bando. Este dilema lo ilustran bien los inmigrantes mexicanos y puertorriqueños en los Estados Unidos" ("Immigrants are judged from opposite extremes . . . and they become less-than-authentic natives of both sides. Their very existence is considered a type of interference and a threat to the identity of each pole. Their efforts to develop certain customs or speech patterns which reflect their material and psychic circumstances within their new sphere are rejected by purists from both sides. Mexican and Puerto Rican immigrants to the U.S. are a good illustration of this dilemma"), 283.

12   Ella and "She" also alternate cultural wor(l)ds in the following scene:

SHE: . . . How about some steamed broccoli . . .
ELLA: . . . arroz . . .
SHE: . . . yogurt . . .
ELLA: . . . frijoles negros . . .
SHE: . . . bean sprouts . . .
ELLA: . . . plátanos fritos . . .
SHE: . . . wheat germ . . .
ELLA: . . . ensalada de aguacate . . .
SHE: . . . raw carrots . . .
ELLA: . . . flan!
SHE: . . . Granola!
ELLA: . . . Tal vez un arroz con pollo, o un ajiaco! (23–24)

13   "My mother once told me that life, especially for a woman was to sew and sing. And I believed it. But now I realize that everyone's life: men's, women's, dogs', cats', turtles', really is to eat and take a crap. In other words, the same old shit."

14   Also, Ella is de-mystifying the corniness of love relationships in boleros; such a double reading produces a humorous situation.

15   In another scene of confrontation, Ella complains of "She"'s presence and dependence on her: "(*Exasperated*) Ay, Dios mío, ¿qué habré hecho yo para merecérmela? ¡Es como tener un . . . un pingüino colgado del cuello!" (p. 8). Ironically, "She"—the Anglo—is compared to an animal who lives in the ice. The simile works as a catachresis for mediating the Anglo-American self.

16   In the opening scene of the play, "She" notices a story in the newspaper and points out the urban violence and crime scene: ". . . Three people have been shot already. For no reason at all. No one is safe out there. No one. Not even those who speak good English. Not even those who know who they are . . ." (p. 1).

17   Ella has moved twice before: Miami and New Jersey.

18   Ella verbalizes a few times her anxiety to find the map: "¿Dónde habré puesto el mapa?" (p. 5); "Tengo que encontrar ese mapa. Estoy decidida" (p. 21).

19   Bruce-Novoa states the following on assimilation: "Assimilation into another culture is a form of death for those who fear losing their own culture. True, it could be seen as a necessary process for entering the receiving society, but those forced to change may not be convinced. The melting-pot ideal is fine for those who have forgotten the excruciating pain of being melted down and repoured into a different mold. Nor does it make it easier to be told by others that their ancestors endured the same thing," in *Chicano Poetry: A Response to Chaos* (Austin: University of Texas Press, 1982), 8–9.

20   Sandra María Esteves, *Yerba Buena* (Greenfield Center, N.Y.: Greenfield Review Press, 1980), 20.

21   Luis Santeiro, *Intar Now*, no. 3 (Spring/Summer 1987): 1.

22   Richard Rodriguez, *Hunger of Memory* (Boston: Godine, 1982), 5.

Part IV. Latinoamericanas from Other Countries

A Cuban-Panamanian-American-Lawyer-Writer
Now in Connecticut

(Testimonio)

BESSY REYNA

(To Susan,
without whose endless encouragement
I would not be here.)

Whenever someone asks me, "Where are you from?"—I always respond, "Panama." In my case, the place where I was born, Cuba, seems to have had very little connection to the rest of my life. I grew up in Panama; my memories and emotional ties will be always linked to Panama. When I was a small child, my parents decided to leave pre-revolutionary Cuba in search of better employment opportunities and a more peaceful environment. Once we left, I had very little contact with most of my relatives. We never went back to visit. More than ten years passed before I saw my grandfather, who, at seventy-five years of age and on a whim, convinced the revolutionary bureaucracy to let him travel to Panama on the plane carrying the Cuban baseball team, en route to play exhibition games. My father, an avid baseball fan, happened to go to the airport that day "just in case someone I know has joined the delegation." He came home with Grandpa, a surprise I will never forget. Grandpa stayed a week, long enough to make me wonder what it would have been like growing up with him, his tenderness and sense of humor around.

Not having an extended family means having the freedom to choose one's associations. Friendship is very important to me. My best friend from elementary school and I have maintained a relationship that is the closest to having a sister I will ever know.

My upbringing is reflected in my writing, particularly in my short stories. I don't write about family issues; my characters are individuals who meet one another and develop interpersonal relationships; what happens between them is what I am interested in writing about. Having had to say goodbye to so many things so many times in my life has also had an impact on what I write.

It is hard for me to figure out exactly when I started to write. I seem to remember it was in high school during a class. I was so bored, and by then I had finished selecting the signature I would use as an adult, which was usually what I did when I was bored. Signatures are very important in Panama. I used to try to design the *M* in a certain way and the *R* in another way. Maybe developing my signature was my first act of creative writing. We had no encouragement in our school when it came to any artistic endeavor. Art classes were not part of the curriculum. Literature was taught without joy or energy, and we were never required to read contemporary authors. One day I wrote a poem and soon, writing in the middle of a class, while pretending to pay attention to the teacher, became commonplace for me. I really can't remember what it was that I wrote so much about.

There was a library close to my home. I decided to walk in one day, and left with one book, and then others, to the point that going there became part of my daily life. The staff grew to know me and even saved books for me. The books were followed by records. I would borrow both the scripts and the music of a Broadway musical and sit at home, imagining people dancing in colorful costumes. I had never seen a live production, but my father used to take the family to the movies every Sunday. I can't remember the first musical I ever saw. I do remember, however, closing my eyes, listening to the music, and creating my own choreography—of course, without understanding a word of the lyrics in English. Maybe at this time I started developing the imagination that would enable me to write at a later date.

The first consistent writing I did was in a diary someone gave me for my fourteenth birthday. I wrote something every night, creating secret codes, lessening the possibility of giving away any secret. In it, I kept track of movies, things I did or wished for, my "crushes." When the first one was full, I wrote in notebooks. One day, when I was feeling very grown up, I threw them away. Later on, the closest I would ever get to keeping a diary was when I first arrived in the United States. The letters I sent home, I later discovered, were full of descriptions, people, places, the seasons, and my excitement and anxiety at suddenly being surrounded by such a different culture and environment while speaking in a language little known to me till then. One day, while helping my mother clean up her room, I came across all those letters that seemed to pop out of every drawer and, as before, I threw them away. "They belong to me," she kept saying, "you have no right to do that!" It didn't matter. Once again, I was willing to discard my memories.

The first thing I ever published was a poem. One of my best friends had died of leukemia at the age of sixteen. My closest friends and I seemed incapable of speaking about her. It was too painful; something was never the same between us because we were always so aware of her absence. The five of us had always spent our time together, meeting daily after school, hanging out during weekends. One afternoon I went to the cemetery, sitting alone in front of her grave, imagining her pain before her death, remembering the last moments spent together. I went home and wrote, and my writing was different this time. Through the process of writing that poem, I learned to communicate with others without their being present. My life was changed by her death; I suddenly became very aware of how fragile happiness could be. The way I spent my time from then on, what I read, how I perceived things, was transformed.

Becoming a writer in Panama, a country where art is not encouraged, where publishing houses do not exist, and where literary magazines are not published on a regular basis, is extremely difficult. Most writers in Panama publish their work in the few literary pages appearing in newspapers or, if they can afford it, through private printings of their books. After the publication of my first poem, I started to submit poems, short stories, and reviews of cultural events to the newspapers with some frequency. Later on, I would also participate in poetry readings and joined the University of Panama's theater group, which presented plays by American and European writers, and which was invited, in cultural exchange programs, to tour other Latin American countries. I volunteered to edit the literary page in the newspaper, *El Dominical;* I called it *An-ai Purba,* which, in the language of the Cuna Indians of Panama, means "the soul of my friend." During the months that I edited this page, I contacted high school teachers in an effort to encourage young writers to submit their work, and provided a consistent forum for well-known Panamanian writers to publish. Even though I did this work on a volunteer basis, I spent many hours at the newspaper, helping the staff in the design of the page and selecting the material. While working on this, I was also given the opportunity—by the owners of a radio station, willing to donate the air time—to produce a weekly radio show. Roberto Fernández-Iglesias (a writer and close friend) and I developed the format for the show, in which we conducted interviews with local artists and provided news and commentary on local arts events. So, from having grown up without any artistic encouragement or background, I found myself, just a few years after my high school graduation, surrounded by people whose main interest in life was the arts, but who had to make a living mostly as teachers, administrators, or office workers.

To me, being a writer is more than just isolating myself to create something. It also means joining others in helping to create an environment where people can learn to appreciate, enjoy, and participate in the arts. In some way, the same motivation that led me to edit the literary page in Panama resurfaced when I was asked to join a group trying to create *El Taller Literario,* the first Hispanic arts and literature magazine in Connecticut. Once again, I am in the middle of a group of artists and writers, doing volunteer work to provide a bilingual forum for Hispanics in Connecticut and other states, where they can publish their work; organizing poetry readings and art shows for the community, and trying to share our culture with a larger audience.

I first came to the United States to study. I wanted to leave Panama for a while, be on my own. I was tired of the sexism and double standard that is so typical of our culture. I was lucky enough to have been granted a scholarship to study at Mount Holyoke College. I arrived, not knowing anything about the school or the town, having never studied in English before, and fully intending to return at the end of one year. Shortly after my arrival, a coup d'etat imposed a military regime in Panama. Some of my friends were exiled, and the political climate was changed significantly. I stayed, earning a B.A. at Mount Holyoke, an M.A. and a J.D. at the University of Connecticut. During most of my graduate student days I was involved with the local chapter of Amnesty International, as well as with a group of women trying to force the university's administration to establish a Women's Center. It was a long struggle that we eventually won. After the Women's Center was established, a group of us formed the writers' collective and published several issues of *Erato,* a feminist poetry magazine.

Both of my books were published while I was already living in the United States. *Terrarium,* a book of poetry, appeared in 1975, and, in 1978, *Ab Ovo,* a collection of short stories, was published by the Instituto Nacional de Arte y Cultura (INAC) in Panama. Some controversy surrounded *Ab Ovo* simply because one of the stories dealt with homosexuality, and other stories had gender-neutral narrators. Whether the character was a man or a woman was for the reader to decide. Because in Panama there is no literary criticism as such, it is hard for me to apply American standards to whether it was "well received." I know people bought it, and some of the stories were reprinted in both Latin American literary magazines and

Panamanian newspapers. Both volumes contain work written in Panama and Connecticut. The loneliness I felt during my first months in the U.S.A., being completely isolated from everything I had known—my culture, friends, and family—is, I now realize, very much reflected in some of the short stories. Other changes in my life—my involvement with the feminist movement and with social issues—are also reflected.

A few years ago I decided to become a United States citizen. It was a very hard choice to make. I felt as if I were saying goodbye to a part of me, making a commitment to remain in a country whose past and current foreign policy in Latin America opposes everything I believe. I know that I will never be able to be fully integrated into American society. As gender differences exist between men and women, so do ethnic and cultural differences. They will always be with me, no matter where I go. My past shapes my present, leaping out in front of me sometimes in the form of a question when, in the middle of a conversation, someone says, "I detect a slight accent, where are you from?" Somehow, the longer I live in the United States, the more obvious my differences become. Those differences will always be reflected in my writing and in how I live my life.

Even though I have been in the United States for nearly twenty years, until recently I only wrote in Spanish. Strangely enough, during one of my last visits to Panama, I started writing a short story in English. Maybe the need to find some privacy while staying at my parents' apartment, or being able to block out the noise surrounding me, helped me concentrate better in another language. Whatever the reason, I now find myself being more comfortable writing in English. Now, the language I choose for a story depends on the tone or the rhythm of the story.

Until now, I never felt the need to translate my work. I participated mostly in Spanish-language poetry readings, and I continued to publish in Spanish. In November 1986, I was invited to join a group of Central American women writers for a bilingual poetry reading in St. Mark's Church, in New York City. As I walked into the church, I had no idea that close to three hundred people were waiting indoors to hear us and to show their solidarity for the people of Central America. I had never read my work in front of such a large bilingual audience. After reading a poem in Spanish, I would get a response from the Spanish-speaking crowd; then a second wave, just as responsive, would follow the poem in English. It was one of the most exciting experiences I have had in a long time. I felt the same response from audiences in Boston and Cambridge. This experience taught me that feminist and political issues are the same, regardless of language. Up to that moment, I had always wondered whether my work was culturally limited.

There are many things I hope to write about. One of my favorite things to do is to write late into the night while observing the light changing towards dawn. Having a full-time job and many other commitments rarely allows me that pleasure. I now write while the commuter bus takes me to and from work. I observe the passengers and wonder what type of work they do. The groups are very different, depending on which bus I take. I am pretty sure that my next story is going to be about them.

Coventry, Connecticut
June 1987

An Oral History

(Testimonio)

SHEREZADA (CHIQUI) VICIOSO

I started writing when I was very young and found out that the best way to pass Math was to write a poem to the teacher. . . . I began to become aware of the marginalized people in my country when I was an adolescent and worked in the barrios as part of a Christian youth volunteer group. Basically I am a poet, but I also write criticism about women's literature. I began to write in 1978 and published my first book of poetry, *Viajes desde el agua*, in 1981.

Up until about 1977, I regarded literature as a hobby of the petite bourgeoisie, but when I went to Cuba and spoke there with writers whom I very much admired, they showed me that a writer is also a cultural worker. Whereas I took note of this fact on an intellectual level, I realized it on an emotional one only when I went to Africa in 1978. I started writing criticism from 1982 on and published my second book in 1985 (*Un extraño ulular traía el viento*).

Both my books were written for Dominicans and were published in Santo Domingo. I never thought of publishing in the United States because, as a Latina, I felt unable to deal with the publishing establishment in that country. My first book was presented at the Las Américas bookshop and other places for Latinos in New York. After all, New York is the second most important city for Dominicans. The island has six million

The above interview with Dominican poet Chiqui Vicioso was taped and subsequently translated by Nina M. Scott at the Segundo Congreso de Creación Femenina, University of Mayagüez, Puerto Rico, on Nov. 17, 1987. Sincere thanks go to the staff of the University of Mayagüez who aided in the making of the tape.

inhabitants and half a million live in New York. Economically, it's the most important. I never felt far from Santo Domingo when I lived in New York.

I first came to the United States in April 1967. Initially, I had wanted to be a lay nun and work in the barrios. Marriage repelled me, especially when I looked at my aunts, practically all of whom were divorced. I couldn't stand the idiocy of the whole scene: the danger of getting mixed up with someone when you were thirteen or fourteen, worrying about not having a boyfriend when you were sixteen. To me, becoming a nun was my path to freedom. I also wanted to study medicine. The one year I planned to stay eventually became seventeen.

My mother, who had left a year earlier, said I should go to the States in order to improve my English and to get to know the world before embarking on becoming a nun. I was very angry with her at the time, but she was right.

I come from a very special family with an intellectual background. On my father's side, my grandfather was a journalist and a writer, and my father is a poet and a well-known composer. My mother is a better poet than I am, but has never dared to write. She is the daughter of a peasant woman who worked in a tobacco factory and a Dominican oligarch who owned the factory and literally bought her when she was sixteen. My mother is a hybrid of two very distinct classes. I felt this when I went to school in Santiago.

In spite of having studied English in school, I found out, on my arrival in New York, that I didn't know very much. Like most Dominicans who come to the United States, I went to work in a factory: first a hat, and then a button factory (the acetone in which we had to wash the buttons damaged my eyes so that I have had to wear glasses ever since). I went to night school for a while, and then was accepted into a city-sponsored intensive English program, where I was paid to study.

My next job was as a telephone operator, and I quickly acquired a reputation as being extremely courteous to the customers, as my English still wasn't all that good and I said "Thank you" to everyone, even if they insulted me. Then Brooklyn College opened its doors to minority students. They responded to a policy, initiated under the Johnson administration, whereby colleges were paid federal funds to admit minorities. I was one of eight Dominican students admitted to Brooklyn College.

Since there were only eight of us, and it was very tough to survive in such a racist atmosphere, we joined up with other minority students, principally Puerto Ricans, Blacks, other people from the Caribbean—we formed a Third World Alliance.

This was a real threshold for me; I had never known the people from

Barbados or Trinidad, etc. My concept of the Caribbean, up to that time, had been limited to the Spanish-speaking part, and I discovered my identity as a *caribeña* in New York.

I was also racially classified at Brooklyn College, which was an interesting experience for me. In Santo Domingo, the popular classes have a pretty clear grasp of racial divisions, but the middle and upper-middle classes are very deluded on this point. People straighten their hair and marry "in order to improve the race," etc., etc., and don't realize the racist connotations of their language or their attitude. In the United States, there is no space for fine distinctions of race, and one goes from being "trigüeño" or "indio" to being "mulatto" or "Black" or "Hispanic." This was an excellent experience for me. From that point on, I discovered myself as a Caribbean *mulata* and adopted the Black identity as a gesture of solidarity. At that time, I deeply admired and identified with Angela Davis, and ever since then, I have kept on identifying myself as a Black woman.

This opened another door; I learned about Frantz Fanon and other Caribbean theoreticians, and that finished Europe for me. I learned about the triangular trade and how we had financed Europe's development. I realized that capitalism was an impossible model to follow in our development. For me, this was discovering a universe. I only became a feminist much later.

When I first became more radical I was very much put off by feminism and people like Gloria Steinem and Betty Friedan—to me they were representatives of the white U.S. middle class who were busy telling us how *we* were being screwed by machismo. In a first stage I rejected this and, up to a point, I also had a false sense of solidarity with our men, who were racially oppressed as well. I felt that if we women criticized our men, we were only providing the racists with ammunition. This created a conflict of loyalties for me.

Discovering myself as a woman came much later. First I had to discover that I was part of a certain geographical area, and then, that I was Latin American. The great majority of the Latin American exiles converged on New York at that time—the Argentinians, the Uruguayans, the Chileans (Allende fell during those years)—so that, for me, New York became a kind of great doorway to this Latin American world.

Being in New York was very essential to my development. I would not be the woman I am today had I not gone to New York. I would have been the classic *fracasada* (failure) in my country because I know that I would not have found happiness in marriage and having children. I would have been frustrated, unhappy in a marriage, or divorced several times over because

I would not have understood that within me was a woman who needed to express her own truths, articulate her own words. That, in Santo Domingo, would have been impossible.

Nevertheless, for the first ten years that I lived in New York, I was engulfed by a great silence; I could write nothing at all. The only poem I salvaged from this era was one about two young Puerto Ricans, aged sixteen and seventeen, who were shot by a bartender they had robbed of $100. I saw an article about it in the paper and it made me terribly sad. The poem ends with the line, "sadness has never come so cheaply." New York was, for me, a crushing kind of silence.

Still, all these experiences were being stored up inside of me. It's that kind of a process; things go in stages.

It was going to Africa that restored my essence as a *caribeña* for me. I went for three and a half months to work on coordinating the first meeting of ministers of education of the Portuguese-speaking African nations, and discovered Amílcar Cabral, the outstanding African cultural and revolutionary theoretician. Up to that point, I had never understood the important role that culture plays in effecting change. This was a central experience for me.

When I returned to the States, I was a different person; I suffered from severe depressions, which I now realize marked the death of one Chiqui and the birth of another. I figured the only thing that could save me was to return to the university, so I decided, at that point, to get an M.A. in Education from Columbia. I tried to work one more year in New York, but it was no good, and I returned to Santo Domingo.

I was there for four years, until last year, when I returned to the States. Some very difficult things happened during that time. The man with whom I had planned to restructure my life died of cancer. I was working terribly hard in my job as an educational coordinator. Basically, I had a kind of breakdown. I returned to the States to recuperate, and then went back to Santo Domingo. I've been there three months now.

I have really wanted to be a literary critic, yet once again I am denying my condition as a writer. The African experience had awakened me to the terrible problem of illiteracy in my country; 40% of the population is totally illiterate, another 40%, functionally so. I've always moved in this atmosphere of crisis and tension [between the two drives in my life]. Even now, I am teaching not literature but a course on Dominican education at the university.

I had to go back to Santo Domingo because, after a few years, living in the United States gave me a kind of physical malaise. . . . When you first get here from your country, full of strength and energy, you get involved in a first stage of learning, absorbing, discovering. Then comes a time when you have to go back in order to revitalize yourself. If you stay in New York too long, you begin to get worn down by it. Anyone who is in the least sensitive can't help but feel bruised by the destruction of our people. Really. I saw it all the time in the Dominican community. Even though I had already acquired all sorts of New York rituals—I took perfumed baths in a flowered bathtub, swallowed my B 12 vitamins, was into meditation—none of it was doing me any good. I realized I had to leave.

The New York experience, which was so crucial to my discovery of my Caribbean and racial identity, has made me a very, very critical person with respect to my own society. Things I never noticed before, I now see. Like racism, for example. Class differences. Santo Domingo is a very societally structured city. The situation of women is atrocious. I get almost rude about this because I can't stand the kind of sexist behavior that exists in my country. And for that, you pay the price of ostracism. It's really hard. By dint of having lived in the United States, I am considered a "liberated woman," which means that the men feel they have a green light to harass me sexually while the women distrust me. That's the most painful part. You come back to your country with a sense of intimate relationship and find that, for the most part, the principal *machistas* are the women themselves. And that's terrible. You find yourself confronted by an immense hostility that is a product of their own frustration. At first you ask yourself, "what have you done to this woman to have her treat you like this?" And then you realize that you symbolize all the things that she has never been able to do, and perhaps never will: leave the country, study what she wants to. She may find herself tied down by three or four children, a husband that bores her, physical confinement, etc.; and you come along as a woman who can come and go as she wishes, write, be creative and productive, freely elect the man she wants to be with, and you become, for her, an object of hatred. It's really dreadful. And with the men, you represent a challenge to try and get you because you're different, but the real challenge is to dominate you. For the women, you are all they cannot be and that must be destroyed for survival. And you have to understand that so that you don't self-destruct. You can laugh off the first two or three aggressions, but by the fourth time, it really hurts.

As a writer I haven't yet been able to talk about my experiences in the States. At some moment in the future I will. Remember that New York was an experience of great silence for me. I feel that a time will come when I will be able to surmount what happened to me in New York and will be able to write about it. Remember, too, that the things I'm telling you in such a light vein today were wrenching experiences for me, especially discrimination. I still can't talk about it, but because I now have a better understanding of the creative process, I have learned not to push the creative instincts so that they won't become artificial. I know I have to let things come to the surface. The time will come when I'll be able to do it. I've written some sociological essays and some journalistic pieces on New York for a Santo Domingo paper in order to let my people know what's happening there, but in terms of literature I haven't yet been able to draw out what I have inside.

Because so many of my potential readers live in New York, I am definitely moving more and more toward publishing in the United States. I think people on the island would be interested as well. . . . We cannot avoid the "invasion" of the Dominicans from the U.S. The whole country is changing: English is spoken all over—you feel the influence of the Dominicans who come back everywhere. I also think there will be interest in my writing in the States, first of all, because there are so many of us there, and second, because I will approach things with the particular viewpoint of a woman. I have a lot to tell about what New York did to my family. I had to assume a kind of paterfamilias role with respect to my siblings. A lot of it was very traumatic.

However, for the moment I'm more interested in women's issues, and especially in testimonials by Dominican women. I'm working on a book that is a collection of women's testimonials from the four years when I was here earlier. I've collected testimonials from all classes of women: peasants, factory workers, etc. I would like to be the voice of those who have no voice. Later, I'll be able to speak about New York.

In Santo Domingo there is a need to create a market for women's literature. As women, we have not yet discovered our power as consumers of books, but some day, when we discover this, perhaps we'll manifest this power by supporting women who write.

Marjorie Agosín as Latina Writer

NINA M. SCOTT

Eight of Marjorie Agosín's poems are included in the recently published anthology *Nosotras: Latina Literature Today* (Binghamton, N.Y.: Bilingual Review/Press, 1986), a collection of writings that, as the preface states, "focuses on the creative literature of United States Hispanic women. Contributions are present from all of the major U.S. Hispanic groups and a wide range of socioeconomic levels and walks of life."[1] Based on the biographical sketches of the contributors, Agosín appears to be the only Latin American author included in this anthology. The very fact that she figures there at all leads one to envision a rapprochement in the sometimes problematic relations between Latina writers and their Latin American counterparts.

Marjorie Agosín was born in the United States to Chilean parents; she subsequently lived in Chile until the age of fifteen. Although a permanent resident of the United States, she considers herself, first and foremost, a Chilean and devotes considerable time and energy to maintaining her contact with Chile. "I live a schizophrenic life because I live in two countries," she says of herself.[2] She is a writer who has been formed by two cultures and who has been able to achieve success in both. In terms of publication, she is even more international, as her books have appeared in the U.S., Chile, Spain, Mexico, Canada, and England. A closer look at her work serves to illustrate two important subjects: the particular role of a South American author writing from within the United States, and the broader issue of the relationship between Latin American and Latina literature.

In the case of Marjorie Agosín, a combination of unique factors has enabled her to function in two countries and two cultures. The fact that Agosín is a citizen of the United States is very important to her work, for it means that, in spite of her strongly stated opposition to the Pinochet regime, she is able to visit Chile whenever she wishes, enjoying a kind of political immunity not shared by other Chileans in exile. And although Agosín has always passionately identified with her country and writes exclusively in Spanish, she was young enough, when she returned to the United States, to understand this culture and avoid the profound cultural shock from which many of the older exiles suffered.[3] Another important aspect of her particular context is the fact that she completed her higher education in this country and holds a position on the faculty of Wellesley College; the salary she earns there, plus access to academic grants, facilitates her frequent returns to Chile and her ability to keep in touch with that culture, in spite of her now-prolonged residence within the United States.

Agosín shares with Latina writers the status of permanent resident in this country: the voluntary distancing from the dominant Anglo culture and the identification with a Latin heritage. However, in spite of these factors, Spanish-speaking minority writers have not always welcomed her as one of their own. As Eliana Ortega observed in her article on "Hispanic" writers in the United States, most minority women writers identify with the Third World and the working class, voluntarily designating themselves "women of color" as a sign of their marginalization and oppression by the dominant culture.[4] From this perspective they are also distrustful of many Latin American women, seeing them as belonging to the upper classes, an élite that has benefited from both economic privilege and higher education, concluding, therefore, that these women should be excluded from the same context as themselves. As the editors of *Cuentos: Stories by Latinas* stated in the foreword to their anthology:

> The question remains . . . to what extent can most Latin American women writers be considered our literary legacy when so many, like their male counterparts, are at least functionally middle-class, ostensibly white, and write from a male-identified perspective. . . . Class, race, and education, however, as it combines with sex, are much more critical in silencing the would-be Latina writers than discrimination on sex alone.[5]

Marjorie Agosín is fully cognizant of the fact that the fundamental differences between feminist movements in Latin America and the United States rest on factors of class as opposed to gender; she states that the feminist movements of the industrialized world are:

> of the privileged class . . ., composed of women who, for the most part, suffer oppression because of their *sex* but not be-

cause of their class. In Latin America, it is exactly the opposite. . . . Feminism in the Third World . . . is born of a
consciousness of class and is therefore political in origin. It
goes without saying that the liberation of rural women or
working women will not come out of a criticism against men,
who are more or less as oppressed as they are, but will emerge
from a radical, cultural change in the class structure and that
change will have to come directly from women themselves
and not from outside forces or influences.[6]

Agosín would seem to typify the kind of middle- or upper-class
woman that the Latina writers refused to recognize as one of their own.
She has never been economically disadvantaged nor suffered personally
from racial discrimination. However, she does identify closely with many
of the same socio-political issues as the Latina writers. Much like other
privileged women of Latin America (Rosario Castellanos and Elena Poniatowska come immediately to mind), Agosín has felt a strong sense of
responsibility to speak out on behalf of the women of her culture who
have been silenced by dint of class, race, and gender. However, there are
those who would say that even this desire to articulate the voice of another
less privileged woman is an indication of elitism, leaving writers, such as
Agosín, in a catch-22 situation. The problem she faces can be clearly seen
in this early poem, in which she indicates for whom it is she wishes to
write:

> Quién es el público
> señora Mónica?
> serán las doncellas de
> las tazas de té?
>
> . . . .
> Tal vez son la
> Menchu, la Antonia
> y la Julia
> pelando papas
> escuchando la
> estrofa.
>
> Dónde leer?
> en un hotel?
> donde una vez al año,
> se reunen a disecar
> la controversia de la
> imagen fálica del
> lupanar y el bastón?

Leer?
en una costra de papel?

Pero me decido
a que me lean
en un bus
cerca del matadero
y la procesión.[7]

The above example serves to underscore the ironic dilemma in which she finds herself; in spite of wishing to bridge the gap between herself and women of other classes, the very vocabulary she uses to express herself is already a distancing factor.

At the 1982 conference on Latin American Women Writers in the Five College area, Agosín came under verbal fire from some of the participating Latina writers with whom she was on a panel on "Hispanic Literature in the U.S." Accused of being "privileged" and "bourgeois," she was told that she had nothing in common with minority writers. Recalling the event, she asks, "What were they asking me to do? Deny my background? I never picked cotton. I can't write as though I had."[8] Apart from this verbal encounter, there were other manifestations of exclusion: rejection of some of her early work by minority presses and journals, as well as noninclusion in certain meetings or panels dealing with literature written in Spanish in the United States. In response to the exclusion she was experiencing, she wrote the satirical "Defensa de la burguesa":

No fui reina del adobe. Nací en casa de cemento, con
un perímetro de jardín imaginado. No pasé hambre, ni
tuberculosis, no tuve piojos en mi dorado cabello.
Sufrí de Smog, me quebré un pie esquiando, pasé
alergias y neurosis, sufrí indigestiones y abortos.

Nací rubia para luego reforzar el color de los elegidos
colonos del cono sur.

Vestí interioridades de seda, sombreros de tul y turquesas
en el vientre. Asistí regularmente al dentista para limpiar
el ripio de mi ser.

Aprendí el Pop y el Rock. Aunque quería bailar cueca y
hacer el amor a un guerrillero frondoso. . . .

. . . .
Me fui a vivir con los indios, y con Ernesto, pero ellos
expulsaron a la princesa rubia de su santo reino.[9]

This type of rejection seems to have diminished in the past few years, as shown by the inclusion of Agosín's poems in anthologies such as *Nosotras*, whose three editors are of Chicana, Puerto Rican, and Cuban background. Nevertheless, the issue of the inclusion or exclusion of works by Latin American writers within the context of "U.S. Latina literature" has not yet been fully resolved.

There have been a number of well-known Latin American women writers who have lived and written in the United States for extended periods of time. Gabriela Mistral, María Luisa Bombal, and Marta Traba are examples of an older generation, while some of the contemporary writers include Luisa Valenzuela, Lucía Guerra Cunningham, Bessy Reyna, and Cecilia Vicuña, to name a few. Their reasons for choosing to reside in the United States are varied: forced or self-chosen political exile, jobs with far better salaries than in their own countries, spouses or "significant others" whose work keeps them in this country. Some of these women write mainly or exclusively in Spanish and consciously direct their work toward a readership in their own country. Others write in both languages and publish both in the United States and Latin America.[10] The extent of their commitment to, or reaction against, U.S. culture varies.

A look at the evolution of Marjorie Agosín's work may reveal some of the factors that account for her increasing acceptance by Latina writers. A comparison of her early poetry with her most recent works shows an increasing tendency to move from fairly restricted reference points to ones that are much more universal. Principally known as a poet, she is also a literary critic and essayist, with books on Pablo Neruda, María Luisa Bombal, and six Chilean woman writers. She is an outspoken feminist and activist, especially on behalf of the mothers of the *detenidos-desaparecidos* in Chile; with respect to the latter, Agosín has written and lectured widely about the *arpilleristas*, the women who have used folk embroideries as a means of making personal statements against the abuse of human rights in their country:

> Por medio de los rústicos hilos se preserva una memoria colectiva, escrita-cosida por aquellas anónimas y tantas veces ignoradas mujeres. Ellas, al dar cada puntada, se arriesgan, al igual que la escritora que en cada palabra se atreve a ser ella y a decir su verdad.[11]

The aforementioned trajectory, from the specific to the general, can be seen quite clearly in her poetry, as well as a process of moving away from an almost exclusive identification with Chile to a more multifacetic cultural approach. The titles of her earliest works reflect this predominant preoccupation with her South American roots: *Chile: gemidos y cantares* (1977) and the subsequent *Conchalí* (1980), whose title refers to a poor section of Santiago. In these works, there are multiple references to particular geographic locations in Chile, as well as to specific persons related to this world: poets such as Pablo Neruda and Nicanor and Violeta Parra, and rural women such as Antonia Pérez, la Menchu, and la Julia. A good example of this early trend is her "Canto a los profesores de literatura en los Estados Unidos," which explains the significance of Isla Negra, a place closely associated with Pablo Neruda:

> Les contaré que
> la Isla Negra
> no es isla ni
> es negra
> tampoco San Remo
> ni la estatua de la libertad.
> Es un pueblo cerca de San Antonio
> en la quintísima región
> donde se come borda y baila
> y a las cinco de la tarde
> se hace el amor.[12]

In order to grasp the full significance of this stanza of the poem, some knowledge of Chilean geography and culture is essential. For example, Isla Negra is the name of a town on the coast in what the government has officially designated as the fifth geographical region, and is also a place where women produce folk embroideries that have become very famous in Chile.[13]

Four years later, Agosín published a bilingual edition of her poetry, *Brujas y algo más/Witches and Other Things* (1984), translated very ably by Cola Franzen. The very fact that she decided to publish a bilingual edition already signals the fact that she was aiming to reach a reading public that was not exclusively Chilean, or even Spanish-speaking. Nevertheless, the Chilean presence is still very strong, and the nostalgia of exile is a predominant theme:

> Mi país es un astillero
> anclado dentro de mí
> curvándose por entre
> las rodillas y la piel
> aún húmeda de sol.
> Mi país es una frazada de estrellas como viruelas
> una rapsodia de voces nulas

que aparecen para penar a la luna
por el pellejo raptado
a plena luz.

. . . .

Mi país
es mi casa con las llaves
ocultas esperándome,
en la playa.[14]

As opposed to Latin America, the "ready-made" culture of the United States is not viewed kindly ("trepaste hasta la vía andina / para llenarte de cobres, cromosomas, de fusil") but its effect is undeniable and inescapable:

Me paseo por Managua, San Salvador
por la Avenida Providencia en Santiago de Chile
y todos vestimos botas de Cowboy
en un sordo diálogo de Rock and Roll.[15]

Many of the poems in this collection have an overt political emphasis and speak to the abuses of human rights in Chile: the torture and mutilation of human beings, as well as the political prisoners who disappear without a trace within the labyrinths of state bureaucracy. This is exemplified in "Mi nación y los sistemas de correo":

Dirección Insuficiente
casa deshabitada
voló como paloma en soledad
Ausente
Fallecido
Mutilado
Rehusado
Desconocido en los círculos sin salida
No existe tal nombre
DESAPARECIDO.[16]

In spite of foregrounding the situation in Chile, in Brujas Agosín begins to move to a more universal plane when she establishes a parallel with events of the Holocaust: "Oyéme Ana Frank / ¿en verdad creías que todos los hombres eran buenos?"[17] She also speaks to the victimization of the female body in other parts of the world, such as the gang rape of a young woman in a tavern in New Bedford, Mass.: "y ahora como una carne en una carnicería de velorios, / amarrada a la mesa de billar / Ella duerme desnuda."[18] In all of these situations of human victimization, Agosín's strategy is the same: "Yo soy hembra sin fusil / pequeña y de cabellos azules como el ácido . . . / yo juro apoderarme de la palabra / ir con ella por los muros de la ciudad / ir con ella donde anduvo el látigo. . . ."[19]

The appropriation of the word, and of the power to speak out, applies to two other topics as well: sacrosanct literature and female sexuality. In "Boom" she discusses, and to some degree debunks, such canonized authors as Nicanor Parra, Cortázar ("la Maga / . . . érase un poco cursi"), and Borges ("Yo nunca he visto / a ninguno de los dos Borges") while praising María Luisa Bombal ("¿por qué no la leyeron?") and Violeta Parra.[20] The note of female eroticism is another constant in Agosín's poetry:

> Comentan que mis versos
> son eróticos-falocráticos-obscenéticos
> atrévanse no más
> digan la verdad
> soy una poeta caliente
> aficionada a las uvas
> y al tinto.[21]

She is also a destroyer of myths, especially of fairy tales: Snow White ("A Blanca Nieves los enanos / no la tuvieron de adorno"), Little Red Riding Hood ("La Caperucita Roja / tuvo que dormir con un lobo"), and Cinderella ("Quereres"), who had enormous feet[22] and was obliged to be eternally grateful to a man who gave her one shoe and a little bit extra: "el zapato bien le quedó / y esa otra cosa también cupo."[23]

Her latest collections of poetry—*Hogueras* (1986), the poems included in *Nosotras*, and *Mujeres de humo* (1987)—continue with many of the subjects previously mentioned: female sexuality, political protest, and the iconoclasm of myths. But her recent poems are more personally introspective, more serious, and less nationalistic in tone. The fact that both books have already been translated into English and at this writing are due out shortly attests to her appeal to a non-Latin readership; furthermore, *Hogueras* will be published by the Bilingual Review/Press, another indication of Agosín's acceptance as a Latina writer.

Illustrative of her shift toward more global parameters are two poems dealing with the Plaza de Mayo. In "A las locas de la Plaza de Mayo," she takes the Mothers out of their exclusively Argentine context in order to underscore the tragic universality of their grief ("las locas de la Plaza de Mayo / en Buenos Aires, en El Salvador, / en Treblinka"),[24] whereas "Invierno en la Plaza de Mayo" is a love poem with no political references whatever:

Tú también sigues
el destino de mis
manos,
en este día
donde las aves
cantan
en la
Plaza
de Mayo."[25]

Her fascination with the reinterpretation of myths is another constant, especially those that have played a significant role in the determination of women's roles. She takes on Eve/Mary, Don Juan, and the phallus itself; given her interest in the interrelationship between texts and textiles, Agosín is attracted to Ariadne and Penelope, the women weavers of classical Greek mythology. The relationship between Ulysses and his faithful wife is developed in two separate poems. In "Penélope I," Ulysses is the archetypal wandering husband; if it isn't Circe, it's Eurydice, "y Ud. teje y desteje / las horas de la soledad / la ausencia sin piedad." The poet advises her to stop being exploited and to start rebelling: "oiga doña Penélope, / avívese, / y por lo menos venda / una bufandita."[26] "Penélope II" is more somber in tone:

Penélope,
destejiendo una mentira,

. . . .

Penélope,
esposa del insomnio
no tejas regresos
porque hoy nadie
vuelve de
Itaca.[27]

If one examines the topics of many of the other Latina authors from *Nosotras*, especially the section on "Oppression" and "Galanes," it is evident how closely Agosín's verses tie in with their concerns, precisely because she has moved away from the specific and local to a more universal *Weltanschauung*. This is also true with respect to her allegiance to her roots. Rather than defining her homeland strictly in terms of Chile (cf. the earlier "Lejos"), or even Latin America, her outlook now extends beyond national boundaries precisely because she speaks from a woman's perspective:

Mi país
es el aire tan
nuestro
en las noches fugitivas
de Atitlán

. . . .

Mi país
son los gemidos
del hambre,
en la africana noche atrevida
suplicante para que no la olvides.

Como mujer
no tengo
país
tan sólo piedras
y ríos,
una ilusión
sin citadelas.[28]

In her effort to combat divisions of class, age, race, gender, and national origin, Marjorie Agosín's voice has become increasingly global. And it is not only Agosín who has evolved in this direction. Cherríe Moraga, in her introduction to the second edition of *This Bridge Called My Back* (the first edition was published in 1979), has also noted that women of color have moved beyond previous boundaries: "The second major difference a 1983 version of *Bridge* would provide is that it would be much more international in perspective . . . as we begin to see ourselves all as refugees of a world on fire. . . ."[29] Agosín speaks very much to the same point, no matter how different her background:

My voice is the voice of a woman from the middle class, from a bourgeois household, but whose feminist consciousness does not come from the European model of the free and independent woman with genuine economic power . . . [The liberation of women] will come when they understand their true value within their own tradition . . . feeling able to depend on all women for advice, recipes, lore, for ways of living and dreaming. They must understand the miracle it is to drink our wine for communion instead of to forget our solitude and to find oblivion.[30]

In the last sentence, the word "communion" captures the essential thrust behind Agosín's writing, explaining why the exclusion of one

woman by another is anathema to her. For this reason, she strongly
supports the idea of including the work of Latin American women, writing in the United States, in Latina literature, incorporating it into the
curricula of courses dealing with Latina literature. Fundamental differences between those Latinas who were born here and those who have
migrated to this country do exist, and should be pointed out. What is more
important, however, is to move beyond these differences, recognizing a
corpus of Latina literature whose parameters are increasingly inclusive,
and whose discourse is able to accommodate a multiplicity of voices.

NOTES

1 María del Carmen Boza, Beverly Silva, and Carmen Valle, eds., *Nosotras: Latina Literature Today* (Binghamton, N.Y.: Bilingual Press, 1986), 7.

2 Interview, Oct. 2, 1986.

3 For a good resumé of the characteristics of Chilean writers in exile, see Manuel Alcides Jofre, *Literatura chilena en el exilio* (Santiago de Chile: Centro de Indagación y Expresión Cultural y Artística, #76, 1986).

4 "Desde la entraña del monstruo: voces 'hispanas' en EE. UU.," in *La sartén por el mango: Encuentro de escritoras latinoamericanas*, ed. Patricia Elena González y Eliana Ortega (Río Piedras, P.R.: Ediciones Huracán, 1984), 165–66.

5 Alma Gómez, Cherríe Moraga, and Mariana Romo-Carmona, eds., *Cuentos: Stories by Latinas* (New York: Kitchen Table Women of Color Press, 1983), viii. It should be noted that in spite of the message contained in this foreword, two Chileans were among the contributors to this anthology.

6 Marjorie Agosín, "Stories of Night and Dawn: Latin American Women Today," trans. Cola Franzen, *Women's Studies International Forum* 8, no. 5 (1985): 508.

7 Agosín, "Auditorio," in *Conchalí* (Montclair, N.J.: Senda Nueva de Ediciones, 1980), 25:

> Who is the audience,
> Señora Mónica?
> Will it be the young ladies
> of the cups of tea?
>
> . . . .
>
> Perhaps it is
> Menchu, Antonia
> and Julia
> peeling potatoes
> listening to
> the stanza.
>
> Where should one read?
> In a hotel?
> Where once a year
> they get together to dissect

the controversy of the
phallic image of
the whorehouse and the cane?

Read?
On a scarred tissue?

But I have decided
that I will be read
on a bus
near the slaughterhouse
and the procession. (Translation mine)

8   Interview, Oct. 2, 1987.

9   Agosín, *Brujas y algo más / Witches and Other Things*, trans. Cola Franzen (Pittsburgh: Latin American Literary Review Press, 1984), 30:

"Defense of the Middle Class Lady"
I was not queen of an adobe hut. I was born in a house made
of cement with an imaginary perimeter around the garden. I
never suffered from hunger or tuberculosis, I found no lice
in my blond hair. I did suffer from smog, I broke a leg
skiing, I had attacks of allergies and neuroses, endured
indigestion and abortions.

I was born blond so that later I could reinforce the color
of the select settlers of the Southern cone.

I wore silk underclothes, hats of tulle veiling, and a
turquoise stone in my belly button. I went to the dentist
regularly to have the debris of my being removed.

I learned Pop and Rock. Although I wanted to dance the
Cueca and make love to a bushy-bearded guerrilla fighter.

. . . .
I went off to live with the Indians, and with Ernesto, but
they expelled the blond princess from their holy realm.

10   Luisa Valenzuela's career as a writer has taken an ironic turn; the English translations of her works have gone through several printings and her name is well known in the U.S. as an important Latin American writer. In Argentina, her books are out of print and her name is not nearly as well recognized as in this country. (I am indebted to Professor Sharon Magnarelli for this information.)

11   Agosín, "Agujas que hablan: las arpilleristas chilenas," *Revista iberoamericana*, nos. 132–33 (Julio-Diciembre 1985): 524.

By means of the rustic threads a collective memory is preserved, written-sewn by those anonymous and so often ignored women. They take a risk with every stitch, just like the writer who in every word dares to be herself and to tell the truth. (Translation mine)

12   Agosín, *Conchalí*, 23.

> I will tell you that
> Black Island
> is neither black
> nor an island
> neither is San Remo
> nor the statue of liberty.
> It is a town near San Antonio
> in the most fifth region
> where one eats embroiders and dances
> and at five in the afternoon
> makes love. (Translation mine)

13   Unlike the *arpilleras*, the Isla Negra embroideries do not make a political statement.

14   Agosín, "Lejos," in *Brujas*, 84:

> "Far Away"
> My country is a slender pier
> anchored inside me
> curving between
> my knees and my skin
> still damp from the sun.
> My country is a tatter
> of stars like pockmarks
> a rhapsody of useless voices
> that come out to mourn the moon
> through the ravished pelt
> of plain daylight.
>
> . . . .
> My country
> is my house with the keys
> hidden waiting for me
> on the beach.

15   Agosín, "Estados Unidos," in *Brujas*, 78 ("[you] climbed up the Andean way / to fill yourself with copper, chromosomes, guns . . .");

> I walk through Managua, San Salvador
> down Providence Avenue in Santiago de Chile
> and we are all wearing cowboy boots
> amid a deafening dialog of Rock and Roll.

16   Agosín, "Mi nación y los sistemas de correo," in *Brujas*, 70:

> "My Country and the postal system"
> Address Insufficient

house uninhabited
flew away like a lonely dove
Absent
Deceased
Mutilated
Refused
Unknown in circles without exit
Such a name does not exist
DISAPPEARED.

17   Agosín, "Escúchame Ana Frank," in *Brujas*, 72: "Listen to me Anne Frank, / did you really believe that all men were good?"

18   Agosín, "La mesa de Billar en New Bedford, Mass.," in *Brujas*, 36: "and now like a piece of meat being mourned in a slaughterhouse, / bound to the billiard table / She sleeps naked."

19   Agosín, "Los desaparecidos," in *Brujas*, 80: "I am an unarmed woman / small and with hair as blue as acid . . . / I swear to arm myself with the word / take it along the walls of the city/take it where the whip went. . . ."

20   Agosín, "Boom," in *Brujas*, "Maga . . . / was a bit tacky"; "And I have never seen / either one of the two Borges."; "why didn't they read her?"

21   Agosín, "Mis versos," in *Brujas*, 58:

"My Verses"
It's said my verses
are erotic-phallocratic-obscenetic
they only try
to say the truth:
I am a warm poet
fond of grapes
and red wine . . .

22   Agosín, "Quereres," in *Brujas*, 60.

23   Agosín, "Cuentos de hadas y algo más," in *Brujas* 16: "The dwarves didn't keep / Snow White as an ornament"; "Little Red Riding Hood / had to sleep with a wolf"; "The shoe fit her very well / and the other thing fit also."

24   Agosín, "A las locas de la Plaza de Mayo," in *Mujeres de humo* (Madrid: Ediciones Torremozas, 1987), 57: "the crazy women of the Plaza de Mayo / in Buenos Aires, in El Salvador, / in Treblinka . . ." (translation mine).

25   Agosín, "Invierno en la Plaza de Mayo," in *Hogueras* (Santiago de Chile: Editorial Universitaria, 1986), 31–32:

"Winter in the Plaza de Mayo"
You also follow
the destiny of my
hands,
on this day
when the birds

sing
in the
Plaza
de Mayo. (Translation mine)

26   Agosín, "Penélope I," in *Nosotras*, 59: "and you weave and unravel / the hours of loneliness / the absence without pity"; "listen, Lady Penelope / get with it / and at least sell / one little scarf" (translation mine).

27   Agosín, "Penélope II," in *Mujeres de humo*, 40:

Penelope,
unravelling a lie,

. . . .

Penelope,
wife of insomnia
don't weave arrivals
because today no one
returns from
Ithaca. (Translation mine)

28   Agosín, "Los países del humo," in *Mujeres de humo*, 71–72:

"Lands of smoke"
My land
is the air
that is so much ours
in the fleeting nights
of Atitlán

. . . .

My land
is the moans
of hunger
in the daring African night
begging you not to forget it.

As a woman
I have
no country
only stones
and rivers,
a dream
with no citadels. (Translation mine)

29   *This Bridge Called My Back: Writings by Radical Women of Color*, ed. Cherríe Moraga and Gloria Anzaldúa (New York: Kitchen Table Women of Color Press, 1983).

30   Agosín, "Stories of Night and Dawn," 509.

Selected Bibliography

ELAINE N. MILLER AND NANCY SAPORTA STERNBACH

WORKS BY LATINA WRITERS

Acosta, Teresa Palomo. *Passing Time*. Self-published chapbook, 1984. Available from Relámpago Books, P.O. Box 43194, Austin, Texas 78745.

Agosín, Marjorie. *Brujas y algo más/Witches and Other Things*. Translated by Cola Franzen. Pittsburgh: Latin American Review Press, 1986.

———. *Chile: Gemidos y cantares*. Prólogo de María Luisa Bombal. Quillota, Chile: Editorial el Observador, 1977.

———. *Conchalí*. Montclair, N.J.: Senda Nueva de Ediciones, 1980.

———. *Hogueras*. Santiago de Chile: Editorial Universitaria, 1986.

———. *Mujeres de humo*. Madrid: Ediciones Torremozas, 1987.

Anzaldúa, Gloria. *Borderlands/La Frontera: The New Mestiza*. San Francisco: Spinsters/Aunt Lute, 1987.

Bornstein-Somoza, Miriam. *Bajo cubierta*. Tucson: Scorpion Press, 1977.

Candelaria, Cordelia. *Ojo de la Cueva/Cave Springs*. Colorado Springs, Colo.: Maize Press, 1984.

Casal, Lourdes. *Los fundadores: Alfonso y otros cuentos*. Miami: Ediciones Universal, 1973.

———. *Palabras juntan revolución*. La Habana: Casa de las Américas, 1981.

Castillo, Ana. *I Close My Eyes (To See)*. Pullman: Washington State University Press, 1976.

———. *The Invitation*. 2d ed. San Francisco: A. Castillo, 1986.

———. *The Mixquiahuala Letters*. Binghamton, N.Y.: Bilingual Press, 1986.

———. *Otro Canto*. Chicago: Alternativa Publications, 1977.

———. *Women Are Not Roses*. Houston: Arte Público Press, 1984.

Readers will note unusual characteristics in this bibliography. For sheer lack of information we have had to omit complete bibliographic citations of works that went out of print rapidly and some publications of small presses or journals that are no longer in existence. The rather unconventional approach to listing journals with street addresses and zip codes was in many instances essential, given the publishing circumstances.

————. *Zero Makes Me Hungry*. Greenview, Ill.: Scott-Foresman Co., 1975.
Catacalos, Rosemary. *Again for the First Time*. Santa Fe: Tooth of Time, 1984.
Caulfield, Carlota. *34th Street and Other Poems*. Translated by Chris Allen and the author. San Francisco: Eboli Poetry Series, 1987.
————. *El tiempo es una mujer que espera*. Madrid: Ediciones Torremozas, 1986.
Cervantes, Lorna Dee. *Emplumada*. Pittsburgh: University of Pittsburgh Press, 1981.
Chávez, Denise. *The Last of the Menu Girls*. Houston: Arte Público Press, 1986.
Cisneros, Sandra. *Bad Boys*. San Jose, Calif.: Mango Publications, 1980.
————. *The House on Mango Street*. Houston: Arte Público Press, 1985.
————. *My Wicked, Wicked Ways*. Bloomington, Ind.: Third Woman Press, 1987.
Clavijo, Uva. *Entresemáforos: Poemas escritos en ruta*. Colección Espejo de Paciencia. Ediciones, 1985.
————. *Ni verdad ni mentira y otros cuentos*. Miami: Ediciones Universal, 1977.
————. *Tus ojos y yo*. Colección Espejo de Paciencia Ser. Ediciones, 1985.
————. *Versos de exilio*. Miami, 1974.
Cofer, Judith Ortiz. *Latin Women Pray*.
————. *The Native Dancer*. Lieb Schott Publications.
————. *Peregrina*. Golden, Colo.: Riverstone Press of the Foothills Art Center, 1986.
Corpi, Lucha. *Fireflight: Three Latin American Poets*. Berkeley: Oyez, 1976.
————. *Palabras de mediodía/Noon Words*. Translated by Catherine Rodríguez-Nieto. Berkeley: El Fuego de Aztlán Publications, 1980.
Cota-Cárdenas, Margarita. *Noches despertando In/conciencias*. Tucson: Scorpion Press, 1975.
————. *Puppey: A Chicano Novella*, Austin: Relámpago Books Press, 1985.
Domínguez, Sylvia Maída. *La comadre María*. Austin: American Universal Artforms Corp., 1973.
Escandell, Noemí. *Cuadros*. Somerville, N.J.: Slusa, 1982.
————. *Palabras/Words*. Somerville, N.J.: Slusa, 1986.
Esteves, Sandra María. *Yerbabuena*. Greenfield, N.Y.: Greenfield Review Press, 1980.
————. *Tropical Rains: A Bilingual Downpour*. New York: African Caribbean Poetry Theater, 1984.
Flores, Gloria Amalia. *And Her Children Lived*. San Diego: Toltecas en Aztlán Publications, Centro Cultural La Raza, 1974.
Gaitan, Marcela T. *Chicano Themes: Manita Poetry*. Minneapolis: Chicano Studies, University of Minnesota, 1975.
Galindo, Mary Sue, Maria Limón, and Jesse Johnson. *Merienda Tejana*. Austin: Relámpago Books Press, 1985.
Gonzales, Rebecca. *Slow Work to the Rhythm of Cicadas*. Fort Worth: Prickly Pear Press, 1985.
Hernandez Tovar, Inés. *Con razón corazón*. San Antonio: Caracol, 1977.
Herrera, María Cristina, and Leonel de la Cuesta, eds. *Itinerario ideológico: Antología de Lourdes Casal*. Miami: Instituto de Estudios Cubanos, 1982.
de Hoyos, Angela. *Arise, Chicano! and Other Poems*. Translated into Spanish by

Mireya Robles. San Antonio: M & A Editions, 1976. Also Bloomington, Ind.: Backstage Books, 1975.

———. *Arise, Chicano y Chicano Poems for the Barrio*. 1975.

———. *Chicano Poems for the Barrio*. Bloomington, Ind.: Backstage Books, 1975.

———. *Selected Poems/Selecciones*. Translated by Mireya Robles. Xalapa: Universidad Veracruzana, 1976.

———. *Woman, Woman*. Houston: Arte Público Press, 1985.

Islas, Maya. *Sola . . . desnuda . . . sin nombre*. New York: Editorial Mensaje, 1974.

———. *Sombras papel*. 1978.

Jaramillo, Cleofas M. *Romance of a Little Village Girl*. San Antonio: Naylor Publishing Co., 1955.

Mendell, Olga. *Adiós*. Chapbook, 1983.

Mohr, Nicholasa. *El Bronx Remembered: A Novella and Stories*. New York: Harper and Row, 1976.

———. *Felita*. New York: Dial Press, 1979.

———. *In Nueva York*. New York: Dial Press, 1977.

———. *Nilda*. New York: Harper and Row, 1973.

———. *Rituals of Survival: Woman's Portfolio*. Houston: Arte Público Press, 1985.

Mora, Pat. *Borders*. Houston: Arte Público Press, 1986.

———. *Chants*. Houston: Arte Público Press, 1984.

Moraga, Cherríe. *Giving Up the Ghost: Teatro in Two Acts*. Los Angeles: West End Press, 1986.

———. *Loving in the War Years: Lo que nunca pasó por sus labios*. Boston: South End Press, 1983.

Moreno, Dorinda. *La mujer es la tierra: La tierra de vida*. San Francisco: Casa Editorial, 1975.

Niggli, Josefina. *Mexican Folk Plays*. Chapel Hill: University of North Carolina Press, 1938.

———. *The Ring of General Macías*. In *20 Prize-Winning Non-Royalty One-Act Plays*, compiled by Betty Smith. New York: Greenberg Publisher, 1943.

Ornelas, Berta. *Come Down From the Mound*. Phoenix: Miter Publishing Co., 1975.

Pereira, Teresinha. *Hey Mex! & Andale Rosana!* Boulder, Colo.: Backstage Books, 1978.

———. *Poems of Exile and Alienation*. Translated by Robert Lima. Boulder, Colo.: Anvil Press, 1976.

Pineda, Cecile. *Face*. New York: Viking–Penguin, 1985.

———. *Frieze*. New York: Viking–Penguin, 1986.

Ponce, Mary Helen. *Taking Control*. Houston: Arte Público Press, 1987.

Portillo Trambley, Estela. *The Day of the Swallows*. In *Contemporary Chicano Theater*, edited by Roberto Garza. Notre Dame: Notre Dame University Press, 1976.

———. *Rain of Scorpions and Other Writings*. Berkeley: Tonatiuh International, 1975.

———. *Sor Juana and Other Plays*. Ypsilanti, Mich.: Bilingual Press, 1983.

———. *Trini*. Binghamton, N.Y.: Bilingual Press, 1986.

Prida, Dolores. *Beautiful Señoritas and Other Plays*. Houston: Arte Público Press, forthcoming.

———. *The Beggars Soap Opera*. Unpublished manuscript. 1979.

———. *Coser y Cantar*. Unpublished manuscript. 1981.

———. *Crisp!* Unpublished manuscript. 1981.

———. *La era latina*. Unpublished manuscript. 1980.

———. *Juan Bobo*. Unpublished manuscript. 1981.

———. *Pantallas/Screens*. Edited by Luis González Cruz, forthcoming.

———. *Savings*. Unpublished manuscript. 1985.

Quiñonez, Naomi. *Sueño de Colibrí/Hummingbird Dream*. Los Angeles: West End Press, 1985.

Ríos, Isabella. *Victuum*. Ventura, Calif.: Diana Etna, 1976.

Rivera, Marina. *Mestiza: Poems*. [Tucson], Grilled Flowers Special Issue, 1977.

———. *Sobra*. San Francisco: Casa Editorial, 1977.

Rivero, Eliana. *Cuerpos breves*. Tucson: Scorpion Press, 1977.

———. *De cal y arena*. Sevilla: Aldebarán, 1975.

Robles, Mireya. *En esta aurora*. San Antonio: M & A Editions, 1976.

———. *Hagiografía de Narcisa la Bella*. Hanover, N.H.: Ediciones del Norte, 1985.

———. *Tiempo artesano*. Barcelona: Editorial Campos, 1973.

———. *Time, the Artisan*. Translated by Angela de Hoyos. Austin: Dissemination Center for Bilingual Bicultural Education, 1975.

Romero, Lin. *Happy Songs, Bleeding Hearts*. San Diego: Toltecas en Aztlán Publications, 1974.

Roybal, Rose Marie. *From Envidia, to la Llorona*. Denver: Southwest Clearing House for Minority Publications, 1973.

Sánchez, Carol Lee. *Conversations From the Nightmare*. Berkeley: Casa Editorial Publications, 1975.

Sánchez, Pilar. *Symbols*. San Francisco: Casa Editorial, 1977.

Sapia, Yvonne. *The Fertile Crescent*. Tallahassee, Fla.: Anhinga Press, 1983.

———. *Valentino's Hair: Poems*. Samuel French Morse Poetry Prize Ser., 1987.

Silva, Beverly. *The Cat*. Ypsilanti, Mich.: Bilingual Review Press, 1986.

———. *The Second Street Poems*. Ypsilanti, Mich.: Bilingual Press, 1983.

Tafolla, Carmen. "La Malinche." In *Encuentro Artístico Femenil*, 41–42. Austin: Casa/Tejidos Publications, 1978.

———. *To Split a Human: Machos, Mitos y la Mujer Chicana*. San Antonio: Mexican American Cultural Center, 1985.

Tafolla, Carmen, Cecilio García-Camarillo, and Reyes Cárdenas. *Get Your Tortillas Together*. San Antonio, Tex.: S/A Publications, 1976.

Taylor, Sheila Ortiz. *Faultline*. Tallahassee: Naiad, 1982.

Umpierre, Luz María. *En el país de las maravillas*. Bloomington, Ind.: Third Woman Press, 1985.

———. *The Margarita Poems*. Bloomington, Ind.: Third Woman Press, forthcoming.

———. *Una puertorriqueña en Penna*. San Juan, P.R.: Masters, 1979.

———. *Y otras desgracias/And Other Misfortunes*. Bloomington, Ind.: Third Woman Press, 1985.

Valdés, Gina. *There Are No Madmen Here Tonight*. San Diego: Maize Press, 1981.

Vallbona, Rima de. *Mujeres y agonías*. Houston: Arte Público Press, 1981, 1982.

———. *Noche en vela*. Houston: Arte Público Press, 1982, 1985.

———. *Polvo del camino*. Houston: Arte Público Press, 1985.

———. *Las sombras que perseguimos*. Houston: Arte Público Press, 1983.

Valle, Carmen. *De todo lo que da la noche al que la tienta*. Manuscript.

———. *Diarios robados*. Buenos Aires: Ediciones de La Flor, 1982.

———. *Glenn Miller y varias vidas después*. Puebla: Premiá Editora, S. A., 1983.

———. *Un poco de lo no dicho*. New York: Editorial La Ceiba, 1980.

Vicioso, Sherezada (Chiqui). *Un extraño ulular traía el viento*. Santo Domingo: Alfa y Omega, 1985.

———. *Viaje desde el agua*. Santo Domingo: Visuarte, 1981.

Vigil, Evangelina. *The Computer Is Down*. Houston: Arte Público Press, 1987.

———. *Nade y Nade*. San Antonio: M & A Editions, 1978.

———. *Thirty an' Seen a Lot*. Houston: Arte Público Press, 1982.

———, ed. *Woman of Her Word: Hispanic Women Write*. Houston: Arte Público Press, 1983.

Villanueva, Alma. *Bloodroot*. Austin: Place of Herons Press, 1977.

———. *Life Span*. Austin: Place of Herons Press, 1984.

———. *Mother, May I?* Pittsburgh: Motheroot Publications, 1978.

———. *Poems: Third Chicano Literary Prize*. Dept. of Spanish and Portuguese. Irvine: University of California, 1977.

Viramontes, Helen. *The Moths and Other Stories*. Houston: Arte Público Press, 1985.

Zamora, Bernice. "Notes from a Chicana 'COED.'" *Caracol* 3 (1977): 19.

———. *Restless Serpents*. Menlo Park: Diseños Literarios, 1976.

Zavala, Iris. *Barrio doliente*. Santander, Spain: La Isla de los Ratones, 1964.

———. *Escritura desatada: Poemas, 1970–1973*. Santurce, P.R.: Ediciones Puerto, n.d.

———. *Kiliagonía*. México: Premiá, 1980.

———. *Poemas prescindibles*. New York: Antiediciones Villa Miseria, 1971.

———. *Que nadie muera sin amar el mar*. Madrid: Visor, 1982.

ANTHOLOGIES

Algarín, Miguel, and Miguel Piñero. *Nuyorican Poetry: An Anthology of Puerto Rican Words and Feelings*. New York: William Morrow, 1975.

Bearing Witness/Sobreviviendo: An Anthology of Writing and Art by Native American Latina Women. Calyx (Oregon) (Spring 1984).

Boza, María del Carmen, Beverly Silva, and Carmen Valle. *Nosotras: Latina Literature Today*. Binghamton, N.Y.: Bilingual Press, 1986.

Canto al Pueblo. Phoenix: Arizona Canto al Pueblo, 1980.

Castenada Shular, A., et al. *Literatura chicana: Texto and Contexo*. Englewood Cliffs, N.J.: Prentice-Hall, 1972.

Chicano Literature: A Reference Guide. Westport, Conn.: Greenwood Press, 1985.

Empringham, Toni, ed. *Fiesta en Aztlán: Anthology of Chicano Poetry*. Santa Barbara, Calif.: Capra Press, 1982.

Fisher, Dexter, ed. *The Third Woman: Minority Women Writers of the United States.* Boston: Houghton Mifflin, 1980.

Keller, Gary D., and Francisco Jiménez, eds. *Hispanics in the United States: An Anthology of Creative Literature.* Special double issue of *Bilingual Review/Revista Bilingüe* 6, nos. 2–3 (1979).

Moraga, Cherríe, and Gloria Anzaldúa, eds. *This Bridge Called My Back: Radical Writings by Women of Color.* Watertown, Mass.: Persephone Press, 1981.

Moraga, Cherríe, Alma Goméz and Mariana Romo-Carmona, eds. *Cuentos: Stories by Latinas.* New York: Kitchen Table, Women of Color Press, 1983.

Partnoy, Alicia, ed. *You Can't Drown the Fire: Latin American Women Writing in Exile.* Pittsburgh: Cleis Press, 1988.

Ramos, Juanita, ed. *Compañeras: Latina Lesbians.* New York: Latina Women's Educational Resources, 1987.

Randall, Margaret. *Breaking the Silences: 20th Century Poetry by Cuban Women.* Vancouver, Wash.: The Pulp Press Book Publishers, 1982.

Sánchez, Rosaura, ed. *Requisa 32.* San Diego: UCSD Chicano Research Publications, 1979.

Siete poetas. Tucson: Scorpion Press, 1978.

Silén, Iván. *Los paraguas amarillos: Los poetas latinos en New York.* Ypsilanti, Mich.: Bilingual Review Press, 1983.

JOURNALS

Agenda: A Journal of Hispanic Issues. National Council of La Raza, 1725 Eye Street, NW, Suite 210, Washington, D.C. 20006.

The Américas Review (formerly *Revista Chicano-Riqueña*). University of Houston, Houston, Texas 77004.

Atisbos: Journal of Chicano Research. P.O. Box 2362, Stanford University, Stanford, California 94305.

Aztlán: Chicano Journal of the Social Sciences and Arts. Chicano Studies Center, UCLA, Los Angeles, California 90024.

Caracol. P.O. Box 7577, San Antonio, Texas 78207.

Carta Abierta: Keeping an Eye on the Chicano Literary World. Department of Romance Languages, University of Washington, Seattle, Washington 98195.

Chismearte. P.O. Box 30128, Los Angeles, California 90030.

Con Safos. P.O. Box 31085, Los Angeles, California 90031. Ceased publication.

La Cucaracha. P.O. Box 5034, Pueblo, Colorado 81002.

De Colores: Journal of Emerging Raza Philosophies. Pajarito Publications, 2633 Granite NW, Albuquerque, New Mexico 87104.

    Vol. 2, no. 3 (1975). Issue devoted to La Chicana. Contains: Noemí Lorenzana, "Transcending the Old and Carving out a New Life and Self-Image"; Erlinda González, "La muerte de un refrán"; Maxine Baca Zinn, "Chicanas: Power and Control in the Domestic Sphere"; Lupe Aguinaga, "World Women's Challenge—New Society Based on Justice and Peace."

Vol. 3, no. 3 (1977). "La Cosecha: Literatura y la Mujer Chicana." Edited by Linda Morales Armas and Sue Molina.

Entrelíneas. Penn Valley Community College and University of Missouri-Kansas City, 3201 Southwest Trafficway, Kansas City, Missouri 64111.

Escolios: Revista de Literatura. Creación-Teoría-Crítica. Roberto Cantú, ed. California State University, 5151 State University Drive, Los Angeles, California 90032.

El Espejo/The Mirror. Romano y Ríos. (1969).

Explicación de Textos Literatios/Hispanic Press. Vol. 15, no. 2 (1986–87). Special issue on Literatura hispana de los Estados Unidos.

Frontiers: A Journal of Women's Studies. Vol. 5, no. 2 (Summer 1980). Special issue on La Chicana: "Chicanas in the National Landscape."

El Fuego de Aztlán. 3408 Dwinelle Hall, University of California, Berkeley, California 94720. Vol. 1, no. 4 (Summer 1977). Bernice Zamora, guest editor. Issue dedicated to La Chicana.

El Gato Tuerto. Carlota Caulfield, ed. P.O. Box 210277, San Francisco, California 94121 (Summer 1987). Special issue: "Hispanic Women Poets in the United States."

El Grito: Journal of Contemporary Mexican American Thought. Quinto Sol Publications, P.O. Box 9275, Berkeley, California 94709. Vol. 7, no. 1 (September 1973). Special issue: "Chicanas en la literatura y el arte."

El Grito del Sol: A Chicano Quarterly. Tonatiuh International, Inc., 2150 Shattuck Avenue, Berkeley, California 94704. Vol. 2, no. 3 (July-September 1977). Special issue on Chicana writers.

Hijas de Cuauhtémoc: Encuentro Femenil. Available on Microfilm, Chicano Studies Library, University of California, Berkeley, 94720; Latin American Center Library, University of Texas, Austin 78712.

Imagine: International Chicano Poetry Journal. 645 Beacon Street, Suite 7, Boston, Massachusetts 02215. Vol. 2, no. 1 (Summer 1985). "Edición Feminista."

La Luz. 800 East Girard, Suite 314, Denver, Colorado 80231. Vol. 4, no. 2 (May 1975).

Maize: Notebooks of Xicano Art and Literature. P.O. Box 8251. San Diego, California 92102.

Mango. Lorna Dee Cervantes, ed. 329 South Willard "A," San Jose, California 95126.

MELUS: Journal of the Society for the Study of Multi-Ethnic Literature of the United States. Joseph Skerrett, ed. 272 Bartlett Hall, University of Massachusetts, Amherst, Massachusetts 01003.

El Nahuatzen. 310 Calvin Hall, University of Iowa, Iowa City, Iowa 53342.

Nuestro. Nuestro Publications, 1140 Avenue of the Americas, New York, New York 10036.

La Palabra: Revista de Literatura Chicana. J. S. Alarcón, ed. Department of Foreign Languages, Arizona State University, Tempe, Arizona 85281. Vol. 2, no. 2 (otoño 1980).

Papeles de la Frontera. José Varela Ibarra, ed. P.O. Box 422, El Centro, California 92243.

Quill. Frank del Olmo. "Voices for the Chicano Movement." No. 40 (December 1971).

Rayas: Newsletter of Chicano Arts and Literature. Cecilio García-Camarillo and José Armas, eds. P.O. Box 7264, Albuquerque, New Mexico 87264.

La Raza Magazine. El Barrio Communications Project, 2808 Altura, Los Angeles, California 90031.

Revista Chicano-Riqueña (Now *The Américas Review*). Arte Público Press, University of Houston, University Park, Houston, Texas 77004. Vol. 6, no. 2 (Spring 1979). Chicana poetry.

Somos. Los Padrinos of Southern California, P.O. Box 5697, San Bernardino, California 92412.

El Tecolote. P.O. Box 40027, San Francisco, California 94140.

Tejidos: A Bilingual Journal for the Stimulation of Chicano Creativity and Criticism. P.O. Box 7383, Austin, Texas 78712. Vol. 1, no. 3 (Summer 1974).

Third Woman. Norma Alarcón, ed. Indiana University, Bloomington, Indiana 47401.

Xalman. 601 East Montecito Street, Santa Barbara, California 93103.

RESEARCH ON LATINA WRITERS

Acosta Belén, Edna. "Conversations with Nicholasa Mohr." *Revista Chicano-Riqueña* 7 (1980):35–42.

Alarcón, Justo S. "La nueva poesía in *Bajo cubierta* de Miriam Bornstein-Somoza." *Third Woman* 2 (1984):57–63.

Alarcón, Norma. "Chicana's Feminist Literature: A Re-Vision through Malintzín/ or Malinche: Putting Flesh Back on the Object." In *This Bridge Called My Back.* 2d ed., edited by Cherríe Moraga and Gloria Anzaldúa. New York: Kitchen Table, Women of Color Press, 1983.

———. "Interview with Cherríe Moraga." *Third Woman* 3 (1986):126–34.

Azize, Yamila. *Luchas de la mujer en Puerto Rico, 1898–1930.* Río Piedras, P.R.: Editorial Cultural, 1985.

Barradas, Efraín. "Conciencia feminina o consciencia social: La voz poética de Sandra María Esteves." *Third Woman* 1 (1982):31–34.

———. " 'Entre la esencia y la forma': El momento neoyorquino en la poesía de Julia de Burgos." *Explicación de Textos Literarios* 15, no. 2 (1986–87):138–52.

Billings, Linda M., and Alurista. "In Verbal Murals: A Study of Chicana History and Poetry," *Confluencia* 2, no. 1 (Fall 1986):60–68.

Bornstein, Miriam. "La poeta chicana: Visión panorámica." *La Palabra: Revista de Literatura Chicana* 2 (1980):43–66.

———. "The Voice of the Chicana in Poetry." *Denver Quarterly* 16 (Fall 1981):28–47.

Bruce-Novoa, Juan. "Bernice Zamora y Lorna Dee Cervantes: Una estéticia feminista." *Revista Iberoamericana* 51, nos. 132–33 (July-December 1985):565–73.

———. *Chicano Authors: Inquiry by Interview.* Austin: University of Texas Press, 1980. Not devoted exclusively to Chicanas but includes them.

———. *Chicano Poetry: A Response to Chaos.* Austin: University of Texas Press, 1982.

———. "Sheila Ortiz Taylor's *Faultline:* A Third Woman Utopia." In *Rewriting the U.S. Canon: Chicano Literature.* Albuquerque: University of New Mexico Press, forthcoming.

Cabrera, Luis. *Diccionario de aztequismos.* México: Ediciones Oasis, 1975.

Candelaria, Cornelia. "Another Reading of Three Poems by Zamora." *MELUS* 7, no. 4 (Winter 1980):102–4.

———. *Chicano Poetry: A Critical Introduction.* Westport, Conn.: Greenwood Press, 1986.

———. "La Malinche: Feminist Prototype." *Frontiers* 5, no. 2 (1980).

Cárdenas de Dwyer, Carlota. "Commentary." *La Luz* 4, nos. 8–9 (November-December 1975):8.

———. "Literary Images of Mexican-American Women." *La Luz* 6, no. 11 (1977):11–12.

Castillo, Adelaida del. "Malintzín Tenepal: A Preliminary Look into a New Perspective." Part I of *Essays on La Mujer,* edited by Rosaura Sánchez. Los Angeles: UCLA Chicano Studies Center Publication, 1977.

Córdova, Marcella, and Rode Marie Roybal: *Bibliografía de la Chicana/Bibliography on the Chicana.* Lockwood, Colo.: Marcella C. Córdova, 1973.

Cota-Cárdenas, Margarita. "The Chicana in the City as Seen in Her Literature." *Frontiers: A Journal of Women's Studies* 6 (1981):13–18.

Cotera, Marta. *The Chicana Feminist.* Austin: International Systems Development, 1976.

———. "Chicana Identity." *Caracol* 2, no. 6 (February 1976):14–15, 17.

———. *Diosa y Hembra: The History and Heritage of Chicanas in the U.S.* Austin: Information Systems Development, 1976.

Darío Salaz, Rubén. "The Chicana in American Literature." *La Luz* 4, no. 3 (June 1975):28.

Desai, Parul. "Interview with Bernice Zamora, a Chicana Poet." *Imagine: An International Chicano Poetry Journal* 2 (1985):26–39.

Dowling, Lee. "Point of View in Rima de Vallbona's, 'La sombra que perseguimos'." *Revista Chicano-Riqueña* 13 (1985):64–73.

Enríquez, Evangelina, and Alfredo Mirandé. "Liberation, Chicana Style: Colonial Roots of Feministas Chicanas." *De Colores: A Bilingual Quarterly Journal of Chicano Expression and Thought* 4, no. 3 (1978):7–21.

Fernández-Olmos, Margarite. "From the Metropolis: Puerto Rican Women Poets and the Immigration Experience." *Third Woman* 1 (1982):40–51.

Flores, Juan. "Back Down These Mean Streets: Introducing Nicholasa Mohr and Louis Reyes Rivera." *Revista Chicano-Riqueña* 7 (1980):51–56.

Gonzales, Sylvia. "The Chicana in Literature." *La Luz* 1, no. 9 (January 1973).

González-Berry, Erlinda, and Tey Diana Rebolledo, "Growing Up Chicano: Tomás Rivera and Sandra Cisneros." *Revista Chicano-Riqueña* 13 (1985):109–19.

Gutiérrez-Revuelta, Pedro. "Género e ideología en el libro de Sandra Cisneros: *The House on Mango Street.*" *Crítica: A Journal of Critical Essays* 1 (Fall 1986):48–59.

Herrera-Sobek, María. "The Acculturation Process of the Chicana in the Corrido." *Proceedings of Pacific Coast Council on Latin American Studies* (1982):23–34.

———, ed. *Beyond Stereotypes: The Critical Analysis of Chicana Literature.* Binghamton, N.Y.: Bilingual Press, 1985.

Hull, Gloria T. "Reading Literature by U.S. Third World Women." Wellesley College: Center for Research on Women, 1984. Working paper no. 141.

Jensen, Richard, José Angel Gutiérrez, and John C. Hammerback. *A War of Words: Chicano Protest of the 1960s and 1970s*. Westport, Conn.: Greenwood Press, 1985. Not exclusively on Chicanas.

Jímenez, Marilyn. "Contrasting Portraits: Integrating Materials about the Afro-Hispanic Woman into the Traditional Curriculum." Wellesley College: Center for Research on Women, 1983. Working paper no. 120.

Lagos Pope, María Inés. "A Space of Her Own: *The Second Street Poems* by Beverly Silva." In Beverly Silva. *The Second Street Poems*. Ypsilanti, Mich.: Bilingual Press, 1983.

Lavis, Marvin. "Rita Mendoza: Chicana Poetess." *Latin American Literary Review* 10 (1977):79–85.

Longeaux y Vásquez, M. E. "The Mexican-American Woman." In *Sisterhood Is Powerful*, edited by Robin Morgan. New York: Vintage Books, 1973.

López Sáenz, Lionila. "Machismo, No! Igualdad, Sí." *La Luz* 1, no. 2 (May 1972):19–20.

Lucero, Marcela. "Resources for the Chicana Feminist Scholar." In *For Alma Mater: Theory and Practice in Feminist Scholarship*, edited by Paula Treichler, Cheris Kramarae, and Beth Stafford, 393–401. Urbana: University of Illinois Press, 1985.

Lucero-Trujillo, Marcela Christine. "The Dilemma of the Modern Chicana Artist and Critic." In *The Third Woman*, edited by Dexter Fisher, 324–32. Boston: Houghton Mifflin, 1980.

Madrigal, Sylvia. "*Emplumada*: A Female Pen in Flourish." *Imagine: International Chicano Poetry Journal* 1, no. 1 (1984).

Maier, Carol. "The Poetry of Ana Castillo." *Letras Femeninas* 6, no. 1 (Spring 1980).

Mandlove, Nancy. "In Response: An Introduction to *Y otras desgracias/And Other Misfortunes* by Luz María Umpierre-Herrera," ix–xiii. Bloomington, Ind.: Third Woman Press, 1985.

Márquez, Evelina, and Margarita Ramírez. "La tarea de la mujer es la liberación." In *La otra cara de México: El pueblo chicano*, edited by David K. Maciel, 173–81. México: Ediciones el Caballito, 1977.

Matilla, Alfredo. "Breve visión panorámica de las letras puertorriqueñas en los Estados Unidos." *Explicación de Textos Literarios* 15, no. 2 (1986–87):19–31.

Medina González, Esther. "Sisterhood." *La Luz* 4, no. 5 (September-October 1975):7.

Mirandé, Alfredo, and Evangelina Enríquez. *La chicana*. Chicago: University of Chicago Press, 1979.

Molina de Pick, Gracia. "Reflexiones sobre el feminismo y la Raza." *La Luz* 1, no. 4 (August 1972):58.

Monda, Bernadette. "Interview with Lorna Dee Cervantes." *Third Woman* 2 (1984):103–7.

Mora, Magdalena, and Adelaida R. del Castillo, eds. *Mexican Women in the United States: Struggles Past and Present*. Los Angeles: Chicano Studies Center, UCLA, 1980.

Morales, Alejandro. "Terra Mater and the Emergence of Myth in *Poems* by Alma Villanueva." *Bilingual Review/Revista Bilingüe* 7 (1980):123–42.

Nieto, Consuelo. "The Chicana and the Women's Rights Movement." *La Luz* 3, no. 6 (September 1974):10–11, 32.

Nieto Gómez, Ana. "Chicana Feminism." *Caracol* 2, no. 5 (January 1986):3–5.

Olivares, Julián. "Seeing and Becoming: Evangelina Vigil, *Thirty an' Seen A Lot.*" In *The Chicano Struggle: Analyses of Past and Present Efforts,* edited by John A. García, Theresa Córdova, and Juan R. García. Binghamton, N.Y.: Bilingual Press, 1984.

Ordóñez, Elizabeth J. "Chicana Literature and Related Sources: A Selected and Annotated Bibliography." *Bilingual Review/Revista Bilingüe* 7 (1980):143–64 (code 0–25).

———. "The Concept of Cultural Identity in Chicana Poetry." *Third Woman* 2 (1984):75–82.

———. "Sexual Politics and the Theme of Sexuality in Chicana Poetry." In *Women in Hispanic Literature: Icons and Fallen Idols,* edited by Beth Miller, 316–39. Berkeley: University of California Press, 1983.

Ortega, Eliana. "Desde la entraña del monstruo." In *La sartén por el mango,* edited by Patricia Elena González and Eliana Ortega, 163–69. Río Piedras, P.R.: Huracán, 1984.

Phillips, Rachel. "Marina/Malinche: Masks and Shadows." In *Women in Hispanic Literature: Icons and Fallen Idols,* edited by Beth Miller. Berkeley: University of California Press, 1983.

Quintanales, Mirtha. "Loving in the War Years: An Interview with Cherríe Moraga." *Off Our Backs* (January 1985):12–13.

Randall, Margaret. "Una Conciencia de Mujer: Review of *Borderlands/La frontera: The New Mestiza.*" *The Women's Review of Books* 5, no. 3 (December 1987):8–9.

Rebolledo, Tey Diana. "Abuelitas, Mythology and Integration in Chicana Literature." *Revista Chicano-Riqueña* 11 (1984):148–58.

———. "The Bittersweet Nostalgia of Childhood in the Poetry of Margarita Cota-Cárdenas." *Frontiers* 5 (Fall 1980):31–35.

———. "Game Theory in Chicana Poetry." *Revista Chicana-Riqueña* 11 (1983):159–68.

———. "The Maturing of Chicana Poetry: The Quiet Revolution of the 1980s." In *For Alma Mater: Theory and Practice in Feminist Scholarship,* edited by Paula Treichler, Cheris Kramarae, and Beth Stafford, 143–58. Urbana: University of Illinois Press, 1985.

———. "Soothing Restless Serpents: The Dreaded Creation and Other Inspirations in Chicana Poetry." *Third Woman* 2 (1984):83–102.

———. "Witches, Bitches, and Midwives: The Shaping of Poetic Consciousness in Chicana Literature." In *The Chicano Struggle,* edited by John A. García, Theresa Cordova, and Juan R. García, 166–77. Binghamton, N.Y.: Bilingual Press, 1984.

Ríos, Herminio, and Octavio Romano, eds. *Chicanas en la literatura y el arte.* Berkeley: Quinto Sol, 1974.

Rivero, Eliana. "Escritura chicana: La mujer." *La Palabra: Revista de Literatura Chicana* 2 (Fall 1980):2–9.

———. "La mujer y la raza: Latinas y Chicanas." *Caracol* 4, no. 4 (December 1977).

Rocard, Marcienne. "La Chicana: Du Stéréotype a l'Auto-définition et a l'Auto-détermination." In *Femmes des Ameriques*, 141–53. Toulouse: Université de Toulouse-Le Mirail, 1986.

———. "The Remembering Voice in Chicana Literature." *Americas Review* 14 (1986): 150–59.

Rodríguez, Alfonso. "Tragic Vision in Estela Portillo's *The Day of the Swallows*." *De Colores: Journal of Chicano Expression and Thought* 5, nos. 1–2 (1980):152–58.

Rodríguez de Laguna, Adela. *Imagenes e identidades: El puertorriqueño en la literatura*. Río Piedras, P.R.: Huracán, 1985. Not exclusively devoted to women.

Salazar Parr, Carmen. "The Chicana in Literature." In Eugene E. Garcia et al., *Chicano Studies: A Multidisciplinary Approach*, 122–34. New York: Teachers College Press, 1984.

———. "Surrealism in the Work of Estela Portillo." *MELUS* 7, no. 4 (Winter 1980):85–92.

Saldívar, José D. "Sandra Cisneros' *The House on Mango Street*." *MELUS*, forthcoming.

Sánchez, Marta Esther. *Contemporary Chicana Poetry: A Critical Approach to an Emerging Literature*. Berkeley: University of California Press, 1985.

———. "Inter-Sexual and Intertextual Codes in the Poetry of Bernice Zamora." *MELUS* 7, no. 3 (Fall 1980):55–68.

Sánchez, Rita. "Chicana Writer Breaking Out of Silence." *De Colores* 3, no. 3 (1977):31–37.

Sánchez, Rosaura, ed. *Essays on La mujer*. Los Angeles: Chicano Studies Center, UCLA, 1977.

Seator, Lynette. "Emplumada: Chicana Rites-of-Passage." *MELUS* 11 (Summer 1984):23–28.

Sontag, Iliana. "Hacia una bibliografía de la poesía femenina chicana." *La palabra: Revista de Literatura Chicana* 2 (1980):91–109.

Sosa Riddell, Adalijiza. "Chicanas and El Movimiento." *Aztlán* 5, nos. 1–2 (1975): 155–65.

Umpierre, Luz María. "La ansiedad de la influencia en Sandra María Esteves y Marjorie Agosín." *Revista Chicano-Riqueña* 11 (1983):139–47.

———. "Interview with Cherríe Moraga." *Americas Review* 14 (1986):54–67.

Umpierre-Herrera, Luz María. *Nuevas aproximaciones críticas a la literatura puertorriqueña*. Río Piedras, P.R.: Editorial Cultural, 1983.

Valdés Fallis, Guadalupe. "The Liberated Chicana—A Struggle Against Tradition." *Women: A Journal of Liberation* 3, no. 4 (1974):20–21.

Vallejos, Tomás. "Estela Portillo Trambley's Fictive Search for Paradise." *Frontiers* 5 (1980):55–58.

Vidal, Marta. *Chicanas Speak Out*. New York: Pathfinder Press, 1971.

Vigil, Evangelina, ed. *Woman of Her Word: Hispanic Women Write*. Special issue of *Revista Chicano-Riqueña* 11 (1983).

Vowell, Faye Nell. "A MELUS Interview: Estela Portillo-Trembley." *MELUS* 9 (Winter 1982):59–66.

Yarbro-Bejarano, Yvonne. "Cherríe Moraga's *Giving Up the Ghost*: The Representation of Female Desire." *Third Woman* 3 (1986):113–20.

————. "Introduction." *The Moths and Other Stories*, by Helena Maria Viramontes. Houston: Arte Público Press, 1985.

————. "*Teatropoesía* by Chicanas in the Bay Area: Tongues of Fire." *Revista Chicano-Riqueña* 11 (1983):78–94.

Zamora, Bernice. "Archetypes in Chicana Poetry." *De Colores* 4, no. 3 (1978).

————. "The Chicana as a Literary Critic." *De Colores* 3, no. 3 (1977):16–19.

Notes on Contributors and Translators

NORMA ALARCÓN is assistant professor of Latin American and Chicano literatures in Ethnic Studies at the University of California at Berkeley. She is also publisher and editor of *Third Woman* and Third Woman Press.

YAMILA AZIZE VARGAS was born in Río Piedras, Puerto Rico. On a Ford Foundation Fellowship, she studied at the University of Pennsylvania, where she was awarded a Ph.D. in Hispanic studies in 1980. Her articles have appeared in several reviews and journals in Puerto Rico and the U.S. Her book, *La mujer en la lucha (1898–1930)* (a history of feminism in Puerto Rico), was published by Editorial Cultural in 1985. She has been assistant professor of Spanish literature of the University of Puerto Rico at Mayagüez and, since August 1987, has been chairperson of the Center of Women's Studies at this university's Cayey campus.

JUAN BRUCE-NOVOA is a professor of Latin American and Chicano literatures at Trinity University, Texas. He is the author of *Chicano Poetry: A Response to Chaos, Chicano Authors: Inquiry by Interview, La sombra del caudillo, en su primera versión,* and *Inocencia perversa,* as well as of numerous articles, among them ones on Elena Poniatowska, Julieta Campos, and Chicana writers. He helped to cofound ADE-CLAN (Association pour la Diffusion et l'Étude des Cultures Latines en Amérique du Nord) in Paris. *Retrospace, Collected Chicano Essays* is currently being prepared for publication.

DENISE CHÁVEZ is a native of Las Cruces, New Mexico, where she makes her home. She is a playwright and a poetry and fiction writer who continues to explore the Southwest landscape. Her book *The Last of the Menu Girls* was published in 1986 by Arte Público Press. Her play *Novenas Narrativas* is currently on tour in the Southwest. At present, she is at work on a novel, *Face of an Angel.*

SONIA CRESPO VEGA was born in New York City of Puerto Rican parents. When she was sixteen her family returned to Puerto Rico, where she completed her high school education and went on to major in English at the Río Piedras campus of the University of Puerto Rico. She now lives in Cabo Rojo and is assistant professor of

English at the Mayagüez campus of the University of Puerto Rico, where she has taught since 1974.

JANICE DEWEY teaches "Women in Western Culture" and "Introduction to Women's Studies" at the University of Arizona in Tucson. Her research focuses on Latin American women writers and feminist issues in Latin America, Latin American and tribal folklore, and lesbian-feminist theory and writing. She has published articles on Borges and Nahuatl literature and myth and is presently seeking a publisher for her study of the myth of the Amazon woman in Latin American literature and culture.

SANDRA MARÍA ESTEVES, Puerto Rican Dominican American poet, born and raised in the Bronx, is widely published in numerous anthologies and literary journals throughout the United States. She published her first collection of poems, *Yerba Buena* (Greenfield Review Press), in 1980, and *Tropical Rains: A Bilingual Downpour* (African Caribbean Poetry Theater), in 1984. She is the recipient of poetry fellowships from CAPS, in 1980, and the New York Foundation for the Arts, in 1985. Ms. Esteves is currently the executive artistic director of the African Caribbean Poetry Theater, a Bronx-based, nonprofit arts organization that is producing dramatic theater and literary events throughout the Bronx, New York City, and East Coast areas.

JANET N. GOLD is a doctoral candidate in Latin American literature at the University of Massachusetts/Amherst. She has translated works of Latin American women writers and has focused her own research on these writers. She has published articles on Latin American literature in *Hispanic Journal* and elsewhere. Currently, she is working on a dissertation on Latin American women writers of the nineteenth century and their autobiographical experience as travelers.

ASUNCIÓN HORNO–DELGADO is a doctoral candidate in Hispanic literatures at the University of Massachusetts and a teacher at Smith College. Her publications include her book, *Primeros poemas* (Zaragoza: Institución Fernando El Católico, 1983), as well as critical studies on Carlos Fuentes and Rafael Humberto Moreno-Durán. Currently, she is working on Hispanic women poets. She organized the original panel at the Tenth Symposium of Spanish and Portuguese Bilingualism at the University of Massachusetts/Amherst, which gave rise to this book.

ELLEN MCCRACKEN is associate professor of comparative literature at the University of Massachusetts/Amherst. Her research interests include Latin American literature, women and mass culture, and literary theory. Her book, "From *Mademoiselle* to *Ms.*: Decoding Women's Magazines," is under final revision.

ELAINE N. MILLER is currently head of the reference department at the Smith College Library. She has a Master of Arts in library science and a Master of Arts in Ibero-American studies from the University of Wisconsin. Before working at Smith she was a reference librarian at the State University of New York at Albany and assistant librarian in the Latin American Collection, University of Florida.

NICHOLASA MOHR was born in New York City's El Barrio of Puerto Rican parents and currently resides in Brooklyn. She is the author of six books of fiction for adults and children. Her most recent works include *Rituals of Survival: A Woman's Portfolio* and *Going Home*. She is the recipient of the American Book Award for excellence in literature, a Jane Addams Peace Award, and numerous other awards, and was a National Book Award finalist..

ELIANA ORTEGA was born in Chile and is a permanent resident of the U.S. She teaches Latin American and Latina/o literature at Mount Holyoke College and has published articles on Latina and Latin American women poets. She is the coeditor (with Patricia González) of *La sartén por el mango* (Río Piedras: Huracán, 1984) and is currently working on a book of criticism about Chilean women poets.

DOLORES PRIDA was born in Caibarién, Cuba, and currently resides in New York, where she is the editor of *AHA Hispanic Arts News*, a publication of the Association of Hispanic Arts. In addition to her numerous plays, she has also written two books of poetry: *Treinta y un poemas* and *Women of the Hour*. Presently, she is at work on several new plays, including *Fantasy Island* and *The Electric Maraca*.

BESSY REYNA was born in Cuba and resided in Panama until 1968, when she came to the U.S. Her works include *Terrarium*, a book of poems, and *Ab Ovo*, a collection of short stories, as well as numerous pieces published in both English and Spanish in this country and Latin America, including her contributions to *Ixoc Amar-Go: Central American Women's Poetry for Peace*, ed. Zoe Anglesey (Penobscot, Maine: Granite Press, 1987). She is presently serving as editor of *El Taller Literario*, the first Connecticut-based Hispanic arts and literature magazine.

ELIANA RIVERO was born in Cuba and has been teaching Spanish-American literature at the University of Arizona since 1967. She has published three books and over thirty-five articles in the area of Hispanic literature, especially on poetry and women poets. Her most recent research has been an NEH-sponsored project on U.S. Hispanic writers (written with Tey Diana Rebolledo) entitled *Unsung Women: The Identity of Chicana Literature*. She has also published her own poetry in two books (*De cal y arena*, and *Cuerpos breves*) and in several collections, among them *Woman of Her Word: Hispanic Women Write, Nosotras: Latina Literature Today*, and *Bearing Witness/Sobreviviendo: An Anthology of Writing and Art by Native American/Latina Women*.

LOURDES ROJAS was born in Barranquilla, Colombia, and has been a permanent resident of the United States since she was eighteen. She teaches Latin American and Latina/o literature at Colgate University. Currently, she is at work on a project concerning the Latin American woman essayist.

ALBERTO SANDOVAL was born in Santurce, Puerto Rico, and has been residing in the United States since 1973. His research concentrates on Juan Ruiz de Alarcón as a Baroque Colonial playwright but also includes marginal groups in the theater, such as the representation on Indians and Moriscos in Golden Age drama and Latinos on Broadway. His bilingual book of poetry, *Nueva York tras bastidores/New*

York Backstage, is forthcoming. He teaches Peninsular literature at Mount Holyoke College.

NINA M. SCOTT was born in Hamburg, Germany, and came to the U.S. when she was nine. She is professor of Spanish at the University of Massachusetts/Amherst, with research interests in the comparative literature of the Americas and Latin American women writers, especially Sor Juana Inés de la Cruz, Rosario Castellanos, and María Luisa Bombal.

NANCY SAPORTA STERNBACH teaches Latina/o and Latin American literature at Smith College. She has published articles on Latin American women's movements and literature, both in the U.S. and in Latin America. She is currently at work on Latin American women's testimonial literature and a project concerning the Latin American woman essayist.

MARY JANE TREACY is associate professor of Spanish at Simmons College in Boston. She did graduate work on the Spanish theater of the Golden Age and, since that work, developed a passion for contemporary Latin American and Chicana women's writing. She has edited *Campo Abierto: Lecturas sociopolíticas de Hispanoamérica,* and her work has appeared in *Hispania, Imagine,* and *Modern Language Journal,* among others.

SHEREZADA (CHIQUI) VICIOSO is a poet, literary critic, and educator from the Dominican Republic and the author of two books of poetry: *Viajes desde el agua* (1981) and *Un extraño ulular traía el viento* (1985). She lived in New York for seventeen years, where she attended Brooklyn College and Columbia University. At present, she is residing in Santo Domingo and has edited a book on Julia de Burgos entitled *Julia, la nuestra.*

HELENA MARIA VIRAMONTES was born in East Los Angeles, California, in 1954 and currently lives in Los Angeles. She has been the coordinator of the Los Angeles Latino Writers Association, literary editor of *XismeArte Magazine,* and winner of several literary competitions, including the University of California at Irvine's Chicano Literary Contest. Her book, *The Moths and Other Stories,* was published by Arte Público Press in 1985.